Backdoor Lawmaking

Backdoor Lawmaking

Evading Obstacles in the US Congress

MELINDA N. RITCHIE

OXFORD
UNIVERSITY PRESS

OXFORD
UNIVERSITY PRESS

Oxford University Press is a department of the University of Oxford.
It furthers the University's objective of excellence in research, scholarship,
and education by publishing worldwide. Oxford is a registered trade mark of
Oxford University Press in the UK and in certain other countries.

Published in the United States of America by Oxford University Press
198 Madison Avenue, New York, NY 10016, United States of America.

Library of Congress Cataloging-in-Publication Data

Names: Ritchie, Melinda N., author.
Title: Backdoor lawmaking : evading obstacles in the US Congress /
Melinda N. Ritchie.
Description: New York : Oxford University Press, [2023]
Identifiers: LCCN 2023007297 (print) | LCCN 2023007298 (ebook) |
ISBN 9780197670484 (hardback) | ISBN 9780197670491 (paperback) |
ISBN 9780197670507 (epub)
Subjects: LCSH: United States. Congress—Rules and practice. |
Executive-legislative relations—United States. | Administrative
agencies—United States. | Legislation—United States. | Government
accountability—United States. | Bureaucracy—United States.
Classification: LCC JK585 .R57 2023 (print) | LCC JK585 (ebook) |
DDC 328.3/4560973–dc23/eng/20230309
LC record available at https://lccn.loc.gov/2023007297
LC ebook record available at https://lccn.loc.gov/2023007298

DOI: 10.1093/oso/9780197670484.001.0001
DOI: 10.1093/oso/9780197670491.001.0001

Printed in Canada by Marquis Book Printing

For Jason

Contents

Acknowledgments

I am grateful to be writing the last words of this book at the Library of Congress, across the street from the book's subject. Completing the book in this setting seems fitting; the origins of the idea for the book developed while I was a congressional staffer working in the US House of Representatives over a decade ago. Since that time, I have been the grateful recipient of generous support and kindness from many people I respect and admire. I appreciate having the opportunity to acknowledge them here.

I am thankful for the insight and thoughtful feedback of many individuals who read drafts of chapters or provided assistance throughout my time working on this project. The project began in the Department of Political Science at the University of Illinois, Urbana-Champaign, where it benefited from the valuable feedback of Brian Gaines, Gisela Sin, Scott Althaus, Bill Bernhard, Jeff Mondak, Bob Pahre, and Matt Winters. I am also grateful for the early support and friendship of Amanda Cronkhite, Katie Francis, Gina Martinez, Matt Powers, Bryce Reeder, Ashly Townsen, Tarah Williams, Andy Bloeser, David Hendry, and Sunhee Park.

I cannot fully express my gratitude to Tracy Sulkin and Jim Kuklinski, who dedicated countless hours, financial support, and invaluable contributions to this project. Tracy's guidance and keen insight was critical at key points during this project. Jim spent multiple Saturdays sitting in his office with me helping with drafts or talks. I am only one of many grateful recipients of his dedicated mentorship across the discipline; he serves as the standard-bearer of scholarship and mentorship for us. I often find myself today saying things to my students that he used to say to me.

I am so thankful for my colleagues at the University of California, Riverside, where I spent the beginning of my career. Jenn Merolla has been such an inspiration and support. She is an exemplary scholar, colleague, and human being. Kim Dionne always knows what to say when I need it the most. Her support has given me the confidence to bring this project home. I am particularly grateful to Ben Bishin, who read and commented on several chapters and other work numerous times and always provided critically needed feedback. Thanks to Nick Weller, who read and commented on several chapters. I am grateful to my UCR colleagues and friends who provided guidance on the project and support over the years: Marissa Brookes, Yasemin Irepoglu Carreras, Miguel Carreras, Steven Liao, Noel Pereyra-Johnston, Dan Biggers, Loren Collingwood, Bronwyn Leebaw, John Cioffi, Ben Newman, Indridi Indridason, and Kevin Esterling. Thanks to Shaun Bowler for taking the time to stop by my office to offer enthusiasm for this project and to make me laugh.

I am grateful for the support of my home institution, the Department of Political Science at The Ohio State University, particularly Jan Box-Steffensmeier, Greg Caldeira, William Minnozi, Alex Acs, Nicole Yadon, Amanda Robinson, and Erin Linn. I owe a special thanks to Michael Neblo for his feedback on the project, guidance, and warm support.

The project benefited immensely from the scholarly communities that welcomed me over the years and the institutions that provided financial assistance for this research. Vanderbilt University's Center for the Study of Democratic Institutions, Princeton University's Center for the Study of Democratic Politics, and the John W. Kluge Center at the Library of Congress provided me the space and time to finish the book. Special thanks to Annelise Russell, who had the unenviable role of helping me through the project's final days at the Kluge Center. Financial support for this project was provided by a Congressional Research Grant from the Dirksen Center during its early days.

I received valuable feedback from audiences at several institutions including the Bedrosian Center at the University of Southern California Sol Price School of Public Policy, the University of Maryland, American University, the Virtual American Executive Politics Seminar, the University of North Carolina, Chapel-Hill, and the American politics speaker series at the Harvard Kennedy School.

I owe special thanks to the small community of scholars who have been working on related projects at the same time. My work has benefited immensely from discussions with Kenny Lowande, Russ Mills, and Nicole Kalaf-Hughes.

I am so grateful for the support and friendship of Hye Young You. Hye Young has been persistently and enthusiastically supportive of my work for years. She read and commented on every chapter of the book and served as a moderator at my book workshop. She is an all-around amazing human being.

Several wonderful individuals have offered support and feedback along the way. I am thankful for the contributions of Jim Curry, Danielle Thomsen,

Erinn Lauterbach, Sharece Thrower, Marc Heatherington, Dave Lewis, Jeff Jenkins, Jenny Mansbridge, Jon Rogowski, Brandice Canes-Wrone, Chuck Cameron, Ken Meier, Gleason Judd, Frances Lee, Sam Kernell, Nara Pavão, Jeff Harden, Jesse Crosson, Chinbo Chong, Steven White, Charlotte Cavaillé, Kris Miler, Jason MacDonald, Susan Webb Yackee, David Karol, David Miller, and Gary Hollibaugh. I am particularly grateful for the valuable feedback from the participants at my book workshop. Thanks to Daniel Carpenter, Sarah Binder, and Alan Wiseman. I owe special thanks to Alan, who read and commented on every chapter.

Engaging with undergraduate research assistants has been one of my greatest joys while working on this project, particularly when I have the opportunity to watch them go on to succeed in incredible careers of their own. Valuable research assistance was provided by Sharon Moraes, Diana Perez, Victoria Yao, Sigrid Ohnesorge, Alexandra Lynn, Claire Marks, Devin Main, Justin Cheng, Jade Henry Kang, and Jacob Luthi. I also owe a special thanks to Jaylin McClinton. I also appreciate the research assistance and feedback of current and former graduate students, Michelangelo Landgrave, Steph DeMora, and Nick Jenkins.

I am grateful to my fantastic editor, Angela Chnapko, for her early and constant enthusiasm for this book. I cannot imagine having a better editor and appreciate her confidence in the project. I thank Alexcee Bechthold and the professionals at Oxford University Press who guided this book to completion.

Finally, I am grateful to Jason Coronel for his unrelenting support and confidence in this project. Without Jason's encouragement in the early stages, this project never would have been more than a final paper for a graduate seminar. He makes sure that I laugh every single day. As I reminded him whenever I needed his feedback on a draft, this book is dedicated to him.

List of Figures

List of Tables

1

Introduction

> I have discovered that smart bureaucrats are able to work magic.
> They are able to take care of a problem that the law would apparently
> normally prohibit, but they will do it without breaking the law.
> I didn't bother to ask how it was done. I didn't want to know.[1]
>
> Senator Robert Packwood (R-OR)

Senator Amy Klobuchar was determined to get the gray wolf off the Endangered Species List. The Minnesota Democrat clashed with environmentalists opposed to delisting the wolf, a move that would strip it of the federal protections established by the Endangered Species Act of 1973.[2] Aside from the conflict over wolves, Klobuchar had near-perfect scores from environmental organizations, but she faced pressure from rural Minnesotans to delist the wolf because it was an increasing hazard to livestock.[3] The Endangered Species Act barred farmers from defending their sheep and cattle from the wolf's attacks, threatening their livelihood. Delisting proponents argued that the wolf was no longer in danger of extinction and did not warrant continued federal protection. The controversy over the wolves was one of a string of divisive issues that forced the senator to navigate the clashing interests of environmentalists and her constituents living in the conservative, rural region of northeastern Minnesota.[4]

Senator Klobuchar, one of the most effective lawmakers in Congress, did not introduce legislation to remove the gray wolf from the Endangered Species List.[5] She used a less orthodox approach that students won't find in their textbooks on Congress. She pressured the federal agency tasked with implementing the Endangered Species Act to delist the gray wolf instead.

Rather than introduce legislation, Klobuchar requested that the US Fish and Wildlife Service remove the gray wolf from the Endangered Species List through rulemaking, a process by which federal agencies, having been delegated authority from Congress, can make policy changes unilaterally. The senator weighed whether to pursue the issue legislatively or through agency

Backdoor Lawmaking: Evading Obstacles in the US Congress. Melinda N. Ritchie, Oxford University Press.
© Melinda N. Ritchie 2023. DOI: 10.1093/oso/9780197670491.003.0001

action but believed that administrative action was preferable to legislation. She reserved delisting the gray wolf legislatively as "Plan B."[6] However, she threatened to introduce legislation if the agency did not advance rulemaking. In fact, the US Fish and Wildlife Service delisted the gray wolf as Klobuchar requested using procedural maneuvers that a federal court would later rule were unlawful.[7]

Why did Senator Klobuchar choose agency action over legislation? The senator's behavior is representative of an overlooked strategy used by savvy legislators to avoid obstacles in Congress and to evade public scrutiny. Klobuchar's choice to pursue policymaking through the bureaucracy in lieu of the legislative process is not unique; this strategic sidestepping is pervasive and widespread across members of Congress.

This book reveals how members of Congress use the federal bureaucracy as a backdoor for policymaking. Legislators exploit the bureaucracy for two strategic reasons. First, by substituting agency procedure for congressional action, lawmakers persuade agencies to accomplish what they fail to achieve through the legislative process. Second, the bureaucracy offers lawmakers a less visible way to represent controversial interests. In short, this backdoor policymaking allows members of Congress to evade accountability and to bypass the legislative process established in the US Constitution.

Inter-branch policymaking offers important implications for democratic governance and representation. Legislators pressure agencies to make policy changes that would not pass Congress, thus undermining the collective authority of Congress and the lawmaking process. Critically, lawmakers are exploiting the obscurity of administrative procedure to evade public scrutiny, thereby threatening democratic accountability. Finally, although a large majority of legislators try to influence agency policymaking, powerful lawmakers—those with the most resources and influence within Congress— are the most capable of exploiting it, thus subverting the ideals of equality in democratic representation.

Some readers might wonder how such unorthodox policymaking could possibly be legal. Of course, Article I of the US Constitution gives the authority to legislate solely to Congress. Yet, law in the United States is largely and increasingly made by government officials who are generally unknown to the American public rather than the members of Congress whom voters chose on Election Day. In fact, more public policy is now made through federal agency regulations than congressional statute.[8] In effect, while civics textbooks depict the bureaucracy as merely implementing laws drafted and passed by Congress, in practice, unelected bureaucrats who work in federal agencies make policy with the full force of law.[9]

The expansion of the bureaucracy's power has raised concerns over the last century. Some scholars have expressed alarm over the inability of democratically elected officials to control politically unresponsive and unaccountable bureaucrats. Others argue that the public is better served by the policy expertise of career civil servants and the continuity offered by agencies insulated from political influence.[10] Debates about who actually controls the bureaucracy—Congress or the president—have also dominated scholarship on the separation of powers.

The emphasis of these scholarly debates on inter-branch power struggles neglects the quiet collusion taking place through informal backchannels spanning branches of government.[11] As I demonstrate, members of Congress and agencies regularly interact, coordinate, and collaborate on matters of public policy through informal channels. Using the Freedom of Information Act, I obtained records that reveal how members of Congress pressure agencies to influence policy. Agencies, in turn, are responsive to individual legislators because they want to build support in Congress for their budgets and priorities and avoid angering lawmakers.[12] These records uncover an interdependent relationship that threatens to undermine the separation of powers.

While these inter-branch negotiations have long been a feature of policymaking in the United States, this book is particularly important considering the challenges facing democracies in the twenty-first century. The expansion of the federal bureaucracy means that unelected agency officials have increasing power over policies that touch every aspect of life in the United States. Unelected bureaucrats are now an integral and undeniable feature of policymaking. This expansion of agency policymaking has led to the development of an interdependent relationship between agencies and members of Congress who use informal backchannels to evade the separation of powers system in which the institution of Congress alone was endowed with authority to legislate.

Yet, the normative implications of these inter-branch exchanges are not straightforward. While this strategic exploitation of the separation of powers is likely to alarm many, some readers may find my descriptions of legislators' tenacity in pursuit of policy objectives an encouraging take on the state of representation in Congress. Many constituents would likely prefer a representative who advocates for their interests across branches of government to one who surrenders following the failure of her legislation.

Moreover, agencies fail to fully implement laws on the books, do not always honor the spirit of legislation, and advance policies—even legally sound policies—that could have negative consequences for particular districts and groups. Consider, for instance, the Food and Drug Administration's labeling decisions that made the US population vulnerable to the opioid crisis.[13] Similar concerns of a troubled implementation process plagued the Dodd-Frank Act.[14] Federal laws on a range of issues—including immigration, marijuana regulation, and the marketing of food products—are not fully enforced, often with the blessing of many lawmakers and to the consternation of others. On the other hand, agencies sometimes implement policies that have little grounding in statute.[15] Whether lawmakers follow up with agencies to push for timely implementation or to inform them of unforeseen costs can have serious implications for representation.[16]

I return to these normative trade-offs throughout the book and weigh them in the final chapter. The conclusions we draw about the normative implications depend largely on aggregate patterns of inter-branch behavior. Readers can judge for themselves as they assess the evidence to follow.

It may be that the growth and increasing complexity of government and the society it regulates "has undermined the assumption that representation and lawmaking legitimately take place only in the legislature" (Mansbridge 2019, 303). Given the increasing polarization and gridlock in a Congress seemingly incapable of passing a budget without stopgap legislation, legislators cannot limit themselves to their Article I powers if they hope to provide adequate representation and good governance.

Back-Channel Policymaking

Journalists, scholars, and the public focus on policymaking within the halls of Congress, scrutinizing how legislators vote, the bills they write, and their statements in committee hearings. In practice, however, members of Congress are not confined to the lawmaking process established in the Constitution or even to the House and Senate chambers. In short, legislators are not limited to legislating.

This book introduces a previously neglected strategy legislators use to influence public policy outside of the formal legislative process and beyond the public eye, which I refer to as *back-channel policymaking*. Members of Congress exploit the bureaucracy's control over policy implementation using informal channels of communication with agencies.

In fact, agencies receive thousands of letters, emails, phone calls, and meeting requests about matters of public policy from members of Congress every year. These interactions span issues from marijuana regulation, challenges for same-sex couples, occupational safety, immigration, trade, and fracking. Legislators use informal channels of communication to make policy appeals to agencies for two strategic reasons.

First, lawmakers pressure agencies to make policy changes that they were unable to accomplish through the legislative process. For example, in 2003, a band of lawmakers led by Senator Ted Kennedy (D-MA) urged the Food and Drug Administration (FDA) to require that pharmaceutical companies use anti-counterfeit technologies for prescription drugs imported from Canada even though the related legislative provision had passed in the House but had not made it into the Senate version of the legislation. The provision, which was opposed by the biotechnology industry, was cut from the final version of the legislation. Despite failure in Congress, Senator Kennedy continued to push for the requirement through agency regulations.[17]

Second, members of Congress also use informal channels of inter-branch communication to advance contentious issues. For instance, in the summer of 2009, Senator Robert Byrd (D-WV), a longtime proponent of a coal mining process called mountaintop removal mining, contacted the US Department of Labor (DOL) about the hazards of the practice.[18] If such contact had been publicly known, it would have been highly controversial in the coal-dependent state of West Virginia. In fact, when Senator Byrd went public with his concerns about mountaintop removal mining in December of that year, it shocked and angered even his close acquaintances, some of whom suggested he was confused in his old age. Then-Governor Joe Manchin's response was that the 92-year-old senator's articulated new position was a "misunderstanding." What the West Virginia public did not realize was that Senator Byrd's changing views on mining were not as head-spinning as they seemed. The elder statesman had expressed his concerns through backchannels until he was ready to go public.[19] While legislative action—such as introducing a bill or participating in a committee hearing—is useful for taking a public stand, discreet interactions with agencies, coupled with opaque administrative processes, make back-channel policymaking a valuable tool for lawmakers on contentious issues.

These examples demonstrate a common but largely unrecognized means of policymaking and representation. Participation in Congress does not end with a vote. Nor is a legislator's influence restricted to committees and the chamber floor. Lawmakers use agency policymaking as a substitute for legislative action.

Overview of the Argument

Why would members of Congress turn to the bureaucracy to influence policy when they have the formal power to legislate? The bureaucracy's expansive system of regulations and policymaking tools offers opportunities for accomplishing legislators' policy objectives in ways that, ironically, would be difficult for a lawmaker to achieve through the legislative process. The average legislator struggles to gain influence in Congress, stymied by institutions, hierarchy and leadership, polarization, and gridlock. With less than 5% of bills becoming law, if legislators "were major league baseball hitters, then they would have struck out swinging many times over" (Anderson, Box-Steffensmeier, and Sinclair-Chapman 2003, 364).[20] Obstacles within the formal legislative process drive legislators to take advantage of the bureaucracy's discretion as an alternative venue for policymaking.

Like presidential signing statements, these informal communications have no formal authority. Instead, they are signals of legislators' preferences as well as the intensity of their preferences. If a legislator signals to an agency that an issue is a priority for them, the agency risks retaliation if it is unresponsive to the signal. Lawmakers vote on agency budgets and programs and can create challenges for the administration by hauling agency heads in for oversight hearings, holding up presidential appointees (in the Senate), and obstructing agency priorities. In this way, members of Congress use their formal powers as lawmakers as leverage to exploit the substantial discretion of the bureaucracy.

The bureaucracy offers lawmakers another advantage as well. As readers might imagine, the nuts and bolts of administrative policymaking receives much less attention than happenings in the Capitol Building. While the spotlight on Congress can be useful for seeking credit for accomplishments and taking a public stand, it is a detriment when dealing with controversial issues. Legislators' actions on divisive issues can attract negative headlines, anger stakeholders, and provide challengers with campaign fodder for the next election. The obscure nature of administrative procedure, on the other hand, is ideal for representing interests that are costly to represent publicly, and the informal nature of legislators' communication with agencies helps keep it off the books. Consequently, legislators have more control over who finds out about their efforts in the bureaucratic venue than in the legislative process.

As a whole, this unorthodox policymaking allows lawmakers to avoid obstacles in Congress and to evade public scrutiny. Taking a step back, back-channel policymaking demonstrates a broader and fundamental lesson about members of Congress. Legislators are rational actors who respond strategically to constraints in pursuit of their interests in ways that test and undermine the formal institutions that grant them authority.

Scholarly Perspectives on the Relationship between Congress and the Bureaucracy

Despite its importance, the scholarly literature has neglected this strategic policymaking behavior. There are several reasons for this oversight. The first involves divisions in the literature that have been shaped by methodological approach. The second is related to the lack of conceptual clarity for important concepts that define the relationship between Congress and the executive branch. Third, scholars have focused on the formal powers of legislators. Finally, the congressional literature has been guided by data availability and, thus, has concentrated on the visible aspects of congressional activity, making the behind-the-scenes policymaking that serves as the foundation for Congress difficult to study.

Of course, the idea that legislators attempt to influence the bureaucracy is not new. However, substantive and methodological divisions in the literatures on Congress, bureaucratic politics, and separation of powers led to categorizations that did not fully recognize the consequential policy interactions between legislators and agencies. Instead, scholars assumed legislator interactions with agencies were primarily electorally motivated casework and pork, or they concentrated on Congress' institutional mechanisms for reining in shirking agencies.

The Congressional-Bureaucratic Relationship:
Keystone of the Washington Establishment

Classic work in the study of Congress may have established the perception that informal exchanges between legislators and agencies are cheap talk rather than meaningful efforts to influence public policy. Fiorina's prominent book, *Congress: Keystone of the Washington Establishment* (Fiorina 1977), continues to serve as the foremost authority on the relationship between individual members of Congress and the bureaucracy. Seeking to explain incumbency advantage, Fiorina argues that the growing federal bureaucracy allows legislators to win over constituents by providing programs, services, and help with personal problems—such as benefit denials and delays in receiving Social Security checks—that result from the bureaucracy's complexity (i.e., casework or constituency service). Thus, in Fiorina's view, members of Congress interact with the bureaucracy to build their "personal vote," the personalized connection with constituents that attracts electoral support. He describes an exploitative system involving legislators trading influence on policy for casework and pork, a more electorally valuable currency. In short, Fiorina argues that the relationship between members of Congress and the bureaucracy is focused on electorally valuable casework and pork, overlooking the important policy interactions between legislators and agencies.

Arnold's (1979) work on interactions between Congress and the bureaucracy reaches much the same conclusions.[21] However, he approaches the question from the point of view of the bureaucrats, highlighting the benefits that accrue to them from the system. His study of congressional influence over the geographic allocation of federal expenditures finds that bureaucrats strategically consider the preferences of legislators when distributing grants in order to build coalitions of support in Congress. Arnold leaves open the possibility that a legislator's influence over the bureaucracy extends beyond casework and grants to issues of national policy, but leaves the research task to "another time, another place, and perhaps another writer" (216). However, while subsequent scholarship has advanced research on casework (Cain, Ferejohn, and Fiorina 1990; Johannes 1984; Parker 1980) and expenditures (Bertelli and Grose 2009; Stein and Bickers 1997), it has neglected the question of whether the interactions between individual members of Congress and the bureaucracy are also consequential for policy.

"Congress is a 'they' not an 'it'"

Scholars have underappreciated the role of inter-branch policymaking outside of the traditional perspectives on congressional oversight. Instead, they have focused on how lawmakers use formal mechanisms—including statute, agency design and procedure, committee oversight and hearings—to ensure agency compliance with the collective goals of Congress or "legislative intent."[22] This approach fostered a tendency to assume legislators' policy interactions with agencies are naive expressions of legislative intent instead of recognizing lawmakers as rational actors behaving as independent agents in the bureaucratic venue.[23]

This emphasis on collective notions of legislative intent is driven largely by early approaches to the study of the separation of powers. Principal-agent theory, long the dominant approach, prompted formal models with a unitary Congress as principal. Legal scholarship required discerning legislative intent by which statute should be assessed. It has also been driven by a focus on formal mechanisms of control, a context dominated by the institutions and organization of Congress.[24]

Yet, as Shepsle memorably points out, "Congress is a 'they' not an 'it.'" The opening paragraph of his article by this title is worth quoting (with apologies to student athletes):

> An oxymoron is a two-word contradiction. The claim of this brief paper is that legislative intent, along with military intelligence, jumbo shrimp, and student athlete, belongs in this category. Legislative intent is an internally inconsistent, self-contradictory expression. Therefore, it has no meaning. To claim otherwise is to entertain a myth (the existence of a Rousseauian great law giver) or commit a fallacy (the false personification of a collectivity).[25]

Even when two legislators vote "yea" on a bill, we cannot assume they had the same intention for the statute. Building on Shepsle's argument, legislators are self-interested rational actors who, I would argue, have little concern for or even necessarily an awareness of a collectively defined intent. Why, then, would we expect legislative intent to drive their behavior toward agencies? From the legislator's perspective, she engages with the bureaucracy as a free agent rather than as a member of a legislature, party, or committee, although, notably, her ability to influence an agency is entirely a product of her membership within these same institutions. While this view is consistent with Fiorina's rational choice approach, scholars have been slow to apply this same logic to how individual legislators engage with the bureaucracy beyond constituency service and pork.[26]

This book departs from previous scholarship by arguing that lawmakers' relationship with the bureaucracy is driven not by legislative intent but in subversion of it. The focus on institutional authority—whether defined by committees, the current majority, or the coalition that enacted legislation—has overshadowed how individual lawmakers exploit the bureaucracy to evade legislative institutions and advance their own objectives. Of course, legislators act through their committees and party structure to oversee the bureaucracy, but they participate unilaterally in the bureaucratic venue as well. The pursuit of the institutional (collective) intent of Congress is concentrated within its formal institutions rather than through unconstrained, informal channels.[27]

This theoretical distinction offers different implications for assessments of representation and governance. The principal-agent framework assumes congressional control of the bureaucracy is important for democratic governance and representation. However, my framework suggests that legislators' influence over agencies undermines the authority of Congress. I revisit and develop these implications throughout the book.

The Tip of the Iceberg: The Focus on Visible Policymaking

Another reason for the neglect of this strategic behavior is congressional scholars' focus on the chambers of Congress. When considering legislators' policymaking behavior, scholars have concentrated on the lawmaking process *within* Congress. For many years, attention was almost entirely on roll-call voting. Eventually congressional scholars pushed into territory beyond up-or-down votes, considering bill introductions, co-sponsorships, floor speeches, and committee participation (e.g., Hall 1996; Koger 2003; Maltzman and Sigelman 1996; Schiller 1995; Sulkin 2005, 2011). However, we know very little about how lawmakers try to influence policy outside of the legislative process. Examining policymaking behavior beyond the halls of Congress is a natural next step.

The focus on formal legislative participation is likely also driven by data availability. While roll-call voting records, bill sponsorship and co-sponsorship, and floor speeches are easily available in the public record, finding data on informal participation is more challenging. Obtaining the records and data presented in this book required an important law known as the Freedom of Information Act.

The Freedom of Information Act and Back-Channel Communications Dataset

Members of Congress value back-channel policymaking, in large part, because it is discreet and concealed from public scrutiny behind the curtain of inconspicuous administrative policymaking. However, this also means that this strategic behavior is difficult to study because it takes place behind the scenes. As a result, the informal interactions between lawmakers and agencies have largely been a black box. This book offers records and data that allow us to examine this strategic behavior for the first time. Under the Freedom of Information Act (FOIA), I obtained records of over 100,000 contacts, including letters, faxes, emails, phone calls, and meetings, between members of Congress and ten cabinet departments during the George W. Bush and Obama administrations. I employ a mixed-method approach to use these unique records in qualitative and quantitative analyses.

First, this book offers a novel dataset constructed from these records of communication. I analyze over 65,000 contacts between members of Congress (US senators and House members) and the US Departments of Labor (DOL), Energy (DOE), and Homeland Security (DHS) spanning the Bush and Obama administrations (2005–2012). These data are used in rigorous statistical analyses in four chapters of the book. The dataset includes indicators identifying legislators' objectives when contacting agencies and a unique measure of how agencies prioritize communication from legislators.

Second, this book includes case studies and qualitative accounts from ten agencies, including the US Trade Representative, and the Departments of Agriculture, Commerce, Education, the Interior, Health and Human Services, Transportation, Labor, Homeland Security, and Energy. These primary source materials allow me to trace the interactions between particular members of Congress and agencies to flesh out how these communications function as part of a lawmaker's overarching strategy for policymaking.

Organization of the Book

This book is organized to present readers with a clear understanding of what communication members of Congress engage in with the bureaucracy, why legislators make policy appeals to agencies, how agencies respond to legislators' appeals, and why inter-branch policymaking is important for representation and democratic governance. The book is structured as follows.

Chapter 2 develops the theory of back-channel policymaking to explain why and how obstacles in the legislative process drive members of Congress to exploit agency policymaking. This inter-branch strategy offers lawmakers two advantages. First, it allows members of Congress to circumvent obstacles in the legislative process by substituting agency policymaking for legislative action. Second, the discreet nature of back-channel communication allows legislators to represent contentious interests that would be costly for them to represent publicly. Taken together, legislators take advantage of agency policymaking to advance their policy objectives while evading accountability.

The chapter also explains the role that agencies play in these inter-branch relationships. Agencies have an incentive to respond favorably to legislators because agencies are dependent on Congress for their budgets, programs, and priorities. This interdependent relationship between lawmakers and agencies leads to collaboration and negotiation over legislation and agency policymaking.

Chapter 3 explains the origins and nature of the data used in the book and the challenges to the Freedom of Information Act. The chapter first details the history and recent developments of the FOIA. Then, I describe how the quantitative dataset was constructed from the FOIA records. I discuss the classification of inter-branch communication into categories used in the book's quantitative analyses. Chapter 3 also provides descriptive statistics about legislators' communication with agencies over time, chambers, and agencies.

Chapter 4 presents a typology and qualitative accounts from the records themselves. This chapter focuses on the content of lawmakers' communication with agencies. I provide qualitative case studies that allow me to trace communications from their origins through their outcomes. This qualitative approach offers several novel insights that are not discernible from the empirical analyses in subsequent chapters.

In Chapter 5, I confront and systematically dispel several misconceptions about the relationship between members of Congress and the bureaucracy using empirical evidence. First, I show that inter-branch policy interactions are not confined to committees or leadership, as was previously assumed. In fact, nearly all members of Congress contact agencies about policy. Legislators regularly communicate with agencies about policy and have done so largely under the radar of congressional scholars. Second, conventional wisdom suggests lawmakers' policy appeals to agencies are cheap talk rather than a meaningful reflection of policy interests. In contrast, I find that legislators' policy communication with agencies is related to their policy priorities, and the legislators who are the most focused on advancing legislation through the formal lawmaking process also interact more frequently with agencies about policy. Third, previous work has overlooked the importance of these interactions by equating them with requests for information or congressional oversight, as traditionally characterized. Another long-held belief assumes that lawmakers do not contact agencies about matters of public policy to any meaningful degree, assuming, instead, that these communications are constituency service and requests for grants. However, I show that lawmakers' contact with agencies is related to their own policy objectives while accounting for conventional measures of oversight and, using a placebo test, I demonstrate that policy appeals are distinct from casework and requests for grants.

In Chapter 6, I explain and test a central argument of the book: Members of Congress use informal channels of communication with the bureaucracy to circumvent constraints in the formal legislative process. I present findings suggesting that legislators use the bureaucracy as an alternative policymaking venue when they (1) face constraints in the legislative process and (2) see opportunities for policy influence within the executive branch. Senators contact agencies with policy requests more frequently when they are members of the chamber minority and share the party affiliation of the president. House members' policy interactions with agencies is highest when they are completely shut out of the lawmaking process and lack formal channels of influence.

However, I find that the most powerful members of Congress are in a better position to take advantage of the bureaucracy's backdoor. This finding is important because it suggests that powerful lawmakers have the upper hand over policymaking in both branches of government. I explain how this advantage could be used to circumvent the collective authority of Congress.

In Chapter 7, I explain and test the second central argument of the book. I argue that the bureaucracy provides an alternative, quiet way for legislators to represent controversial interests. I show that, when faced with competing principals of party and constituency, legislators strategically choose less visible, back-channel means for pursuing policy goals. I discuss the implications of these findings for accountability and transparency.

In Chapter 8, I introduce a novel measure of agency responsiveness. This measure is constructed from internal agency notes and documents regarding how it prioritizes contacts from members of Congress and which requests receive the attention of those in power at the agency. My results depart from the findings of previous work using alternative measures and allow me to distinguish between competing theories of agency responsiveness. Rather than rewarding co-partisans of the administration, agencies employ a risk-averse strategy in responding to members of Congress. Agencies are motivated to avoid angering legislators—any legislator—but particularly lawmakers who are motivated and in positions to retaliate against the agency in consequential ways. The chapter's empirical findings offer important substantive contributions on agency decision-making and responsiveness.

In the ninth and final chapter, I discuss the conclusions we can draw from my research and the implications for the study of Congress and inter-branch politics. How should this book change how we study and understand Congress? Given the growth of administrative lawmaking, we can no longer assume that roll-call votes are the most important policymaking activity that a legislator undertakes. Focusing on what members of Congress do in the House and Senate chambers and how they exercise their Article I authority is to fixate on the tip of the iceberg.

Chapter 9 engages with emerging research in democratic theory to consider how the book's conclusions lend insight into the normative trade-offs for representation and democratic governance.[28] Rather than signaling the deterioration of the separation of powers and Congress's constitutional authority to make law, back-channel policymaking may offer the preservation of democratic norms and legitimacy under the inevitable dominance of administrative lawmaking. Given the growth of the nation, an expanded range of public problems and policy issues, and an increase in polarization and gridlock, legislators' policy appeals to agencies—which now comprise the majority of law—serve as a channel for maintaining democratic norms.

Conclusion

This book represents a significant departure from the prevailing framework on Congress, bureaucracy, and separation of powers. The growing influence and autonomy of the bureaucracy has been the focus of legal scholars and political scientists concerned about Congress's preservation of Article I powers. How does Congress rein in the bureaucracy? How does Congress maintain oversight over the executive branch?

Yet, separation of powers—commonly thought to serve as a constraint on the legislative branch—serves as a backdoor for lawmakers to skirt the collective authority of Congress. Legislators are not concerned with bureaucrats shirking the institutional authority of Congress and statutory obligations. Instead, they harness agency policymaking in order to evade the institutional authority of Congress themselves.

Members of Congress are incorporating agency policymaking into a broader strategy of policymaking that spans branches of government. Lawmakers use agency regulations as a substitute for legislative action, collaborate with agencies to delay and block the implementation of law until new legislation is passed, and obtain legislative language from agencies. This inter-branch strategy for policymaking is far hazier than the separation of powers described in the Constitution.

2

A Theory of Back-Channel Policymaking

Congressional candidates make big promises on the campaign trail. Once elected, however, legislators are limited in their opportunities to advance their priorities in Congress. Even the most tenacious lawmakers confront bicameralism, partisan gridlock, gatekeeping by committees, chamber procedures and norms, leadership's control of the agenda, and 534 other members of Congress, all with their own priorities and interests. Moreover, legislators must represent diverse constituencies with conflicting positions on a wide range of issues. What strategies do lawmakers have for navigating these challenges?

Even casual observers of Congress know how legislators use logrolling and legislative procedures to overcome obstructions or to obstruct the policies of their colleagues.[1] Yet, our knowledge is largely confined to tactics used within the halls of Congress. We know less about how these strategies extend across branches of government.[2] Do members of Congress strategically use external institutions to advance their policy agendas, and, if so, how?

The central argument of this book is straightforward: Legislators do not limit themselves to the legislative process. When legislators confront obstacles in Congress, they shift to the federal bureaucracy as an alternative venue for policymaking. For the reasons I explain in this chapter, the bureaucracy is often a more promising venue for lawmakers.

Statutory policymaking, where Congress initiates a policy change from the status quo through legislation, is not the only way to make policy. Alternatively, agencies have been delegated authority from Congress, which allows them to establish policy changes unilaterally.[3] Of course, agency action is subject to correction by the court or Congress, but agencies are at times able to take actions that would not pass statutory thresholds but that neither the court nor Congress would—or could—overturn. Moreover, once policy changes are established, it becomes more difficult to reverse them using administrative action.[4] Consider, for example, DHS guidance (predating Obama's executive order) that protects childhood arrivals to the US and Justice Department policies deferring to state cannabis laws. While neither

Backdoor Lawmaking: Evading Obstacles in the US Congress. Melinda N. Ritchie, Oxford University Press.
© Melinda N. Ritchie 2023. DOI: 10.1093/oso/9780197670491.003.0002

the Dream Act nor the decriminalization of marijuana could have passed Congress at the time, agencies were able to establish policies with similar objectives.[5] Previous research has focused on how agency autonomy stymies congressional control of the bureaucracy but has neglected to consider how lawmakers use agency discretion to evade the institutions and procedures of Congress themselves.

The federal bureaucracy's extensive authority over policy provides opportunities for individual lawmakers to influence policy outside of the legislative process. The bureaucracy offers several advantages: First, agency policymaking does not require the prior approval of Congress. Second, agency policymaking is discreet and often evades the scrutiny of the public, interest groups, Congress, and even the president. Third, agencies have reason to be responsive to legislators. Under conditions that limit legislators' efforts in Congress, the bureaucracy is the more favorable venue for lawmakers to pursue policy objectives.

The purpose of this chapter is to develop a theory of back-channel policymaking. This theory explains why members of Congress engage with the bureaucracy on matters of policy, how these back-channel interactions allow legislators to evade constraints in Congress and within their constituencies, and when lawmakers are most effective at taking advantage of agency policymaking. This theoretical framework offers specific predictions about variations in legislator and agency behavior that I will test in the empirical chapters to follow.

Conventional Wisdom about Policymaking

The prevailing view among the public portrays policymaking as existing within the chambers of Congress. Journalists and congressional scholars focus most of their attention on lawmakers' participation during formal proceedings on the floors of the House and Senate. Pundits debate upcoming votes, and scholars study what makes legislators effective at advancing their bills through the legislative process. Indeed, the congressional literature on policymaking has been traditionally dominated by work on roll-call votes. This focus on the legislative process is appropriate as legislation continues to be the primary vehicle for passing important and consequential laws such as the Affordable Care Act (ACA), the USA PATRIOT Act, and the First Steps Act. However, around the same time that these laws were enacted, important administrative law—including requirements to reduce copper and lead in drinking water;[6] a regulation protecting miners from noise-induced hearing loss;[7] and the contraception mandate, which is often mistakenly assumed to be in the text of the ACA—went into effect.[8] The inattention to how legislators influence policy outside of the chambers of Congress is not in keeping with how policymaking has changed over the past several decades.

Today, policy is made mostly through agency regulations rather than through congressional statute (e.g., Eskridge and Ferejohn 1992; Warren 2011). Agencies have substantial influence over policy due to the growth in society, the expansion of the federal government, and the discretion granted to them by Congress. While Congress benefits from delegating to the bureaucracy and the policy expertise of agencies (Bawn 1995; Epstein and O'Halloran 1999; Huber and Shipan 2002), an important line of research considers Congress's struggle to maintain control over the bureaucracy through tools, such as committee oversight (Aberbach 1990; Dodd and Schott 1979; Hall and Miler 2008; McGrath 2013; Shipan 2004), agency design and administrative procedure (Balla 1998; McCubbins, Noll, and Weingast 1987, 1989), appropriations committee reports (Bolton 2022), limitation riders (MacDonald 2010), and federal advisory committees (Balla and Wright 2001). Yet, some scholars argue that the legislature remains limited in its ability to control bureaucratic drift and that agencies have developed their own strategies for evading the scrutiny of Congress (e.g., Potter 2019).

While the bureaucracy's expansion subverts Congress's institutional authority, individual legislators exploit the bureaucracy's discretion to pursue policy goals of their own. As discussed in Chapter 1, the traditional framework assumes the relationship between Congress and the bureaucracy is driven by the institutional or collective intent of Congress. This perspective characterizes inter-branch interactions as congressional oversight— Congress correcting agencies that have violated legislative intent. In other words, Congress passes a bill, the president signs the bill, and Congress works to ensure that the bureaucracy implements that law as intended. In contrast, my theoretical framework asserts that legislators use the bureaucracy's influence over policy to pursue individualistic policy goals apart from the intent of Congress and party.[9] Rather than enforcing bureaucrats' adherence to Congress, legislators exploit agency policymaking to evade the institutional authority of Congress themselves.

That is not to say that lawmakers' policy requests to the bureaucracy always conflict with the presumptive intent of Congress. Legislators often contact agencies to ensure they are implementing laws properly and efficiently. However, while a legislator may intervene to ensure that an agency is implementing her bill as she intended, she might also ask that the agency forgo implementing sections of her colleague's bill. In other words, when a legislator contacts the bureaucracy to ensure a law is being implemented, it is not motivated by a general concern for congressional oversight, but by a desire to see that his bill—which he wrote, cosponsored, and worked on in his committee—is implemented. The Dodd-Frank Act, for instance, provoked intervention from legislators—some demanding it be strengthened and others that it be weakened—during its implementation.[10] Legislators pressuring agencies to take diametrically opposed courses of action cannot all be pursuing a singular legislative intent. As Hall (1996) described the motivation of legislators' participation, "Individuals act to pursue their interests, not promote the functioning of the group" (56). In short, legislator interactions with the bureaucracy are tied to their own policy goals rather than conventional depictions of oversight.

I argue that this behavior is motivated by the same general goals that guide participation in Congress, such as voting, committee work, and introducing and cosponsoring bills.[11] For example, when a member of Congress has demonstrated her policy interests through her legislative activities, it should guide her interactions with the bureaucracy. However, back-channel policymaking differs from previously studied channels of policy influence in important and strategic ways that predict how frequently and under what circumstances legislators choose the bureaucracy as a policymaking venue.

Why the Bureaucracy?

My general argument underlying why members of Congress make policy appeals to the bureaucracy is simple: They are constrained from accomplishing their policy goals within the formal lawmaking process. If members of Congress were always able to accomplish their policy goals via the legislative process, we would not expect them to make policy appeals to the bureaucracy to any meaningful degree. All legislators face constraints in Congress. However, legislative obstacles and the tools lawmakers have to overcome them can vary based on the legislator's status in Congress and her constituency. Opportunities for influencing policy through the executive branch may be particularly important for legislators who are the most constrained from influencing policy and representing their constituencies within the legislative process.

To understand the motivation behind back-channel policymaking, it is important first to recognize the bounds of legislators' influence within Congress. While members of Congress have several legislative tools they can choose from to participate in policymaking, the lawmaking process is riddled with obstacles that can prevent them from advancing their policy preferences and representing their constituencies. Lawmakers participate in the legislative process by voting (e.g., Kingdon 1973; Miller and Stokes 1963; Poole and Rosenthal 1991), introducing and cosponsoring bills (e.g., Koger 2003; Sulkin 2005, 2011), and working within their committees (e.g., Hall 1996). Despite these outlets for participation, individual legislators' influence within the lawmaking process is limited.

I propose two ways that constraints in Congress motivate lawmakers to shift to the bureaucracy as an alternative policymaking venue. The first is driven by obstacles to accomplishing policy objectives within the legislative process. When lawmakers face institutional barriers to legislative action, they turn to the bureaucracy, particularly if it is a more promising venue for their policy objectives. For example, if a legislator is in the minority in her chamber but shares a party affiliation with the administration, agency policymaking could be a more worthwhile option.[12] The second pathway is motivated by a desire to evade the visibility of the legislative process. Members of Congress exploit the obscurity of administrative policymaking to represent interests that are costly for them to represent publicly.[13]

In the following section, I develop my theory by focusing on these two types of constraints and generate hypotheses that I test in subsequent chapters. Then, in the remainder of this chapter, I offer theoretical expectations for how agencies respond to legislators' policy requests. In short, it comes down to constraints, capacity, and opportunity.

A Theory of Legislative Constraints

It was 1977 when Fenno identified the campaign strategy of "running against Congress," and yet the promise of going to Washington to make changes is still a staple of election challengers (although, ironically, also of some incumbents) (Fenno 1977, 194). But what capacity does a legislator have to make changes in Congress? Considering the concern among the media, the public, and academics over gridlock and polarization, how capable is the average legislator at influencing policy within the legislative body?

One answer is, not very. Research suggests that members of Congress are limited in their ability to influence policy. When a legislator introduces a bill, it has only about a 3% chance of becoming law (Anderson, Box-Steffensmeier, and Sinclair-Chapman 2003; Casas, Denny, and Wilkerson 2020; Volden and Wiseman 2014). Most bills die in committee and never even see a floor vote.

As Mayhew points out, to the question: " 'But what bills has he passed?' There is no unembarrassing answer" (Mayhew 1974, 60). Despite introducing about a dozen bills every Congress, the average House member sees none of her bills become law during a term. Setting aside ceremonial bills often used to rename post offices, only a quarter of House members introduce legislation that becomes law during a session. In fact, most House members struggle to get one bill of substance passed within their own chamber. Even powerful, well-resourced senators are hard-pressed to advance a single bill to statute, with a majority of senators failing to get a bill of substance into law and only managing to advance one or two bills past the Senate floor. Lawmakers may be able to advance bills by "hitchhiking" them onto omnibus legislation, but successful hitchhiker bills are also rare, becoming statute at about the same rate as stand-alone legislation (Casas, Denny, and Wilkerson 2020). Even savvy members of Congress are stymied by the many veto points of the legislative obstacle course.

Of course, the most direct way lawmakers influence policy is by voting on legislation. Yet, legislators generally do not have much say over what they are voting on and often are not even given enough time to read the legislation before they vote on it (Curry 2015). Moreover, lawmakers have an alarmingly high rate of absenteeism. In 2019, absenteeism rates for some House members included over a third of all votes. Senator Cory Booker (D-NJ) set a Senate record by missing about 65% of votes in 2019 (with Senator Bernie Sanders (I-VT) a close second with 63% missed votes).[14] Of course, absenteeism tends to be higher for presidential candidates like Booker and Sanders. Leading up to the 2016 election, Senator Marco Rubio (R-FL) missed about a third of votes while he was campaigning in 2015.[15] With the exception of presidential candidates and lawmakers with reported health issues, the highest absentee rates are roughly around 10% to 20%.[16]

Given that a legislator's vote in Congress is her only policymaking power recognized in the Constitution, these high absentee rates are puzzling.

Legislators can try to work through their committees, but there are considerable limits for committee members. When studying the Foreign Affairs Committee, Fenno concludes that "... in proportion to members' desires and expectations, their opportunities to contribute to the making of foreign policy are small. The resulting disappointment and frustration tend to drive down the rates of internal participation" and that Foreign Affairs Committee members "function largely as consumers of the executive branch information" (Fenno 1973, 188). Even membership on the Appropriations Committee does not seem to offer control over policy, as suggested by a member of the powerful committee, who told Fenno, "Appropriations is a dog's life. You don't have any influence over policy" (144). In his study of post-reform House committees, Hall (1996) offers a less dire account, concluding that legislators who do participate in their committees and subcommittees have influence, but his empirical findings show low levels of participation overall. He finds that committee participation tends to be low both in terms of attendance and committee and subcommittee voting (34–35). Likewise, informal, behind-the-scenes participation is not widespread, with most legislators playing a negligible role (43).

What stops legislators from playing a role in policymaking? Scholars and the media alike have focused on divided government, polarization, and partisanship, and how these factors might decrease Congress's productivity. Indeed, there has been a steep decline in the number of laws enacted by Congress since the 1970s (Taylor 2013, 71; and see Casas, Denny, and Wilkerson 2020). Mayhew's landmark book (Mayhew, 1991) overturned conventional wisdom by concluding that divided government has little effect on legislative productivity and led to a flood of research debating the impact of divided party control (e.g., Binder 1999, 2003; Howell et al. 2000) and polarization (e.g., Binder 1999, 2003; Jones 2001; Lapinski 2008) on gridlock. However, the public's blame of partisan conflict firmly persists, sustained by events such as the fiscal cliff crisis in January of 2013 and increasingly frequent government shutdowns. News stories about polarization in Congress have increased (Levendusky 2009) with the media overwhelmingly focused on partisan conflict. In 2012, Thomas Friedman wrote in his *New York Times* column that, due to polarization, The United States has "gone from a democracy to a 'vetocracy'—from a system designed to prevent anyone in government from amassing too much power to a system in which no one can aggregate enough power to make any important decisions at all."[17]

But while the media have propagated the notion of gridlock due to partisanship and polarization; congressional scholars have pointed out that there are also a myriad of more elusive, persistent constraints stymieing members of Congress from participating and influencing policy. Both formal and informal constraints intervene through the many choke points within the legislative process. Critically, the constraints of lawmaking affect some lawmakers more than others, leading to the unequal distribution of power in Congress.

The Formal and Informal Constraints of Congress

Earlier work considered whether the informal norms of Capitol Hill limit participation in Congress. For example, lawmakers defer to committee and subcommittee members and do not encroach on committee work when they are not members. As one of Fenno's respondents explained, "It's frowned upon if you offer an amendment in the full committee when you aren't a member of the subcommittee" (Fenno 1973, 95). While there are organizational advantages to such norms (i.e., specialization), this deference keeps legislators from advancing their policy preferences within the committee system. Norms of apprenticeship limit legislators' participation in policymaking and are "very real and confining." A freshman senator "is expected to keep his mouth shut, not to take the lead in floor fights, to listen and learn" (Matthews 1960, 94–95). While more recent work indicates that freshmen legislators' influence has increased in the decades since Matthews and Fenno conducted their studies (e.g., Sinclair 1986, 1989), it is hard to imagine a new legislator accomplishing any policy goals given other limiting factors.

Limitations on junior legislators, for instance, have also been attributed to information and transaction costs (Curry 2015; Hall 1996). All members of Congress have limited time and resources, but some have more resources than others. Participation in policymaking requires information, policy expertise, and "political intelligence" as well as other resources including staff (Hall 1996, 91). Legislators must have the background knowledge, the political savvy, and the staff to pursue their policy goals. Hall points to these constraints as the cause behind the inactivity of freshmen and new committee members. For some members of Congress, these requirements prohibit their involvement in committee and other legislative action.

Legislative institutions and procedures also impede lawmakers' efforts and lead to disproportionate influence across Congress. Congressional leadership wields its authority to control the process, further limiting the rank-and-file's influence. Within committees, rank-and-file members are generally not deeply involved in policymaking, and while the chair may try to accommodate individual members, "ultimately, it is about satisfying the chair rather than figuring out what the rank and file want" (Curry 2015, 56). While the leadership cannot prevent legislators from introducing and cosponsoring bills, it can constrain their bills from coming to the chamber floor for a vote. In fact, leadership has been in the practice of drafting its own legislation behind closed doors for some time (Curry 2015).[18] Leadership's control of the process makes being a member of Congress feel "more like being a powerless cog in a sputtering machine" (Drutman 2018).

Legislators have control over how they vote, but congressional leadership controls the rules of the game. When members of Congress decide how to vote, they are limited to dichotomous choices structured by leadership, at times along extreme partisan lines. Leadership decides what they vote on (e.g., Aldrich 1995; Cox and McCubbins 1993, 2005; Harbridge 2015; Rohde 1991) and what information the rank-and-file have about legislation prior to the vote (Curry 2015). Leadership is also known to attach entire bills onto other omnibus legislation, leading legislators to vote for policies they would not have favored as stand-alone bills.

By preventing legislators from offering amendments, leadership stifles the rank-and-file's capacity to propose modifications to legislation on the chamber floor.[19] These limitations on individual lawmakers span both chambers of Congress and are on the rise. The Rules Committee, under the tight grip of House leadership, increasingly issues closed rules, which do not allow for amendments. The 114th Congress (2015–2016) was the last time an open rule was issued, and nearly half of rules were closed to all amendments in recent congresses (Wolfensberger 2018).[20] Even in the supposedly individualistic Senate, what are referred to as majoritarian exceptions, such as using budget reconciliation to avoid the filibuster, have diminished the power of the individual senator and bolstered majority party control (Reynolds 2017).

In short, congressional leaders define the terms of legislative deals, while rank-and-file lawmakers are limited to voting up-or-down on a slate of bills that have been arranged by leaders. Lee Drutman summarized the dismal state of the lawmaker:

> Now everything moves through party leadership, which is increasingly writing bills on its own, cutting out committees, and giving rank-and-file members no opportunity for input. Most members are kept in the dark until the last minute and then forced to vote on legislation they had no role in crafting, with no opportunity to even look at it until right before the votes.

As a result, "individual members are now primarily interchangeable parts in a series of party-line votes" (Drutman 2018).

The Constraints of the Public Record

While the obstacles I have described thus far constrain legislators from advancing policies, lawmakers are also limited by the public nature of the legislative arena. The spotlight on many policymaking activities, including roll-call votes, bill introductions, and cosponsorships, can be costly for members of Congress because they do not have control over the visibility of their participation. Visibility within the context of Congress is defined by the "ease with which an outside actor (e.g., an interest group, an electoral constituency) can determine that a member voted against its interests" and is particularly costly for legislators who are pulled in different directions (Covington 1987, 49). Research suggests, for instance, that legislators are extremely concerned with the electoral consequences of voting (Arnold 1990; Mayhew 1974; Fiorina 1974; Jacobson 1987; Kingdon 1973). Legislators try to avoid "wrong votes" (Arnold 1990; Kingdon 1973) or votes that conflict with their "home style" (Fenno 1978). The cost of visibility also applies to bill introductions, which can draw opposition from constituents, organized interests, and other legislators. Moreover, a "campaign opponent or an interest group can point to a senator's bill as easily as they can point to a roll-call vote" (Schiller 1995, 189). Information about how a legislator votes and the bills she sponsors is readily available to the media, party leaders, other legislators, voters, and election challengers who can use the legislator's activities against her in a future campaign.

The spotlight on Congress is particularly challenging for roll-call voting decisions because legislators are forced to take a position without room for ambiguity and without control over issue selection. Each roll-call vote presents a dichotomous choice offering "only two sides—yea or nay—so a representative cannot be all things to all people" (Arnold 2004, 92). Voters sometimes punish legislators who vote with their party (Ansolabehere, Snyder, and Stewart 2001; Canes-Wrone, Brady, and Cogan 2002), particularly on divisive issues (Carson et al. 2010). But some scholars (e.g., Aldrich 1995; Cox and McCubbins 1993; Rohde 1991) argue that voting with one's party can offer benefits in the long run. Thus, legislators are presented with a trade-off when voting.

This point identifies the limit of roll-call votes in particular. Voting is one way of representing a constituency, and it is often not ideal for legislators who seek to represent diverging interests within their districts and states. Legislators must make a dichotomous decision, and the choices have been limited, at times along extreme partisan lines.

The conflict between party affiliation and constituency interest is further complicated by subgroups within a constituency. A constituency is not homogeneous, and legislators do not perceive it as a uniform entity (Fenno 1977, 1978). Subgroups of constituencies can influence a legislator's decisions depending on the issue in question (Arnold 1990; Fiorina 1974; Kingdon 1973; Bishin 2009) or the party affiliation of the legislator and subconstituency (Bishin 2000). Constituencies contain numerous, often diverging, interests. Even when a legislator votes the preference of the majority of his constituents, there are subgroups that are not represented by his vote. Conflicting subgroups within a constituency may lead legislators to act strategically by representing various parts of the constituency in different ways (Bishin 2009).

Some scholars argue that members of Congress make strategic decisions based on the visibility of various outlets of participation. Research suggests, for instance, that the risks associated with widespread visibility can influence legislators' decisions about cosponsorship. Legislators are less inclined to cosponsor bills involving contentious policy issues when there is a good chance the various segments of their constituencies will find out about it (Koger 2003). In short, legislators avoid public legislative action when representing interests that are costly for them to represent publicly.

In fact, several scholars have produced evidence that the costs of visibility lead members of Congress to pursue less visible strategies when they face cross-pressures. For example, cross-pressured legislators delay and avoid public position-taking (Box-Steffensmeier, Arnold, and Zorn 1997; Cohen and Noll 1991; Glazer et al. 1995). Cross-pressured majority party members also avoid signing discharge petitions on legislation they cosponsored, an indication of support for party leadership (Miller and Overby 2010). Conflicted members of the president's party have higher rates of absenteeism than consonantly pressured members on votes that are important to the president, and they strategically use less visible procedures (e.g., interim motions) to show support for the president's policies (Covington 1987). Other work finds that legislators respond to redistricting by adjusting their positions on votes that are visible to their new constituencies but continue to toe the party line on less visible, procedural votes that allow the party to control the agenda (Crespin 2010). This literature consistently finds that cross-pressured legislators strategically exploit less visible channels to satisfy competing principals.

The Advantages of Back-Channel Policymaking

The constraints of the legislative process highlight the advantages of agency policymaking. First, agency policymaking does not require authorization by Congress. Congress's delegation of authority to the bureaucracy allows agencies to make the first move and establish policy changes unilaterally (Ferejohn and Shipan 1990). These policy changes are, of course, subject to legislative and judiciary correction. Congress can reverse agency action, but collective action problems in Congress make legislative action difficult. The courts can determine agency actions are inconsistent with the law.[21] However, judiciary correction requires that an agency action be brought to the court's attention. Moreover, in *Chevron v. Natural Resources Defense Council* (1984) ("Chevron"), the Supreme Court ruled that the courts should give wide deference to agencies, and courts applying Chevron often side with agencies—what is commonly referred to as "Chevron deference" (Eskridge and Ferejohn 1992; Hume 2009; see Potter 2019, 28, also see Wiseman and Wright 2020).[22] This autonomy could make agency policymaking more promising grounds for advancing a lawmaker's interests than the legislative process, particularly if the legislator's objective does not clash with the agency's or the administration's priorities.[23]

While the courts have occasionally found political pressure from members of Congress to be inappropriate,[24] the judicial treatment of legislators' informal communications with agencies is hazy, and it is not clear that agencies or members of Congress adhere to court guidance. While members of Congress may communicate their policy preferences to agencies when there are no pending proceedings and as part of public rulemaking proceedings, it is less clear whether off-the-record communications are allowed once formal proceedings are underway. Based on DC Circuit Court rulings in the leading cases on ex parte communications, the court's reasoning recognizes the inevitability of congressional pressure on agencies and that legislators' communications with agencies are a reasonable and necessary aspect of their duties as representatives. However, the court has delineated limits for the content of such communications and how they should be treated. Communications from members of Congress should be confined to the merits of the issue and should not threaten retaliation.[25] In addition, agencies must record such communications in the public record. In a leading case on ex parte contacts during rulemaking that involved meetings between Senator Robert Byrd and the EPA, the court summarized its reasoning:

> We believe it entirely proper for Congressional representatives vigorously to represent the interests of their constituents before administrative agencies engaged in informal, general policy rulemaking, so long as individual Congressmen do not frustrate the intent of Congress as a whole as expressed in statute, nor undermine applicable rules of procedure. Where Congressmen keep their comments focused on the substance of the proposed rule ... administrative agencies are expected to balance Congressional pressure with the pressures emanating from all other sources. To hold otherwise would deprive the agencies of legitimate sources of information and call into question the validity of nearly every controversial rulemaking.[26]

Although the court's reasoning may support democratic norms while recognizing the inevitable dominance of administrative law, it raises some concerning implications. In short, the court's "reasoning recognizes that congressional pressure on agencies is ubiquitous, but its expectation that agencies will be able to balance congressional pressure against pressure from other sources may be somewhat unrealistic" (Beermann 2006, 50). Some legal scholars have argued that allowing "members of Congress the freedom to 'vigorously' press the interests of their constituents in private meetings with agency personnel provides those members with a powerful tool for shaping agency action to their preferences" (Beermann 2006, 50). By allowing these informal communications but overlooking the inevitable political pressure and implicit retaliatory threats, the court may, in fact, give license to back-channel policymaking.

Second, while lawmakers' actions in Congress are under a microscope, agency policymaking—and legislators' direct appeals to agencies—avoid public scrutiny. How lawmakers vote, the bills they sponsor, and what they say on the chamber floor and in committee hearings is covered by the press, included in public record, and often even televised. Voting and bill sponsorship records are easily accessible online, and there are unlimited journalistic interpretations of legislators' actions in the media.

However, the direct contact lawmakers have with agencies is not readily public. Obtaining the records and information for this research required dozens of Freedom of Information Act (FOIA) requests, a persistent back-and-forth with FOIA officials, requests for fee waivers, appeals after agencies denied requested fee waivers, and, in many cases, waiting several months to receive the records. Even then, this onerous process produces thousands of pages of documents that require careful examination. As I discuss in Chapter 3, some members of both parties of Congress are now even trying to block agencies from releasing their communication records.

Adding to the secrecy, agency policymaking involves opaque processes that are not widely covered in the press. In fact, scholars find that there is widespread ignorance and unawareness of agency policymaking and that "even lawyers and people who work for the federal government tend not to understand the rulemaking process unless they have been personally involved in some way" (Farina et al. 2011, 9).[27] Obfuscating within an often impenetrable process, bureaucrats strategically use procedures to avoid the attention of the public and even Congress and the president, allowing them to restrict participation and scrutiny (Potter 2019).

This lack of transparency creates the ideal backchannel for lawmakers seeking to influence policy quietly. Members of Congress may choose to publicize their efforts to influence agencies, but they have much more control over dissemination. Legislators can submit press releases about their contact with agencies to all the media outlets on their distribution list or use social media to publicize it widely. Alternatively, members of Congress may want to publicize their involvement with agency policymaking more narrowly by emailing their supporters or the beneficiaries, reaching out to an interest group or industry newsletter, or making a speech to an organization. They may even decide to remain silent about their activity altogether and wait to see if the issue is raised during the next election (or try to keep their activity quiet until after an election).

I am not arguing that the public could never be made aware of these inter-branch communications. Of course, legislators are known to publicize their communications with agencies themselves when it suits their interests. It is also possible that opposition groups or investigative journalists (not to mention, political scientists) could obtain and publicize a legislator's letter or email to an agency. In Chapter 3, I describe instances when members of Congress clearly did not intend for their contact with agencies to become public.

Rather, I am arguing that back-channel communication is a more discreet means for representation because it is less accessible and more costly to publicize without the consent of the legislator. Lawmakers have more control over the visibility of their communication with agencies in comparison to other policymaking activities. As scholars of political communication have pointed out, members of Congress choose among the variety of communication tools and media available to them based, in part, on the legislator's ability to control the message and a targeted audience (Russell 2021, 60–1). Newsletters and speeches, for instance, allow a legislator to have control over the message and a targeted audience while television appearances are more likely to reach a broad audience but require the lawmaker cede control.[28]

Part of what makes back-channel policymaking quiet is not simply the accessibility or control over dissemination, but the obscurity and inscrutability of the processes and content of administrative policymaking. Opposition groups and newspapers have limited capacity and incentive to track and examine hundreds of thousands of communication records across agencies and translate administrative regulation and procedure into language that the average citizen will understand. It is less costly and more efficient for them to focus on the public activities and positions of legislators.

For comparison, we also see members of Congress representing divisive interests on procedural roll-call votes. Procedural roll-call votes are public and can also be used by newspapers and opposition groups. Yet, we still observe legislators using procedural votes as a quieter way of representing controversial interests that are less favored within their constituencies (Crespin 2010). Like back-channel policymaking, procedural votes are useful as a quieter means of representation—though they are even more public than inter-branch communications—because the processes are more complicated and less comprehensible by the general public and more difficult to use in an attack ad.

Finally, agencies have an incentive to be responsive to lawmakers. Agencies are motivated to be responsive to lawmakers' requests as a way of building good will and accruing allies in Congress to support the agency's interests, including support for the agency's budget, programs, and legislative priorities (Carpenter 2001; Ritchie and You 2019). Of course, agency policymaking is not without limits. Legislators' informal appeals to agencies are not legally binding and have no formal authority. Instead, these appeals serve as signals of a legislator's preferences and preference intensity. In other words, these appeals indicate what a lawmaker wants and how motivated she is to pursue the issue further if the agency does not comply. The impact of these appeals depends on the credible threat that the agency will incur costs for noncompliance or benefits for responsiveness.

These costs of noncompliance may result from formal or informal action by the legislator. Members of Congress can initiate demanding oversight including requiring agency heads to testify in committee hearings. If lawmakers are unable to achieve their objectives through agency policymaking, they may resort to legislative action that would compel the agency to comply with the legislator's preference. As mentioned earlier, such legislation is unlikely to pass, but agencies are very risk-averse and would prefer to comply with a legislator's request voluntarily rather than face the prospect of new legislation. New legislation raises the risk of demanding statutory obligations from the agency if it passes or, even if it does not pass, could draw public attention and scrutiny to the issue. In fact, lawmakers do not need to evoke formal authority to retaliate against an agency. Legislators can use their authority and notoriety as members of Congress to draw public ire and scrutiny to the agency by attacking it, or the administration, in the press. Agencies have an incentive to avoid negative press attention, which can lead an agency head to lose his job and damage his reputation (e.g., FEMA Administer Michael Brown) (Lewis 2008, and see Carpenter 2001, 2010). Reputational costs for an agency often translate into reputational costs for the president as well. Consider, for example, the negative press attention

President George W. Bush received after criticism of FEMA's response to Hurricane Katrina.

Of course, agencies face pressures from multiple directions or principals, including organized interests (Carpenter and Krause 2012). Organized interests are often well-resourced and savvy lobbyists of agencies, but we know from recent research that interest groups lobby members of Congress, not only to influence legislation, but because of the influence legislators have over agencies. In fact, over 50% of lobbying following a bill's passage targets members of Congress, not agencies (You 2017). This statistic suggests that organized interests allocate substantial resources to lobby Congress to influence the implementation of legislation. Indeed, the records I use in this book show that industries are sometimes behind the appeals legislators make to agencies. For example, during the Obama administration, the US Department of Labor began an initiative to crack down on hospitality employers for violations of unfair labor practices. My records show that several members of Congress from both sides of the aisle contacted Labor Secretary Hilda Solis to urge her to stop the initiative at the request of the hotel and hospitality industry.[29] In short, organized interests often enlist legislators to lobby agencies on their behalf.[30]

Why would organized interests ask legislators to lobby agencies on their behalf when they are capable of lobbying agencies themselves? Despite the expertise and resources organized interests have to influence agencies, legislators wield leverage over agencies that organized interests do not. First, unlike organized interests, legislators' informal requests to agencies are tied to formal threats of retaliatory action including oversight, and budgetary and statutory authority that can be used to reorganize an agency or cut programs. Second, although individual legislators—or even a substantial group of lawmakers—do not have legal authority absent statutory thresholds, individual legislators' preferences offer the pretense of legal authority that organized interests do not. Empirical work (Ban and You 2019) showing that the Securities and Exchange Commission cited comments from members of Congress more than other organizations in the final rules for the Dodd-Frank Act offer support for this argument.

Needless to say, the president and presidential appointees play an important role. It is more challenging for an agency to comply with legislators' requests if they conflict with the priorities of the agency's other principal, the president. Moreover, while agencies have preferences of their own (Carpenter 2001), the presidential appointees who populate agencies may also want to help co-partisans or like-minded legislators (Bertelli and Grose 2009). On the other hand, appointees have an incentive to avoid angering lawmakers who already have reason and the capacity to punish the administration, such as senators who could hold up confirmation hearings in retaliation.[31]

Moreover, as "Congress is a 'they' and not an 'it,'" the same applies to agencies. Communications from members of Congress can be used by agency officials to persuade their colleagues during the course of decision-making. Agency decisions are generally not made by a single individual but are collaborative efforts of teams within the agency. Disagreements among the many players involved in an agency decision are the result of a diverse range of preferences, areas of expertise, professional roles and objectives, and personal incentives (Carpenter 2010, 2001; Carpenter and Krause 2012; Quirk 2014). Agency officials do not always agree with one another on the best course of action. There are often differences of opinion among bureaucrats about what action to take or how fast to act. Bureaucrats look for indicators to use to pressure their colleagues at the agency to accept their positions.[32] Policy appeals from members of Congress provide a signal that there is some political support for an action—whether a change in policy or even a pause in enforcement—which can be used as leverage within an agency's internal debates.[33]

Despite the advantages that agency policymaking offers lawmakers, working though the bureaucracy is not costless for legislators. Just as some legislators are more limited than others in Congress, not all lawmakers have the capacity to take advantage of agency policymaking.

The Limits of Back-Channel Policymaking

In the previous section, I focused on the constraints of legislative action and the advantages of working through the bureaucracy. However, there are also limitations to and costs for back-channel policymaking. While legislative constraints motivate members of Congress to reach out to the bureaucracy with their policy concerns, not all legislators have the capacity to take advantage of this alternative approach to influencing policy. This second consideration in my theory of back-channel policymaking distinguishes between what motivates back-channel policymaking from what facilitates it. Are some legislators more capable of getting what they want from the bureaucracy?

I break this question down into two stages. First, has the legislator contacted the agency? Legislators cannot successfully influence policy through the bureaucracy if they do not first contact an agency. Second, once a legislator contacts an agency, how successful are they at achieving policy change through the bureaucracy? These two stages are intertwined. As such, it is important to consider what factors facilitate both stages of back-channel policymaking. Before considering which legislators are most successful at influencing policy via the bureaucracy, we must know which legislators actually reach out to the bureaucracy with their policy concerns. Knowing which legislators try to use back-channel policymaking can also lend insight into which ones are successful at it.

Like participation within Congress, back-channel policymaking is facilitated by information and policy expertise, political intelligence, and resources. These factors can affect both a legislator's ability to communicate with the bureaucracy about a policy request as well as the likelihood that the agency will respond favorably to her request. For example, a member of Congress must have some knowledge about the policy area in order to make a credible request. Moreover, while introducing or cosponsoring a bill is an obvious way to pursue a policy goal, some legislators might not even recognize communicating with the bureaucracy as an option or know which agency to contact. Likewise, legislators' networks may facilitate inter-branch communication. Lawmakers are more likely to reach out to an agency if they have a personal relationship with the agency head or have sat across from her in committee hearings over the years. A learning process also likely plays a role; legislators increasingly employ the backchannel as they learn that it is an option. Of course, any policymaking activity requires time and resources, and a large staff that can collect information, recognize instances in which back-channel policymaking could be a strategic option, and contact and keep up with an agency would clearly facilitate participation.

Lawmakers' perceptions of whether their efforts in the bureaucratic venue would be successful may also factor into deciding whether to expend limited time and resources to become involved in agency policymaking. If, for example, the agency's mission or the administration's agenda conflicts with the legislator's objective, she may decide it is not worthwhile to pursue it through agency policymaking. In short, while constraints in Congress may motivate lawmakers to seek alternative ways to pursue their objectives, they may decide the bureaucratic venue is not promising either. Thus, much like interest group lobbying, members of Congress are more likely to work through the bureaucracy of a "friendly" administration that shares their party affiliation or interests. A legislator's perception of her likelihood of success may not be an accurate reflection of how agencies respond to lawmakers, but it is likely to affect the lawmaker's decision to initiate contact.

How do agencies decide how to respond to legislators' policy appeals? Do agencies favor some lawmakers over others? Do some lawmakers have advantages that shoot them to the top of an agency's priority list? Recent research suggests that, given unlimited resources, agencies try to be responsive to all members of Congress because any legislator could make life difficult for an agency (Ritchie and You 2019). But some lawmakers have outsized influence over an agency's fortunes, giving agencies the incentive to prioritize some legislators over others.

In this way, the formal power of lawmakers within the legislative arena can translate into informal influence with the bureaucracy. Agencies have strong incentives to respond favorably to a legislator's request if the legislator has the potential to repay the agency in the form of support for the agency's budget, programs, and other policies in the legislative arena. A legislator's capacity to reciprocate is tied to her status and position in the legislative process. A legislator who has limited influence within the legislative process is unlikely to be able to reciprocate in comparison to a powerful member of Congress.

Indeed, previous research suggests that power in Congress translates into power with the bureaucracy. For example, agencies favor legislators with influence over their budgets and programs when geographically allocating funds (Arnold 1979). Agencies have been shown to privilege members of committees with jurisdiction or oversight (Arnold 1979; Bang and Hollibaugh 2022), key legislators required to build coalitions of support (Arnold 1979; Carpenter 2001), and members of the majority party (Kernell and McDonald 1999; Levitt and Snyder 1995). It seems, then, that lawmakers need influence in one venue to have influence in the other.

A Framework of Back-Channel Policymaking

The implications of this Catch-22 are important for questions of representation and power in Congress. If powerless lawmakers use the bureaucracy as a way of advancing policy despite obstacles in Congress, it could mitigate the unequal power distribution in Congress. However, it may be the case that already powerful members of Congress are using the bureaucratic backdoor to amass even more control over policy. In short, the rich get richer.

Thus, it is important that we consider what motivates back-channel policymaking in conjunction with what facilitates it. While the limitations of the legislative process motivate members of Congress to shift to agency policymaking, the lawmakers who are the most constrained from influencing policy in the legislative process may be the least capable of taking advantage of agency policymaking. Two distinct hypotheses can be derived from this theoretical discussion, one focusing on motivation and the other on capacity.

First, the *legislative constraint hypothesis* states that members of Congress make policy appeals to the bureaucracy when they face obstacles in the legislative process and need an alternative way to influence policy. In Chapter 6, I examine obstacles related to institutions and status that prevent legislators from influencing policy.

Although all members of Congress—even members of leadership—face constraints, not all legislators are equally capable of taking advantage of agency policymaking. While lawmakers facing legislative constraints might have the most need for an alternative way to influence policy, they may not have the resources to contact agencies or the power to influence them. The same limitations that constrain them in the lawmaking process might also prevent them from engaging with the bureaucracy. Instead, lawmakers who already have power within Congress may be the most capable of using the backchannel. I refer to the hypothesis that a legislator's policy appeals and success with the bureaucracy is dependent on her status and power in Congress as the *capacity hypothesis*. I consider this hypothesis by examining legislators' appeals to agencies in Chapter 6 and then how agencies respond to legislators' appeals in Chapter 8.

These first two hypotheses focus on the incentives and constraints of members of Congress, but agency incentives—and lawmakers' anticipation of agency incentives—factor into a legislator's decision about whether to make appeals to the bureaucracy as well. Even if lawmakers are stymied by obstacles in Congress, they may not want to expend limited resources by appealing to the bureaucracy if they think it is unlikely to be worthwhile. Building off the legislative constraint hypothesis, I consider the *bureaucratic advantage hypothesis* that legislators will make policy appeals to the bureaucracy when constrained in the legislative process *and* when they anticipate that the bureaucracy is a more promising venue for accomplishing their objectives. Lawmakers are unlikely to appeal to agencies if their requests are likely to be rejected because of a conflict with the administration's priorities. Critically, this hypothesis is in direct conflict with expectations derived from previous theories of oversight and assumptions that lawmakers are focused on reining in shirking agencies and hostile administrations.

Alternatively, legislators may be most likely to require an informal channel for recourse when their party is completely shut out of formal institutions of lawmaking. This may be particularly the case in the US House of Representatives where members are limited by short terms and a constant need to campaign. These limitations lead House members to work through the formal institutions of the chamber—primarily committees and party—and they are heavily dependent on their party's accomplishments, whether in Congress or the White House. If a House member's party is out of power, her last recourse is to push back against the actions of the party in power through informal channels. I identify this prediction as the *obstruction hypothesis*.

My theoretical discussion focused on two distinct types of constraints. The first type is defined by the obstacles that prevent lawmakers from accomplishing their policy objectives and is the focus of the legislative constraint hypothesis. The second type of constraint is defined by the limits of the visibility of the legislative process, which expose lawmakers to public scrutiny and attacks from election challengers. This argument derives the *constituency constraint hypothesis*: Members of Congress make policy appeals to the bureaucracy in order to represent interests that are costly to represent under the spotlight of the legislative process. I consider this hypothesis in Chapter 7 by examining if legislators choose the inconspicuous bureaucratic venue over the exposed legislative arena when representing issues related to contentious conflicts between the various interests a lawmaker is expected to represent.

Finally, when are policy appeals an effective way to influence policy? Legislators may think they have the advantage if they share interests with the administration, but is that actually the case? Agencies may have an easier time responding to the requests of co-partisans of the administration if there is less distance between their preferences. Yet, agencies may be more concerned with the administration's enemies than its friends. My theory suggests that agencies use a risk-averse strategy by prioritizing lawmakers who have both the capacity and motivation to retaliate against the agency. This *retaliation hypothesis* runs counter to assumptions and findings in previous work asserting that agencies reward co-partisans. Of course, whom an agency prioritizes may depend on who is making the decision at the agency. Appointees are likely to be focused on presidential interests, but career civil servants may be concerned with their own policy priorities in addition to the mission of the agency. Moreover, appointees are likely more cognizant of the political sensitivity of their interactions with lawmakers, particularly given that the appointees themselves are often the targets of lawmakers' retaliation. As one senator described, "Again, the solution was going to have to be made by going to the top. The head of the IRS was aghast at the short sightedness of the bureaucrats who had rejected [the senator's favored course of action]."[34] While I am not able to test these personnel differences, I explore them using qualitative accounts in Chapter 4.

Using a rational choice framework, I explain why and when members of Congress make back-channel policy appeals to agencies and how agencies respond to lawmakers' appeals. The testable empirical expectations derived from my theoretical discussion are summarized in Table 2.1.

Table 2.1 Summary of Hypotheses

Legislative constraint hypothesis	Members of Congress make policy appeals to the bureaucracy when they face obstacles in the legislative process and need an alternative way to influence policy.
Capacity hypothesis	The frequency and success of legislators' policy appeals is positively related to her resources, experience, expertise, and institutional position within Congress.
Bureaucratic advantage hypothesis	Members of Congress make policy appeals to the bureaucracy more frequently when they confront constraints in the legislative process and when they anticipate that the bureaucracy is a more promising venue for accomplishing their objectives.
Obstruction hypothesis	Members of Congress make policy appeals to the bureaucracy more frequently when their party is shut out of formal institutions of authority (e.g., Congress and the White House) and their only means of recourse is obstruction through informal channels.
Constituency constraint hypothesis	Members of Congress make policy appeals to the bureaucracy more frequently when they confront cross-pressures on an issue.
Retaliation hypothesis	Agencies prioritize members of Congress who have both the capacity and motivation to retaliate against the agency.

Conclusion

When then-California Attorney General Kamala Harris debated Congress-woman Loretta Sanchez during the campaign for the open Senate seat in California, the future Vice President attacked Rep. Sanchez for having only passed one bill during her tenure in the House of Representatives. "My opponent has passed one bill in her 20 years in Congress, and that was to rename a post office," Harris said from the debate stage. Sanchez responded, "It's pretty obvious to me that my opponent doesn't understand the Congress at all." While Rep. Sanchez lost the Senate race (as well as her House seat, which she gave up to run for the Senate), some observers said Harris's attack on her was misleading.[35] In fact, during her time on Capitol Hill, Senator Harris never passed even one bill into law. True, Harris only spent four years in the Senate before being sworn-in as vice president. Yet, given the track record of the average member of Congress, we can bet that her record may not have looked much different from Rep. Sanchez's if she had remained in Congress. In fact, Harris may have come to regret her attack on Rep. Sanchez had a challenger used it against her when defending her seat.[36]

Obstacles in the legislative process make failure far more common than success in Congress. Campaign challengers often point out how few (if any) bills the incumbent has passed, but it is unlikely the challenger would do much better if elected. The average legislator is not likely to see one of her bills pass even in her own chamber. Advancing policy in the legislative process is difficult. In short, it's harder than it looks.

Yet, members of Congress have demonstrated strategic capacity for evading constraints. Overcoming legislative hurdles often involves procedural maneuvers and backroom deals. In this chapter, I described how the bureaucracy offers savvy lawmakers a way to skirt legislative obstacles—and Congress altogether. Yet, while the bureaucratic venue has its advantages, it has limitations of its own. In subsequent chapters, I test the theory I have laid out about how members of Congress weigh the trade-offs of the legislative process versus the bureaucracy as alternative venues for advancing policy.

Before testing the hypotheses introduced in this chapter, I first describe the original records and data used for the analyses. In Chapter 3, I describe how I obtained the records using the Freedom of Information Act and how I categorize communications and measure policy appeals for the quantitative analyses in Chapters 5 through 8. Chapter 3 also provides initial descriptive statistics from the dataset to give context for the subsequent analyses. These statistics will provide the foundation for the central empirical analyses but are important findings in their own right: Despite their formal power as legislators, members of Congress regularly make policy appeals to a separate branch of government. Chapter 4 offers a qualitative depiction of the nature of the records and what they can tell us about inter-branch communication. The qualitative accounts of Chapter 4 shed light on back-channel appeals in ways that quantitative analyses cannot, offering a narrative about how lawmakers have used informal inter-branch communication to avoid scrutiny, substitute administrative tools for legislative action, and collaborate with bureaucrats as a component of a broader strategy to achieve a policy objective. These depictions are consistent with the analyses I provide in subsequent chapters but offer readers a bird's eye view of these interactions in the wild.

3

The Freedom of Information Act and the War against Transparency

> The Freedom of Information Act should be administered with a clear
> presumption: In the face of doubt, openness prevails. . . . All agencies
> should adopt a presumption in favor of disclosure, in order to renew
> their commitment to the principles embodied in FOIA, and to usher
> in a new era of open Government.[1]
>
> President Barack Obama
>
> [S]omething is desperately wrong with the process. It is either totally
> broken or requests are intentionally being ignored.[2]
>
> FOIA requester

In the politically tumultuous fall of 2017, a bipartisan group of House
members joined forces in a rare act of unity.[3] House leaders took legal action
to try to stop congressional records from being released under the Freedom
of Information Act, a law intended to promote government transparency and
accountability.[4] As described by House General Counsel, the often divided
House leaders "voted unanimously to authorize this intervention . . . to protect the institutional interests of the House."[5] The watchdog organization that
sued for the records characterized the vote differently: "In a rare moment of
bipartisanship, House leaders came together late on a Friday night to try to
block the American people from learning the truth. . . . [I]t speaks volumes
that Congress's first priority is to keep the public in the dark."[6]

What were the records the lawmakers tried to block from being released?
The House leaders tried to block agencies from releasing records of communication from members of Congress. In fact, these types of records are the
source of the data used in this book. In this chapter, I describe how I obtained
these records, how I use them, and what we can learn from them.

These records show that, even during times of gridlock and polarization,
Congress is in constant communication with the executive branch. Agencies

Backdoor Lawmaking: Evading Obstacles in the US Congress. Melinda N. Ritchie, Oxford University Press.
© Melinda N. Ritchie 2023. DOI: 10.1093/oso/9780197670491.003.0003

receive thousands of emails, letters, and phone calls from members of Congress every year. However, the frequency and content of these communications has been a mystery. While the FOIA has existed for decades, there are several challenges that make obtaining the records difficult, time-consuming, arduous, and sometimes even impossible.

One reason these data are difficult to obtain is that members of Congress and the executive branch do not always want their communications to be made public.[7] While elected officials often tout transparency and public accountability, they prefer to have control over the dissemination of their records. In fact, Congress exempted itself from the FOIA statute, only requiring the executive branch to release records.

How, then, did I obtain the congressional records used in this book? While records in possession of Congress are not subject to a FOIA request, when a member of Congress sends an agency a letter or email, it is then in the possession of the agency, not Congress. Likewise, when a senator picks up the phone to call an agency head or meets with the Secretary of Labor, the call and meeting logs and internal agency notes are subject to the FOIA. When an agency makes a record of communications from members of Congress in the agency's internal logs, the logs are subject to the FOIA.[8]

In the lawsuit referenced in the opening of this chapter, the House leaders claimed that congressional records are not agency records and so are not subject to the FOIA and that the release of the records would be a detriment to "the institutional interests of the House."[9] Rep. Jeb Hensarling (R-TX), chairman of the House Financial Services Committee, had sent letters to several agencies cautioning against the release of legislators' correspondence with agencies, arguing that such records are "sensitive and confidential."[10]

This is not to say that congressional communication is always intended to be hidden from public view. To the contrary, legislators often advertise their contacts with agencies in press releases as a way of claiming credit for benefits accrued to their constituencies (Fiorina 1977; Grimmer 2013; Grimmer, Westwood, and Messing 2014; Mayhew 1974). However, press releases and public statements publicizing legislators' interactions with agencies are only accessing the tip of the iceberg.

In this chapter, I describe how I used the FOIA to uncover the informal policy interactions that span branches of government. First, I offer a brief background on the law that made this book possible and describe how I used the FOIA to obtain records. I detail the challenges and ongoing problems with the FOIA process, and the tricks I learned to effectively overcome obstacles to obtaining documents. Second, I describe how I categorized the records and the coding procedure I used to create the novel dataset used in the empirical analyses in Chapters 5, 6, 7, and 8. Finally, I offer some initial descriptive statistics using the dataset that provides the foundation for the rest of the book.

The Freedom of Information Act

This account of the informal dynamics between members of Congress and agencies is made possible by the Freedom of Information Act. Without this important law, this book would not have been written. Without this law, the interactions, collaborations, and informal deals made between these separate branches of government would remain a black box.

The Freedom of Information Act is a federal law allowing anyone to request documents and records from the government.[11] The FOIA was first signed into statute by President Lyndon Johnson on July 4, 1966, and it has been updated with additional legislation and case law several times since.[12] Prior to the FOIA, agencies had substantial discretion over the records and information they released to (or withheld from) the news media and public.[13]

President Johnson was reluctant to sign the law, concerned that government officials must be able "to communicate with one another fully and frankly without publicity,"[14] but he eventually caved to pressure.[15] Publicly, he celebrated the law even though he had continued misgivings, stating at its signing, "a democracy works best when the people have all the information that the security of the nation permits."[16] The first enactment of the FOIA was considered ground-breaking, as only Sweden and Finland had similar disclosure laws, neither of which were as extensive as the FOIA.[17] Not a single agency in the executive branch supported the legislation.[18]

While the original law lacked teeth, the Pentagon Papers and Watergate ushered in new concerns about government transparency and accountability. Public pressure drove Congress to pass legislation to strengthen the FOIA, but not without a fight. Congress overrode President Ford's veto of the legislation in 1974. Additional amendments followed in later years including specific requirements and deadlines for agencies.[19]

FOIA is not without limits. Agencies are not required to release some types of information. The law allows for nine exemptions to protect, for example, personal privacy, national security interests, and geological information regarding wells. However, the agency must justify withholding information under these exemptions. A process for appealing agencies' FOIA decisions to withhold information is available under the law.[20] In addition to the nine exemptions, there are three exclusions that are treated differently from the exemptions. Exemptions must be acknowledged and justified to the requester. However, if requested records are covered by an exclusion under the FOIA, the agency is authorized to "respond to the request as if the excluded records did not exist."[21] The exclusions cover sensitive issues of law enforcement including records that could interfere with enforcement proceedings[22] or expose the identity of an informant if their existence is revealed.[23] The third exclusion relates to a subset of FBI records concerning international terrorism and foreign intelligence.[24]

Fulfilling FOIA requests can be costly, and agencies may recoup the costs of responding to them. Requesters may be charged fees for record searches, review, and duplication. To give a sense of the possible costs, the Department of Health and Human Services reports that fees for a search (not including duplication) generally range from $23 to $83 an hour, but such fees can vary by agency and type of personnel.[25] The law offers fee waivers and reductions for particular categories of requesters, such as the news media and educational institutions,[26] and if the information requested is in the public interest and is not primarily in the requester's commercial interest.[27]

What do the fees and waivers mean in terms of FOIA-related costs to the government? In 2019, the executive branch incurred a total of $486,194,200 in FOIA processing costs and $38,710,513 in FOIA-related litigation costs, for a grand total of well over $500 million. The FOIA price tag for agencies is over two hundred times the amount agencies collected in fees.[28] FOIA is not costless for the American taxpayer.

Today, agencies offer information about how to submit FOIA requests on their websites, and requests can generally be submitted either through online portals or via email. In 1996, FOIA was amended to provide access to documents in electronic formats.[29] Other developments include a practice by some agencies of contracting out FOIA tasks to private companies rather than relying on government FOIA officers.[30] While many of these developments have made it easier than ever to access information about the government, FOIA remains a painful and arduous process in many instances.

FOIA Challenges and Agency (Un)Responsiveness

While administrations extol the value of government transparency, agencies have been criticized for intentionally exploiting delays, exceptions, excessive fees, and other bureaucratic maneuvers to withhold information from the public. These obstacles can make obtaining documents under FOIA challenging or even impossible. Some agencies have earned reputations for consistently failing to produce records. These practices led the House Committee on Oversight and Government Reform to conclude, "Agencies create and follow FOIA policies that appear to be designed to deter requesters from pursuing requests and create barriers to accessing records."[31]

Excessive fees, for example, can be a major hurdle for requesters. Fees can amount to thousands of dollars. In a particularly egregious case, the Drug Enforcement Agency charged $1.5 million dollars for a request![32]

Extensive delays can also present challenges. While FOIA requires that agencies respond to (but not necessarily complete) a request within 20 business days (30 days if the request was submitted to the wrong component),[33] the time limit can be extended depending on the nature of the request.[34] It is not uncommon for agencies to take months or even years to complete a request.[35]

If a requester does not respond to an inquiry by the agency within a specific period of time, the agency may close the request entirely. Some agencies will exploit this rule and others to close cases. A common agency tactic is to send "still interested" letters. Agencies will often simply ask if the requester is still interested in receiving the information and request a confirmation from the requester within a specific period of time (e.g., 20 days). If the requester does not confirm her continued interest in the documents by the deadline, the agency is off the hook for providing the documents. The State Department, in particular, is notorious for long, repeated delays (some nearly a decade) or even not fulfilling FOIA requests at all.[36]

Another abuse of the FOIA is when agencies send hard copies of responses and documents in the mail when the requester explicitly asked for electronic versions of the documents. The Electronic Freedom of Information Act (EFOIA) of 1996 requires that agencies provide records in the format requested (e.g., hard copies, electronic) (Halstuk and Chamberlin 2006). Yet, agencies have been known to disregard format preferences even when explicitly stated in the request. These practices add additional delays and cost and often result in documents that are more challenging for the requester to read or use. More importantly, these are in violation of FOIA statute and principles of government transparency and accountability.

There are remedies, including administrative appeals and lawsuits, but legal recourse bears a substantial burden for the requester.[37] Only a very small fraction of the hundreds of thousands of FOIA requests made each year end in federal court.[38] Hurdles within the FOIA process may lead requesters to abandon their cases long before taking legal action.

The Back-Channel Communication Dataset

Beginning in May 2012, I submitted FOIA requests to federal agencies. I experienced a range of responses to my requests. In the best cases, agencies emailed me the electronic documents I requested within the time frame required by statute. In many other cases, I had to repeatedly call and email FOIA officers to check on the status of my often delayed requests. Unfortunately, this persistence can be a necessity if one ever hopes to receive their requested documents. In some cases, FOIA officers repeatedly denied my requests for fee waivers, despite my persistent calls and insistence that I qualified for the waiver and documentation showing that I had received fee waivers from other agencies. These denials required that I formally submit appeals (which I won). In one particularly frustrating exchange with an agency, I contacted my congressman's district office for help. Using a draft letter I supplied, a congressional staffer emailed the agency.[39] The agency promptly emailed me apologizing for misclassifying my request.

Congressional Correspondence Logs

I requested records of communication between members of Congress and the agency. Agencies have standardized systems for processing and managing correspondence from members of Congress.[40] In response to my FOIA request, I received a type of document agencies maintain for their internal records of the agency's contact with congressional offices, referred to as a congressional correspondence log.[41] While these logs can vary in their format and content, the department logs consistently include the name of the member(s) of Congress who contacted the agency, a summary of the subject of the contact, and a correspondence date.[42] Often agencies list the date the agency responded or is expected to respond. Some agencies include a summary of how the agency responded (or plans to respond) and subsequent correspondence relating to the original contact. The logs list an identifier or control number for each contact, which can be used to make subsequent FOIA requests for copies of the actual letter, email, fax, notes, or other materials associated with the contact. The logs also usually include the name of the individual, agency, bureau, or office to which the contact was addressed. If the legislator contacted the agency on behalf of an organization or individual, that information may also be included (although the names of private citizens are generally redacted).[43] Particularly detailed logs include the type of communication (e.g., letter, fax, email, meeting, phone call), the office and individual to which the contact is assigned, the signature level required for the response, and an internal agency designation of the priority level of the contact. Notes regarding the legislator—including if she is a committee chair or ranking minority member or if she is a member of a committee with jurisdiction over the agency—may be included.[44]

Figure 3.1 shows an example of a page of a congressional correspondence log from the US Department of Homeland Security.[45] As the figure illustrates, the redactions are limited to the specific text that is determined to be exempt from release and include a notation identifying the exemption the agency used to justify the redaction. The redactions shown in the figure are justified under exemption (b)(6) of the FOIA, which protects the information of private individuals (not including government officials). Most of the redactions in the records included in the dataset used in the analyses in this book are concealing identifying private information (usually the names of constituents). Occasionally, the agency will redact text under exemption (b)(4) of the FOIA, which protects commercial and financial information. Fortunately, the information withheld under these exemptions is not necessary for my purposes, and any other exemptions were minimal and did not result in the redaction of information required for my analyses.

These logs are intended for internal use by the agency and provide a summary of the contact that allows agency officials to understand the fundamentals of the original correspondence. I use the summaries of the communication that the agencies produced for their own internal use to construct the dataset, as I describe in the next section. For example, in Figure 3.1, the second row on the second page of the log provides a summary of the letter from Senator Chuck Schumer shown in Figure 3.2. In the letter, Senator Schumer expresses his opposition to the US Customs and Border

Policy Congressional Report
Opened Between 09/01/2008 and 10/31/2008

Line #	WF #	Receive Date	Letter Date	Congress Number	Congressman Name	Sender Name	Constituent	Subject of Request	Component	Due Date
1	792199	9/5/2008	9/5/2008	112th Congress	Congressman Gary L. Ackerman	The Honorable Gary L. Ackerman (b) (6)	The Honorable Gary L. Ackerman (b) (6)	(b) (6) requesting the status of the I-730s filed foe her children, (b) (6)		9/26/2008
2	792638	9/9/2008	9/8/2008	112th Congress	Congressman Gary L. Ackerman	The Honorable Gary L. Ackerman (b) (6)	The Honorable Gary L. Ackerman (b) (6)	(b) (6) regarding the status on interview scheduling fo (b) (6)		9/30/2008
3	792711	9/9/2008	9/8/2008	112th Congress	Congressman Gary L. Ackerman	The Honorable Gary L. Ackerman (b) (6)	The Honorable Gary L. Ackerman (b) (6)	(b) (6) regarding the status of the I-730s for (b) (6)		9/30/2008

Figure 3.1 Congressional correspondence log, US Department of Homeland Security

574	769935	4/29/2008	4/22/2008	112th Congress	Senator Charles E. Schumer	The Honorable Charles E. Schumer	(b)(6)	▮ (b)(6) re: status of her application for employment with the United States Office of Homeland Security/Citizenship and Immigration Services		5/20/2008
575	770141	4/30/2008	4/23/2008	112th Congress	Senator Charles E. Schumer	The Honorable Charles E. Schumer	The Honorable Charles E. Schumer	Writes expressing concern over CBP's decision to alter customs valuation practices based on the "first sale rule".	CBP, ESLIAISON1	5/14/2008
576	765844	4/9/2008	4/2/2008	112th Congress	Congressman David Scott	The Honorable David Scott	The Honorable David Scott	Writes on behalf of his constituent (b)(6) regarding information on his background investigation.	CBP, ESLIAISON1	4/23/2008
577	763949	3/31/2008	3/5/2008	112th Congress	Congressman Robert C. Scott	The Honorable Robert C. Scott (b)(6)	The Honorable Robert C. Scott (b)(6)	(b)(6) regarding his case status		4/21/2008
578	764473	4/2/2008	3/14/2008	112th Congress	Congressman Robert C. Scott	The Honorable Robert C. Scott	The Honorable Robert C. Scott (b)(6)	(b)(6) regarding her case status		4/23/2008
579	769955	4/29/2008	4/17/2008	112th Congress	Congressman Robert C. Scott	The Honorable Robert C. Scott (b)(6)	The Honorable Robert C. Scott (b)(6)	(b)(6) regarding his I-485 application		5/20/2008

Figure 3.1 Continued

CHARLES E. SCHUMER
NEW YORK

COMMITTEES:

JOINT ECONOMIC
BANKING
JUDICIARY
RULES
FINANCE

United States Senate
WASHINGTON, DC 20510

April 23, 2008

The Honorable Michael Chertoff   The Honorable Henry M. Paulson, Jr.
U.S. Department of Homeland Security   Department of the Treasury
Washington, DC 20528   Washington, DC 20220

Dear Secretary Chertoff and Secretary Paulson:

I am writing to express my concerns regarding the January 24, 2008, proposal by U.S. Customs
and Border Protection (CBP) that would alter the way in which the transaction value of imported
articles is calculated and eliminate the so-called "first sale" rule. As I understand it, if CBP's
proposal were to take effect, many U.S. companies would be forced not only to pay increased
import duties, fees and taxes, but also to restructure and possibly eliminate business units that
have been built around this long-standing precedent. For some of my constituents, the extra
costs could reach into the millions of dollars which, ultimately, will be passed on to consumers
and cause more U.S. jobs to be pushed offshore.

New York's apparel industry would be particularly hard hit. The industry injects billions of
dollars into the New York economy and employs tens of thousands of New Yorkers in apparel
design, production, distribution, sales and marketing operations. Fashion industry leaders such
as Jones Apparel, Phillips-Van Heusen, and Carole Hochman Design Group are headquartered in
New York. Clothing retailers, such as Macy's, JCPenney and David's Bridal, employ an
additional 127,000 people throughout the state. The continued health of these and other
companies in the apparel industry, including Perry Ellis, Hanesbrands, Biflex, VF Corporation,
Ariela-Alpha, TellaS Ltd., and Smart Apparel, is critical to the New York economy.
Overturning the first sale rule would come at a significant cost to these companies and, by
extension, at a significant cost to New York consumers and the New York economy.

For approximately 20 years, the courts and CBP have recognized the first sale rule as a viable
appraisement tool. CBP has failed to articulate any overriding need to revisit this issue or the
legal basis for doing so. The claim that CBP has had "difficulty" administering the rule simply
does not ring true with my constituents. The rule has been successfully administered for two
decades and CBP has issued dozens of ruling letters and provided guidance regarding
compliance. Many New York companies have built business plans and vendor relationships
around the first sale rule. This makes CBP's failure to assess the economic impact of the
possible effects of its proposed rule change all the more egregious.

I question the Administration's judgment in imposing what essentially amounts to a tax increase
on consumers and businesses at a time when we are seeking to stimulate the economy to avoid
an extended or deep recession. Since the first sale rule was established as a viable appraisement
method in 1988, it has helped U.S. companies compete in the global marketplace, enabling them

Figure 3.2 Letter from Senator Charles Schumer to Secretary Michael Chertoff
and Secretary Henry Paulson

Protection (CBP) proposal to eliminate a practice known as the "first sale"
rule, which allowed importers to declare a lower import value (resulting
in lower import taxes) when the US importer purchased the goods to be
imported from a foreign middleman for a higher price than that paid by the
middleman.[46] In other words, the US importers were traditionally allowed

to offer savings opportunities to their customers. The rule has resulted in millions of dollars in savings on virtually every type of product purchased from overseas, lowering costs for American consumers and boosting the bottom line of job-creating companies.

New York consumers, workers and businesses would be hit hard by this change. CBP has offered no viable justification for such a significant tax increase on families and businesses and I request that you withdraw this ill-advised proposal immediately. I understand that a number of other Senators have written to you on this issue, but I chose to write to you separately to underscore how important this issue is to the New York economy.

Sincerely,

Charles E. Schumer
United States Senator

cc: W. Ralph Basham
      Commissioner, U.S. Customs and Border Protection

Figure 3.2 Continued

to declare the lower price of the goods from the "first sale" to the middleman as the value of the imports. This change was contentious because, as Senator Schumer notes in his letter, it would have required companies to pay higher import taxes. CBP later withdrew the proposal.[47]

These records provide the universe of contacts between members of Congress and key agencies within the executive branch and are the foundation for the novel dataset used for the analyses in this book. As my theoretical argument focuses on inter-branch communications on public policy, it required that I create a coding scheme to identify contacts that were related to policy issues. I discuss my coding process in the next section. Finally, I close the chapter by offering descriptive statistics about how the communications vary across agencies and over time.

Coding Procedures

The records I obtained under the FOIA contain details on well over 100,000 contacts between members of Congress and the executive branch.[48] Testing my theory of back-channel policymaking required labor-intensive, manual coding of the summaries of each contact as described in the logs. To accomplish this task, I limited the dataset to contacts by members of Congress, both House members and senators, to three cabinet departments between 2005 through 2012 (109th–112th). This time span offers variation in party control of the White House as well as unified and divided government. It includes unified and divided government under President George W. Bush's second term of his presidency and the first term of President Barack Obama.[49] I examine contacts to three agencies: the US Departments of Labor (DOL), Homeland Security (DHS), and Energy (DOE). These three departments offer variation in agency ideology: the DOL leans liberal, DHS leans conservative, and the DOE is generally considered to be ideologically neutral (Clinton et al. 2012). The DOE is also an important inclusion as the issues under its jurisdiction require greater expertise, which could have implications for how legislators intervene with the agency. This framework produces 65,442 contacts in total. Of those contacts, 30,452 were with DHS, 26,984 were with DOL, and 8,006 were with the DOE.

Legislators contact agencies for a variety of reasons, including to assist constituents with casework (Fiorina 1977) and in support of grants for their districts and states (Arnold 1979). I used content analysis to identify policy-related contacts, which required that I read and code agency summaries of more than 65,000 contacts.[50] I coded correspondence as policy-related if it concerned the formation, broad/categorical implementation, or broad/ categorical enforcement of policies (e.g., the department's rulemaking process, regulations, guidance, law, and public problems). I identified policy contact by the following criteria: The legislator or her staff contacted (e.g., via letter, fax, email, meeting, phone call) the agency about a law, agency program or policy, or a national policy issue (i.e., not a grant request, earmark, or casework). While casework (or constituency service) concerns personal matters (or cases) of individual constituents, policy relates to government action on public issues and social problems.[51]

All other communication is coded as either non-policy or grant-related. I categorize communication as involving non-policy activities if it concerns casework, an event invitation, or similarly ceremonial or personal correspondence (e.g., thank you notes, birthday greetings, condolences). I operationalize casework as involving (1) a matter particular to individual constituents or a family or (2) routine assistance customarily conducted by a congressional office's caseworker (e.g., VISA renewals, delayed social security checks, workers' compensation claims).[52] Most correspondence coded as non-policy satisfies both criteria. However, some of this correspondence applies only to the first or the second criterion (such as a request for expedited processing of a business's VISA application). While the category of communication coded as non-policy includes contacts that are not casework (e.g., event invitations, birthday cards), I refer to this category as "casework" throughout the book since casework comprises the vast majority of contacts in this category. I classified communication as a grant request if it involved a request or support for federal funds for a particular project, program, or organization within the district, state, or region. To be clear, while grants are a type of policy—distributive policy—I am using a narrow definition of policy that excludes grants in order to address previous assumptions that legislators only contact agencies about grants (and casework) and not broader types of policy. Moreover, as I discuss in Chapters 2 and 8, there are theoretical reasons to expect differences in how legislators and agencies interact about grants and similar distributive benefits.[53]

Once coded, the total number of policy contacts is 14,921, nearly a quarter of all contacts. Unsurprisingly, the largest category of contacts is casework, comprising 62% of all contacts. Grant requests make up the smallest type of contact at 15%.

Variation in Contact Type across Agencies

The composition of inter-branch communication varies across agencies, as Figure 3.3 illustrates. Casework comprises the smallest category of contacts

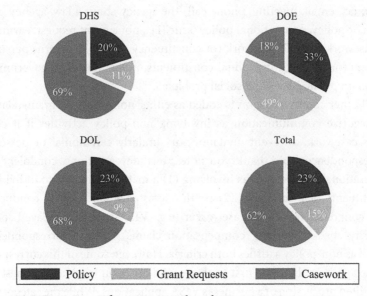

DHS

DOE

20%

11%

69%

18%

33%

49%

DOL

Total

23%

9%

68%

23%

15%

62%

Policy   Grant Requests   Casework

Figure 3.3 Percentage of contact types by select agencies

to the DOE, unlike the DOL and DHS. Instead, the DOE receives a much larger percentage of grant requests (49%) in comparison to the other two agencies. Why might we observe this variation across agencies?

The types of contacts agencies receive differ based on the authority, jurisdiction, functions, and programming of the agency. Some agencies, like the DOE and the US Department of Transportation (DOT) oversee issues—such as initiatives to promote energy efficiency and revitalizing public transportation—that involve several grant and loan programs. The DOE, for instance, has several grant programs for renewable energy and to promote innovations in energy production. Likewise, the DOT receives a higher percentage of grant-related requests in comparison to other cabinet departments because a large part of the DOT's functions involve distributing federal funds for transportation projects. DOL and DHS, on the other hand, have large benefits programs—such as worker's compensation (DOL)—and services—including passport and immigration services (DHS)—that generate more interactions with constituents struggling to obtain benefits and assistance, thus contributing to more casework. This variation in agency functions leads to differences in the types of communications these agencies receive from legislators.

Relatedly, it is important to point out how the agencies included in the dataset for this book may differ from other agencies in terms of the types of contacts they receive. For example, smaller, independent agencies—such as the Armed Forces Retirement Home (AFRH), the Corporation for National and Community Service (CNCS or AmeriCorps), the National Science Foundation (NSF), and agencies that primarily function to distribute services or benefits, such as the Social Security Administration (SSA)—are likely to primarily receive casework rather than grant or policy-related contacts in comparison to the agencies of focus in this book. Departments led by members of the president's cabinet play a greater role in policymaking and receive more policy-related communication than other agencies that primarily deal with services for constituents, like sending out social security checks.

Thus, my selection of agencies likely generates a larger percentage of policy-related communication than if I were to include all federal agencies in my sample. While it is important to make note of this sampling feature, it does not influence the focus of this book, which is not about all contacts between legislators and agencies, but about the neglected policy interactions that we know far less about. That said, I will offer some descriptive information about casework and grant-related contacts and leverage them as placebos to consider the robustness of my results, but the focus of the theoretical arguments, and thus the analyses, is policy appeals. As such, while the policy-related contacts comprise a larger percentage of total contacts than would be the case if I included every federal agency, the percentage of total policy contacts is not critical for justifying their importance.

While it is interesting to observe the breakdown of contacts across these types, one type does not necessarily lend insight into how we understand another. For instance, while casework generally comprises the largest portion of contacts, the volume of casework does not offer any insight into the frequency, regularity, or importance of policy contacts. Casework also outnumbers bill introductions, which we would not interpret to mean that bill introductions are infrequent or less important than casework. Of course, we would expect casework to far outnumber bill introductions. Each legislator has thousands of constituents contacting them every year asking for help with personal problems, and each legislator has at least one caseworker (senators often have several) whose sole responsibility is to manage casework. Likewise, percentages of casework and policy appeals offer limited insight. Like apples to oranges, comparing categories of contacts makes little sense.

In fact, legislators' policy appeals to agencies vastly exceed the number of bills introduced in Congress. In comparison to the 14,921 policy contacts in my dataset, roughly 6,537 bills were introduced in the House and Senate within the same issue areas during the same time period.[54] The average number of policy appeals by senators (22) and House members (7) are far more frequent than bill introductions. The average number of bills sponsored on the same policy issues during the same time period by senators is five, and House members sponsor an average of three bills.[55]

As the figures presented in the next section illustrate, agencies receive thousands of policy appeals from members of Congress every year. Moreover, as I show in Chapter 5, nearly all legislators engage with agencies about public policy. Some lawmakers reach out hundreds of times during a single Congress.

Inter-Branch Contact across Time

How might inter-branch communication vary across time? We might expect differences during divided versus unified government, at the start of a new administration, or following major legislation. Figure 3.4 offers some insight by plotting the number of contacts by year and contact type. Most prominently, there is a clear spike in contacts in 2009. There are a couple of possible explanations for that spike. The first is the change in the political context during 2009. It was the start of the new administration under President Obama and a change in party control of the White House that gave Democrats unified control of government. This could lead to a sudden increase in contacts for a few reasons. Democrats in Congress may have viewed new opportunities for advancing policy or pursuing grants under a more receptive president. Alternatively, Republicans in Congress may have been ready to attack the new Democratic-controlled administration. These two possibilities are not mutually exclusive and may be contributing factors, but other aspects of Figure 3.4 and Figures 3.5, 3.6, and 3.7—which break down the contacts by agency—point to another explanation.

First, the increase in contacts shown in Figure 3.4 is primarily due to a spike in grant requests, although casework also increased in 2009. Policy contact remains relatively steady in comparison. Second, scanning across Figures 3.5, 3.6, and 3.7, the spike in 2009 is most prominent for grant requests received by the DOE. While the political context of the new

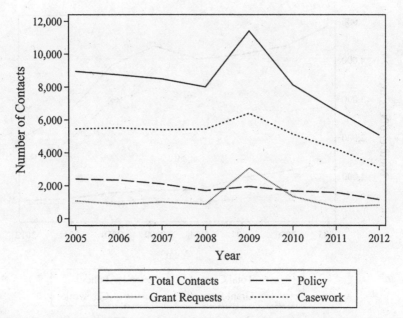

Figure 3.4 Total number of contacts from members of Congress to the US Departments of Labor, Homeland Security, and Energy by contact type, 2005–2012

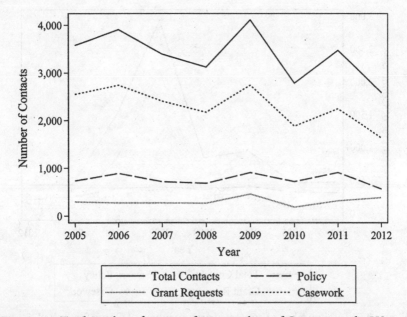

Figure 3.5 Total number of contacts from members of Congress to the US Department of Labor by contact type, 2005–2012

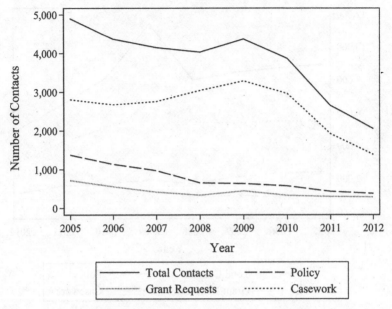

Figure 3.6 Total number of contacts from members of Congress to the US Department of Homeland Security by contact type, 2005–2012

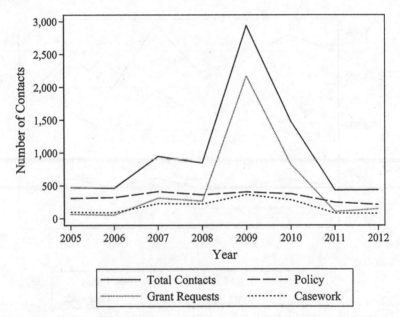

Figure 3.7 Total number of contacts from members of Congress to the US Department of Energy by contact type, 2005–2012

administration may still play a role, the increase is more likely due to the passage of the 2009 stimulus bill—the American Recovery and Reinvestment Act (ARRA)—signed into law by President Obama on February 17, 2009. The $831 billion stimulus package prompted a mad rush by legislators eager to secure stimulus funds for their districts and states. Consequently, agencies with stimulus funds to distribute received thousands of requests from legislators notifying the agency of "shovel-ready" projects. This would explain why the spike in contacts is primarily focused on grants, although casework related to the stimulus also contributed to the increase in total contacts in 2009. Constituents, for example, contacted their legislators (who then contacted the relevant agencies on their constituents' behalf) to inquire whether they could personally benefit from a program funded by the stimulus. Moreover, energy efficiency was a major component of the law—to the tune of $90 billion in clean energy investments and tax incentives—of which the DOE received more than $35 billion. The ARRA's concentration on energy efficiency funding could explain why the spike in grant requests is particularly prominent for the DOE.[56]

Turning to variation of policy communication across congresses, Figure 3.8 reveals a steady decline in policy communication to the DHS but an increase in policy contact to the DOL. One possible explanation for this pattern could be related to the change in party control of the administration and agency ideology. Perhaps legislators are more inclined to contact the conservative-leaning DHS under a Republican administration and the liberal-leaning DOL under a Democratic administration. These contacts could be driven by White House co-partisans in Congress who believe their requests will be well-received or by White House out-partisans who are particularly vigilant of politicization of agencies under such conditions. The DHS, however, shows a decline in all contacts over time, including grants and, to a lesser degree, casework. This decline could be due to the infancy of the nation's youngest department, which had only existed for about two years prior to the start of the dataset.[57] The organization of the newly created DHS may have led to an overall spike in contacts in its early years as its jurisdiction and mission took shape. In comparison, contact with the DOE is relatively steady across congresses, consistent with what we might expect given its reputation for neutrality and expertise. Legislators' contact with the DOE may be driven less by partisan or ideological concerns, with the agency experiencing less meddling given the highly technical nature of its

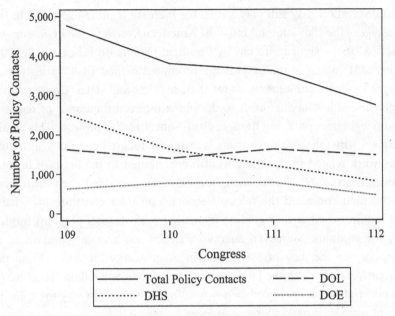

Figure 3.8 Total number of policy contacts from members of Congress to select agencies by Congress, 2005–2012 (109th–112th Congresses)

jurisdiction. I examine some of these explanations further in subsequent chapters.

Conclusion

These data reveal that bureaucrats hear from members of Congress about matters of public policy thousands of times each year. Given the bureaucracy's growing discretion over policy and the rise of administrative lawmaking, understanding these inter-branch policy interactions is important for democratic representation and public accountability. However, scholars, journalists, and the general public fixate on lawmakers' public behavior within the halls of Congress.

The Freedom of Information Act allows us to pull back the curtain from legislators' dealings with the executive branch. Yet, journalists account for less than 10% of FOIA requests. Estimates indicate that universities and scholars comprise the smallest group of requesters, making less than 5% of FOIA requests.[58] Who, then, is seeking government documents? In fact, the bulk of FOIA requests are made by commercial businesses, consulting firms and hedge funds, in particular. Businesses have turned reselling information obtained under FOIA into a profit-making enterprise.[59]

Scholars, however, have been slow to realize the value of the FOIA for their research.[60] The lag in scholars' use of the FOIA is understandable given the challenges I describe in this chapter. It is easier to study legislators' public behavior particularly when they advertise it themselves.

It is important that we do not confine our study of members of Congress to the behaviors that they want us to see. The Freedom of Information Act sheds light on the informal, inter-branch policymaking that occurs behind the scenes. In this chapter, I describe the construction of the dataset that provides the foundation for this book. In the subsequent chapters, I use the dataset to test the theory of back-channel policymaking in quantitative analyses.

First, however, I offer a qualitative accounting of these back-channel, inter-branch negotiations in Chapter 4. When legislators contact agencies about policy, what are they contacting about? What are legislators asking of agencies? I explore the content of lawmakers' policy appeals in the next chapter.

Appendix

Back-Channel Policymaking Codebook

This appendix provides additional details beyond the information in Chapter 3 about how the data used in the empirical analyses were collected and coded.

Compiling the Dataset

I obtained the records described in the coding procedures below under the Freedom of Information Act (FOIA), which allows individuals to request any records from a federal agency (but see the limitations and exceptions described in Chapter 3). Beginning in May of 2012, I submitted Freedom of Information Act (FOIA) requests to several departments including the US Departments of Labor (DOL), Homeland Security (DHS), and Energy (DOE).[61] I requested records of communication between members of Congress and the departments, known within the agencies as congressional correspondence logs. The congressional correspondence logs include details about each contact including the names of the legislators involved, the dates of contact, a summary of the subject of the contact, as well as additional information.

Coding Procedures

In order to produce a dataset for the quantitative analyses in Chapters 5, 6, 7, and 8, the records required labor-intensive, manual coding of the summaries of each contact as described in the logs. In order to accomplish this task, I limited the dataset to contacts by members of Congress, both House members and senators, to the three Cabinet departments between 2005 through 2012 (109th–112th). This time span offers variation in party control of the White House and unified and divided government. It includes unified and divided government under President George W. Bush's second term of his presidency and the first term of President Barack Obama.[62] I examine contacts to three agencies, the US Departments of Labor (DOL), Homeland Security (DHS), and Energy (DOE). These three departments offer variation in agency ideology, as the DOL leans liberal, DHS leans conservative, and the DOE is generally considered to be ideologically neutral (Clinton et al., 2012). This framework produces 65,442 contacts in total. Of those contacts, 30,452 were with DHS, 26,984 were with DOL, and DOE accounts for 8,006 contacts.

Legislators contact agencies for a variety of reasons, including to assist constituents with casework (Fiorina, 1977) and in support of grants for their districts and states (Arnold, 1979). I used content analysis to identify policy-related contact, which required that I read and code agency summaries of the over 65,000 contacts.[63]

All correspondence was coded as policy, grant-related, or non-policy. The "non-policy" category is chiefly comprised of casework/constituency service, and so I refer to the category as casework throughout the book. If there was doubt or uncertainty about whether a contact was about casework or policy, it was coded as casework (i.e., non-policy). If there was uncertainty about whether a contact was about a grant or policy, it was coded as grant-related.

I coded correspondence as policy communication if it concerned the formation, broad or categorical implementation, or broad/categorical enforcement of policies (e.g., the department's rulemaking process, regulations, guidance, law, public problems). Specifically, I identified policy contact by the following criteria: The legislator or her staff contacted (e.g., letter, fax, email, meeting, phone call) with the agency about a law, agency program or policy, or a national policy issue (i.e., not a grant request, earmark, or casework). To be clear, while casework/constituency service concerns personal matters (or cases) of individual constituents, policy relates to government action on public issues and social problems.

All other communication is coded as either non-policy or grant-related. I categorized communication as involving non-policy activities if it concerns casework, an event invitation, or similarly ceremonial or personal correspondence (e.g., thank you notes, birthday greetings, condolences). I operationalize casework as involving (1) a matter particular to individual constituents or a family or (2) routine assistance customarily conducted by a congressional office's caseworker (e.g., labor certification, VISA renewals, delayed social security checks, workers' compensation claims).[64] Most correspondence coded as non-policy satisfies both criteria. However, some of this correspondence only applies to the first or the second criterion (such as a request for expedited processing of a business' VISA application). While the category of communication coded as non-policy includes contacts that are not casework (e.g., event invitations, birthday cards), I refer to this category as "casework" throughout the book as casework comprises the vast majority of contacts in this category.

I classified communication as grant requests if it involved a request or support for federal funds for a particular project, program, or organization within the district, state, or region (e.g., support for the Community-Based Job Training Grant, support for Base Realignment & Closure (BRAC) Phase 1 funds). Contacts coded as a grant request may describe support for a "proposal" or "application" rather than explicitly state it is for a grant. Contacts concerning general funding issues (e.g., funding levels for mine safety or OSHA) were coded as policy rather than as grant requests. Contacts regarding the criteria the agency uses for distributing grants would be coded as policy rather than as grant requests.

To be clear, while grants are a type of policy, distributive policy, I am using a narrow definition of policy excluding grants in order to address previous assumptions that legislators only contact agencies about grants (and casework) and not broader types of policy. Moreover, as I discuss in Chapters 2 and 8, there are theoretical reasons to expect differences in how legislators and agencies interact about grants and similar distributive benefits.[65]

Once coded, the total number of policy contacts is 14,921, nearly a quarter of all contacts. Unsurprisingly, the largest category of contacts is casework, comprising 62% of all contacts. Grant requests make up the smallest type of contact at 15%.

Examples of each category (and each department used in the quantitative analyses) quoted from the congressional correspondence logs (typographical and grammatical errors are from the original logs):

Policy

Department of Labor

- Concerns regarding proposed rule making on Trade Adjustment Assistance (TAA).
- Requests prostate cancer to be added to the list of qualifying cancers under the Energy Employees Occupational Illness Compensation Program Act (EEOICPA).
- Requests that quota on textile imports be reinstated.
- Request the department to implement break time for nursing mothers.
- Regarding the draft of the proposed changes to OSHA's confined space standard.

Department of Homeland Security

- Writes regarding how DHS implements air travel restrictions on passengers with communicable diseases that pose a significant threat to public health.
- Writes regarding concerns with drugs and violence at the U.S.-Mexico border and the need to take greater action.
- Shares concerns regarding need for multi-layered cargo screening process.
- Writes in support of stronger U.S. trade remedy laws regarding Chinese furniture.
- Requesting an assessment of the vulnerability of offshore oil rigs to terrorist attacks or sabotage in light of the Deepwater Horizon oil spill.

Department of Energy

- Writes urging the Department of Energy to suspend temporarily filling the Strategic Petroleum Reserve.
- Asks the DOE to consider broadening the Solid-Stale Energy Conversion Alliance program criteria to include the many highly promising options that natural gas would allow.
- Request a review of the Internal Revenue Service decision to allocate Qualifying Advanced Coal Project tax credits under Section 48A of the Internal Revenue Code to the Integrated Gasification Combined Cycle projects using bituminous coal.
- Requests NNSA deploy M-PONDS technology to validate existing technology funded in FY 06; requests cost-estimate for deploying M-PONDS as part of Mega-ports Initiative for FY 07.
- Urging DOE reconfirm DOE's focus energy conservation & ensure that final ENERGY STAR clothes washer criteria does not include aggressive water-use component will drive consumers away from energy.

Non-Policy/Casework

Department of Labor

- OWCP claim issue.
- Request review of her eligibility for TAA adult education retraining under NAFTA.
- Congratulation on your confirmation as Assistant Secretary of Labor for OSHA.
- Thanks for your birthday wishes & I send our best to you and Sam.
- Request reinstatement of her COBRA coverage due to her severe medical condition.

Department of Homeland Security

- Customer is requesting the status of her husband's I-485 application.
- (b)(6) writes about his product which could be used against terrorist activities as well against hurricanes.
- Writes on behalf of constituent, (b)(6) writes that he has regularly been stopped by customs when returning to the United States. A customs officer remarked to that he is flagged because of a narcotics conviction on his record. (b)(6) states that he was never been convicted on a narcotics charge, and requests an immediate investigation into this matter.
- Writes on behalf of a constituent who wants to know what happened to 1,600 barrels of honey that were confiscated by ICE.
- Constituent, (b)(6) writes regarding Cat Stevens, who converted to Islam some years ago and is now on the "Do Not Enter" list maintained by DHS.

Department of Energy

- Writes regarding constituent radiological contamination incident.
- Expressing concerns of constituent who worked for WSI Oak Ridge Team and feels she was misled regarding benefits such as company service time, medical benefits, vacation accrual and severance packages; requests a detailed explanation.
- Congressman Todd Tiahrt on behalf of constituent is submitting a FOIA requests for information on the dates April 29, 1974 through March 31, 1975, for irradiation reconstruction for the (then) Atomic Energy Commission compound.
- Congratulations on the occasion of her retirement from the Department of Energy and wish her the best of luck in the years ahead.
- Thanks Under Secretary Johnson for sending him the "Best of Volume 10" from her music library.

Grant Requests

Department of Labor

- Support for the Community-Based Job Training Grant.
- Two unsolicited grant proposals to help displaced workers in Maine.
- Support of 3 proposals for the Workforce Innovation in Regional Econ Dev (WIRED).
- NEG support for Base Realignment & Closure (BRAC) Phase 1 Funds/$1.37M Grant.
- Community Based Job Training Initiative Grant for 3D tech in training of coal miners.

Department of Homeland Security

- Writes to support the grant request by the Syracuse Fire Department for funding under the Firefighters Grant Program.
- Requests a timely assessment of communities not yet eligible for assistance under a June 11, 2009 disaster declaration for flooding in Alaska.
- Sen. Bingaman writes in support of providing $800,000 in agency funds for a program entitled "Economic and Social Impacts of Southern Border Security Programs, Threats and Trade-Related Policies and Agreements," proposed by a team of experts from New Mexico State University, Texas A & M and the Border Trade Alliance (BTA).
- Senators Reid and Ensign request assistance regarding grant funding for the Nevada State Fusion Center "Hub", to serve as the primary link to Nevada homeland security organizations and other federal agencies.
- Request assistance with expediting emergency levee repairs in California's Sacramento Valley and San Joaquin Delta.

Department of Energy

- Constituent seeking funding for his proposal to develop solar energy on existing surface mined lands in West Virginia.
- Urge the Department of Energy to consider applying some of the American Recovery and Reinvestment Act funds to address the serious wildfire in Colorado.
- Requests DOE assistance concerning constituent's company, Solar PowerUp and a grant application.
- Commending the Department in outlining funds to Pennsylvania regarding the Energy and Efficiency Block Grant Program as a result of the American Recovery Investment Act.
- Writing on behalf of the City of Homer, Alaska which feels it was improperly denied funding under the American Reinvestment and Recovery Act under the terms of the Energy Efficiency and Conservation Block Grant program.

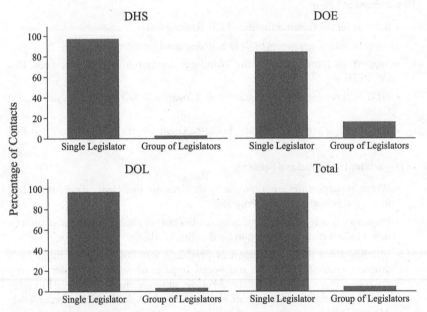

Figure 3A.1 Percentages of contacts originating from a single legislator or group of legislators to select agencies

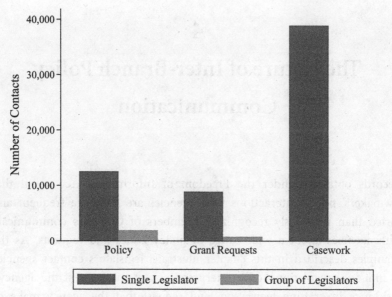

Figure 3A.2 Total number of contacts originating from a single legislator or group of legislators to the US Departments of Labor, Homeland Security, and Energy by contact type

4

The Nature of Inter-Branch Policy Communication

Records obtained under the Freedom of Information Act reveal that lawmakers' policy interactions with agencies are far more frequent and varied than previously recognized. Members of Congress communicate with agencies about a wide range of policy issues and requests. As the examples described in this chapter illustrate, legislators contact agencies to influence regulations, offer interpretations of law, request the agency's assistance in crafting legislation, and request that the agency make or obstruct policy changes using the tools of administrative policymaking. Members of Congress even urge agencies to initiate policies that are lagging in the legislative process (e.g., the Dream Act) in advance (or in lieu) of passage and to delay or suspend implementation of provisions. This chapter presents a qualitative accounting of inter-branch communication that offers insight beyond what can be gained from the quantitative analyses in the subsequent chapters.[1]

While legislators' policy appeals to the bureaucracy are as diverse as the interests and objectives of Congress, I develop a typology presented in Table 4.1 to offer readers a sense of the prominent purposes and strategies that characterize these informal interactions. I focus on three agency tools that legislators' exploit: agency policymaking, information, and enforcement. Legislators' appeals exploit these agency resources for four major objectives: (1) triggering policy changes, (2) obstructing policy changes, (3) involving agencies in coordinated strategies that span both branches, and (4) securing agency intervention with other political actors (e.g., states, the other chamber of Congress). These categories do not represent the universe of policy contacts and are not mutually exclusive; many policy interactions can be multifaceted and complex, as I illustrate in the examples described later in the chapter. However, each of these categories exemplify the largely unrecognized complexity of informal inter-branch negotiations.

Backdoor Lawmaking: Evading Obstacles in the US Congress. Melinda N. Ritchie, Oxford University Press.
© Melinda N. Ritchie 2023. DOI: 10.1093/oso/9780197670491.003.0004

Table 4.1 The Tools and Objectives of Policy Communication

	Tools		
Objectives	Regulation	Information	Enforcement
Request Action	Rep. Bilirakis requested DOT "Consider Rulemaking to Require Automobile Manufacturers to Include Seatbelt Warning devices in Vehicles They Produce."	Rep. Speier contacted DOT to "Request that NHTSA Review the Newest Technology Available on Deceleration Lights for Motorcycle [sic] and Consider Making Lights Legal."	Rep. Baca contacted DHS "requesting that deferred action be granted to those eligible under H.R.2681 The Proud Act [a bill that never became law]."
Block Action	"Rep. Slaughter writes in opposition to the Department of State and DHS's Advanced Notice of Proposed Rulemaking on the Western Hemisphere Travel Initiative, and urges DHS to review the regulation and move to expand the NEXUS and Free and Secure Trade (FAST) programs."	"Ranking Members Don Young, Jim McCrery, and Joe Barton requesting that a quantitative analysis is conducted on the impact of Speaker Nancy Pelosi's energy bill 'H.R. 3221' on domestic oil, natural gas, gasoline and diesel supplies, and prices."	Senator Cornyn "Writes regarding the administration's potential expansion of deferred action or parole to broad classes of illegal aliens currently in the United States. Requests the Secretary's commitment not to use the parole authority to cover large numbers of illegal aliens, even if each case is reviewed individually."
Agency-MC Coordination	Senator Lugar "Expresses concerns about the Environmental Protection Agency's proposed rule to implement the Renewable Fuels Standard expansion passed in 2007; urges EPA to hault [sic] consideration of lifecycle gressnhouse [sic] gas emissions due to lack of sufficiemt [sic] information, and work with Congress to find a workable solution."	Rep. Souder requested DHS "review the attached draft bill and provide any technical assistance that your Department believes may improve it."	Rep. Inglis asked, "Could the DOE exercise its discretion to forestall enforcement of the 2010 commercial refrigerator/freezer standards against self-contained SOC Display Merchandisers while work is progressing on a legislative resolution that would establish credible, reasonable achievable [sic] standards for those products. [sic]"

(continued)

Table 4.1 *Continued*

	Tools		
Objectives	Regulation	Information	Enforcement
Agency Intervention	Rep. Dent wrote to DHS, DOS, and DOJ "regarding lawsuit challenging Arizona's S.B. 1070 and asks that the Administration address sanctuary city practices."	Rep. Franks wrote to DHS "asking the Secretary to encourage the Senate to pass H.R. 5026 the GRID Act during the Lame Duck session."	Rep. Fleming contacted DHHS: "On February 12, 2012, the Washington State House approved legislation requiring all insurance companies to provide coverage for abortion services if they also provide coverage for prenatal care. The Reproductive Parity Act, HB 2330, approved by the House, and its companion bill, SB 6185, approved by a Senate committee, would have far reaching and alarming consequences. Of most importance is the fact that either bill, if enacted as currently drafted, would be a direct violation of the Hyde/Weldon amendment, federal law which protects providers, in this case insurance companies and health plans, against discrimination. It is essential that the administration clearly convey to any state advancing legislation that would impede statutory conscience protections, that doing so would be in direct violation of federal law."

Agency Policymaking and Rulemaking

Members of Congress exploit agencies' unilateral authority to make policy as a resource for advancing their own objectives. This authority is often exercised through a formal process called rulemaking, which agencies use to make policy changes by developing and enacting new rules and regulations. Rulemaking is often opaque, but it is an important way, although not the only way, agencies make policy. In fact, thousands of rules are made each year resulting in binding law created outside of Congress. Many policy changes assumed to be accomplished in Congress are actually legally binding rules issued by bureaucrats within federal agencies (Potter 2019). Rulemaking is an important resource for legislators because it offers them a discreet means to try to influence policy outside of the legislative process.

How does rulemaking offer lawmakers advantages that the legislative process does not? Despite the formal procedure for rulemaking outlined in the Administrative Procedures Act (APA), rulemaking is less tethered to statute and oversight than one might think. Even readers familiar with rulemaking may not realize that most rules are not mandated by statute. Instead, estimates suggest over half of rules, even important rules, emerge from agency discretion (West and Raso 2013). Moreover, even so-called mandatory rules may include discretionary provisions that were "in no way intended by the enacting legislative coalition or stated in statutory language" (Potter 2019, 31). In short, policy changes can be accomplished by agencies without explicit authorization in statue.

Additionally, while the formal rulemaking process includes various stages of review and input (by the OMB and the public), these stages can be sidestepped sometimes.[2] For example, if an agency justifies invoking "good cause," the agency skips the public comment period and starts with an emergency interim final rule (Potter 2019, 62). Likewise, there are exceptions and limitations for government review. The OMB only reviews a fraction of rules that are deemed significant and have an annual economic impact of at least $100 million (Balla and Gormley 2018, 100–1).[3] The 1996 Congressional Review Act (CRA) requires that major rules be submitted to Congress and the Government Accountability Office (GAO) at least 60 days before going into effect, but the CRA was only successfully used once to overturn a rule prior to 2017 (Kerwin and Furlong 2018).[4] Agencies can use these loopholes to avoid scrutiny and advance their interests.

In fact, agencies have developed strategies to weigh the rulemaking process in their favor. Similar to lawmakers' ability to strategically maneuver and manipulate legislative procedures, agencies are skilled at procedural politicking in the bureaucratic venue. How bureaucrats draft rules, control the consultation process, and structure the timing of the rulemaking process allows agencies to achieve their preferred policy outcomes (Potter 2017, 2019). These tools of procedural politicking permit agencies to subvert the preferences of interest and industry groups, Congress, and even the President and OMB by, for example, drafting rules in a way that raises the cost for principals and external actors (e.g., an OIRA desk officer) (Potter 2019, 74).

Paradoxically, while this procedural politicking avoids interference from Congress, individual legislators can harness agency autonomy for their own purposes. Agencies can use procedural maneuvering to fulfill legislators' policy requests, whether the legislator is a collaborative ally or a powerful senator whom the agency wants to keep happy.[5] As one senator described it, "I called the head of the IRS. Another one of the advantages of being a Senator. He immediately took my call. . . . He said it would be taken care of immediately."[6] Given that legislative action generally requires the approval of 218 House members, as many as 60 senators, and the president, this type of inter-branch exchange can be considerably more manageable.

Where Do Rules Come From? How Legislators Shape the Rulemaking Agenda

The origin of rules remains a black box in the literature on rulemaking. There has been virtually no published studies on the origin of rules (see West and Raso (2013) for a rare exception).[7] Of course, agencies must justify a proposed rule with an originating statute, but it is often not clear when a statute requires the promulgation of a rule and what type of rule it requires. In fact, about two-thirds of rules and over half of important rules were agency initiatives that were authorized, but not required, by statute (referred to as discretionary rules as opposed to mandated rules required by statute) (West and Raso 2013).

What, then, inspires agencies to propose rules? What shapes an agency's initiative to exercise its discretion? While some argue that presidents centralize administrative power to accomplish their policy goals, others have found White House influence on rulemaking to be largely reactive rather than focused on initiating new rules (West and Raso 2013). West and Raso suggest that "informal pressures" from members of Congress may be an origin of rules (West and Raso 2013, 512, and see Golden 2003 interviews).

In fact, qualitative evidence from the records described in Chapter 3 suggest that informal policy appeals from members of Congress are one source of the rules agencies propose.[8] For example, in a conversation with Energy Secretary Samuel W. Bodman, Senator Byron L. Dorgan (D-ND) requested that the Secretary "consider undertaking a rulemaking" so that the department could establish a reporting system to more effectively monitor the refining and distribution of fuels.[9] In December of 2004, Senator Maria Cantwell (D-WA) faxed a letter to Department of Health and Human Services (HHS) Secretary Tommy Thompson and Food and Drug Administration (FDA) Acting Commissioner Lester Crawford requesting that the FDA:

> ... proceed with a rulemaking strengthening the ban on agents in animal feed thought to cause bovine spongiform encephalopathy (BSE, also known

as mad cow disease). Remains concerned about the continued delays in regulating these important barriers to prevent the transmission of BSE, and urges publishing, at very least, an interim final rule that will close feed ban loopholes.[10]

Clearly, members of Congress are trying to affect the rulemaking agenda. It has been previously assumed that when a legislator wants to make a policy change, she introduces a bill (or pursues influence in her committees), not recognizing that legislators also view rulemaking as a policymaking venue for their own priorities.

Legislators also lobby agencies on behalf of organizations and industries that petition for a rule. The APA allows individuals and organizations to formally petition an agency to take a regulatory action, and such petitions can be a source of rules (Potter 2019, 31). For example, Senators Lisa Murkowski (R-AK) and Jeff Bingaman (D-NM) emailed Energy Secretary Steven Chu a letter in support of a "petition recently sent to DOE from a large coalition of electric motor manufacturers, energy efficiency advocates and others who have proposed consensus energy conservation standards for electric motors," and urged "DOE to consider the proposal."[11] Petitions such as these can be a source of rules or influence the content of rules.

Outside the Rules

While agencies have strategies for circumventing the requirements of rulemaking, they can also work outside of the rulemaking process altogether. The rulemaking procedures dictated in the APA statute only apply to legislative rules. Interpretive rules and guidance are not subject to the notice-and-comment requirement, which requires agencies to solicit public comment on new rules. Rather than issuing a formal rule, agencies may choose to use guidance documents, agency statements that offer guidelines and details about the agency's position on an issue (Haeder and Yackee 2020). Guidance documents have drawbacks since they are not legally binding, but they are generally satisfactory for establishing compliance and are useful for evading formal review and congressional oversight (Balla and Gormley 2018, 116–117). Guidance documents are also more discreet than rulemaking and are more difficult to track. These advantages likely contribute to the importance of guidance documents for lobbying. In fact, interest groups achieve greater success when lobbying agencies during the guidance document process than formal rulemaking (Yackee 2020). The trade-offs of these various approaches offer agencies options for deciding how to respond to a legislator's policy request.

Accordingly, legislators often ask agencies to make policy changes but leave it to the agency to determine how to make the change. Legislators request what they want to achieve and then ask that an agency issue "the regulations necessary" to change a policy.[12] An agency official involved in rulemaking illustrated this cooperation. When the Senate Majority Leader Harry Reid (D-NV) would contact his agency wanting a policy change, the official and a team of colleagues would discuss the various options for fulfilling the request, whether they actually needed to propose a rule or if they could use a less formal approach. In a nod to the agency's discretion, he also noted that they would sometimes need to communicate with the agency's legal representatives to consider how far they could "stretch the law."[13] Agencies are often in a better position than the legislator to assess potential approaches for accomplishing a legislator's objective because agencies have more expertise in administrative procedures and more information about potential resistance from various interests.

Shaping the Content of Regulations

While legislators may be the source of new regulations, they also shape the rulemaking agenda by intervening to support, obstruct, and shape agency regulations during the rulemaking process. Legislators frequently contact agencies in support of or in opposition to rules or to ask for changes. Sometimes these communications are included in the formal public comment period records, while others are not included in rulemaking documents.[14] Often legislators ask that proposed rules be withdrawn or replaced with a stronger or modified version. For example, Rep. Henry Waxman (D-CA), chair of the Committee on Energy and Commerce, requested that the DOT "Issue A Stronger Rule Regarding Roof Crush Resistance That is More Protective Than the Proposed Rulemaking."[15]

However, legislators will also ask for revised rules that offer loopholes or exceptions, thus weakening a rule. Fifteen Republican House members and senators from Texas, Louisiana, and Oklahoma wrote to "Respectfully

Request That the Department Conduct a Comprehensive Evaluation of the Current Hours-of-Service Regulations and Issue and Exemption Through a Revised Rulemaking for the Oil and Natural Gas Industries."[16] In other circumstances, legislators ask for loopholes to be closed. Rep. John Dingell (D-MI) wrote to the EPA Administrator Lisa Jackson and Secretary of Transportation Ray LaHood to express concerns about regulations intended to limit greenhouse gas emissions in the auto industry. Rep. Dingell, representing the home of the American auto industry, did not write to oppose emission standards for the auto industry, but to critique the proposed loophole given to auto companies based outside the United States. He argued that:

> granting such an exemption strikes me as providing qualifying manufac-
> turers with a district competitive advantage over their competitors, which
> are bound by law to comply with federal emissions standards. As a matter of
> principle, I believe all manufacturers that sell vehicles in the United States
> should be subject to uniform and universally applied regulation.[17]

Legislators try to influence the content of agency regulations by pushing for loopholes or pressuring agencies to eliminate exemptions.

Lawmakers also oppose new rules or regulations altogether. One instance of legislator involvement in policy implementation that captured the public's attention involves a controversy over neglected prosecution for the mislabeling of extra virgin olive oil. Store shelves are lined with many products sold as extra virgin olive oil that actually contain less desirable oil.[18] Interest groups have pressured the USDA to enforce stricter regulations.[19] However, concerned with the impact on regional olive oil producers in New York State, Senator Chuck Schumer wrote to the USDA requesting that the Secretary hold back on imposing regulations, arguing that the proposed change "would dramatically raise testing costs for U.S. olive oil bottlers" and "increase prices for consumers." Senator Schumer also pointed out that the move "would deviate from the internationally-recognized standard, mandate expensive new testing regimes, and require labeling changes." Schumer concluded that the proposed change "seems unnecessary at best and economically harmful at worst."[20] The senator's advocacy on behalf of the olive oil bottlers occurred, not through the legislative process, but via the bureaucracy.

When legislators express opposition to agencies' new policy initiatives, it can be in the early stages of the rulemaking process or even before a rule has been formally proposed.[21] The legislators indicate they heard that the agency was considering or planning to propose a rule, sometimes from a press report. By expressing opposition to proposals early in the policymaking process, legislators can exert negative agenda-setting power by signaling to the agency that there will be resistance if they move forward with the proposal.

Procedural Politicking and the Pace of Rulemaking

Members of Congress can also influence an agency's policymaking agenda by urging the prioritization of issues or asking for delays on rulemaking. In fact, agencies strategically leverage their control over the pace of rule-making to their advantage (Potter 2017, 2019, and see Haeder and Yackee 2022). Legislators try to influence agencies' pace in rulemaking as well, either by urging agencies to fast-track a rule or by asking agencies to delay rulemaking.

Legislators also contact agencies about rulemaking procedures, expressing concerns or asking them to make changes. These contacts can relate to the length of the public comment period, bypassing public comment, or other procedural choices the agency has made. These types of contacts may be most critical when the agency chooses rulemaking procedures that limit review and public input, a strategy agencies use to push through a rule and move policies toward the agency's preference (Potter 2019). One example of such a procedure is an interim final rule, which allows an agency to finalize a rule without public comment. Agencies have significant discretion in such cases, and without public comment, it may be up to individual legislators to represent the concerns of the public or affected interests. However, legislators also request agencies use strategies that bypass public input. Thus, legislators try to take advantage of agencies' procedural politicking for their own purposes.

First, legislators frequently urge agencies to accelerate rulemaking or use procedural maneuvers that bypass the need for public comments or congressional review. For example, in a letter to HHS Secretary Michael O. Leavitt, Rep. Rosa DeLauro (D-CT) asked the Secretary to fast-track a rule to protect against the spread of mad cow disease by issuing an interim final rule, which would expedite the regulation but also bypass public comment and congressional scrutiny:

> As you know in January 2004, following the positive test for a cow in Washington State, both FDA and Secretary Thompson called for an urgent rulemaking to ban cattle blood, poultry litter that can contain cattle tissue, and restaurant plate waste that may contain beef from entering the animal feed stream, and to require feed mills to segregate production lines and equipment for the manufacture of species specific animal feed.
>
> However, in July 2004, Acting Commissioner Crawford changed this plan and issued an Advanced Notice of Proposed Rulemaking (ANPR) calling for a period of comment about the need for a rule, prior to any possibility of an important rule being written, issued for comment and implemented. This action means that we are unlikely to have a final rule for quite some time, and that we risk putting cattle into the food supply that have eaten contaminated feed. Regardless of the purpose of the ANPR, there was nothing to stop FDA from immediately requiring a halt, via an interim final rule, to potential contamination by blood, poultry litter and plate waste.[22]

Notice Rep. DeLauro's criticism of FDA Acting Commissioner's decision to allow the public to comment on the proposed regulation, while requesting that a rule be implemented immediately prior to any public input. This procedural maneuver would not only speed up the regulation but would also cut off any objections from interests (e.g., farmers) that might find the regulation overly burdensome.

However, legislators also express concerns about using these procedural maneuvers when they oppose the regulation. For example, Rep. Barney Frank (D-MA) contacted DHS about the US Coast Guard (USCG, which is under DHS) using an interim final rule to fast-track a regulation and bypassing public comment:

> Expresses concerns regarding USCG decision to publish an interim final rule (Automatic Identification System, Requirement for fishing vessels) that would require fishing vessels which are 65 feet or greater in length to install Automatic Identification System to comply with the Maritime Transportation Act of 2002. Many vessels participating in the managed fisheries within the Mid-Atlantic and northwest are already required to carry a vessel monitoring system at signficant [sic] cost.[23]

Even when interim final rules are not used, legislators criticize agencies for bypassing opportunities for input from the public and stakeholders. Rep. Peter Hoekstra (R-MI) expressed his concerns to DHS about a proposed rule, writing that he was "Disappointed that no public meetings on the proposed rule were held in the Great Lakes region, and would encourage you to hold a public meeting in the Great Lake region before taking any further action on the proposed rule." Rep. Hoekstra "Enclosed written comments from several facilities in my district regarding the TWIC rulemaking."[24] Often legislators will ask for additional hearings, sometimes in specific regions, and for extensions of public comment periods.

In sum, agencies—and legislators trying to influence agencies—have a great deal of discretion over the development of rules and regulations. If a legislator asks an agency to make a policy change, one way the agency may try to be responsive to the legislator's request is by proposing a rule and justifying the proposed rule with existing legislation. Agencies have other tools, like guidance, that skirt rulemaking requirements altogether. Legislators can also pressure agencies to influence or obstruct policy changes either directly or by raising procedural issues. When the literature considers the influence of Congress on agency policymaking, it overwhelmingly focuses on the institutions within Congress (e.g., committees) and formal means of oversight rather than on individual legislators pressuring agencies throughout—and outside of—the rulemaking process (also see Yackee 2012).[25]

Information

Information also plays an important role in legislators' communication with agencies, but not quite in the way assumed by the previous literature, which has characterized the interactions in terms of legislators seeking information from agencies. While legislators do request information from agencies, such requests generally accompany other demands for agency action and signal the legislator's own preferences. The requests for information are not merely for fact-finding or oversight to ensure the intent of Congress. Like legislators' interventions in rulemaking, requests for information are closely tied to the political and policy goals of the legislator.

For example, legislators request information from agencies to use to challenge their rivals' legislation in Congress. This strategy is illustrated by a request sent by the Republican Ranking Minority Members of three House committees, Don Young (R-AK) of the Committee on Natural Resources, Jim McCrery (R-LA) of Ways and Means, and Joe Barton (R-TX) of the Energy Committee, to Energy Information Administration (EIA) Administrator Guy F. Caruso to obtain information to use in their challenges against "Speaker Nancy Pelosi's energy bill," or what Rep. Young referred to as the "no-energy bill" in a press release attacking the legislation.[26] Rep. Young expressed frustration at his minority party status on the critical committee, arguing that the "Republicans on our Committee spent two days fighting each and every provision of this Democratic bill, only to have the Democrats preserve the anti-energy provisions on party line votes." However, he continued to use information about the predicted impact of the legislation to rail against it in press releases and speeches. Agencies are an important source of information that legislators use to support or attack legislation, even when legislators are constrained from influencing the legislation in Congress.

Similarly, legislators will ask a cabinet member or agency head for her opinion on pending legislation, either to use against rival legislation or in support of their own.[27] At times, legislators will request the secretary make a public statement in support of the legislator's bill or to express concerns about pending legislation in hopes that the secretary's statement—and reputation as a more neutral source of expertise—will persuade other political actors and the public.[28] Members of Congress even ask cabinet members to lobby other legislators. Rep. Trent Franks (R-AZ), for example, contacted DHS "asking the Secretary to encourage the Senate to pass H.R. 5026 the GRID Act during the Lame Duck session," using the Secretary to lobby the other chamber of Congress.[29]

Importantly, legislators ask agencies to review their legislation and offer expertise or opinions and even ask agencies to draft legislation.[30] These requests are often characterized as collaborations on legislation.[31] While there has been evidence of agency-originating bills at the state level (Kroeger 2021), little attention has been paid to agency-drafted legislation across levels of government (but see Walker 2017). However, concerns have been raised as to the constitutional implications of agencies writing legislation.[32]

When making voting decisions, legislators ask agencies about how they plan to implement legislation if it passes.[33] For example, prior to voting on a continuing resolution (CR) to fund the remainder of the 2007 fiscal year (H.J.Res.20), Senators John McCain (R-AZ) and Tom Coburn (R-OK)—both famously critical of earmarks—wrote to Secretary Bodman to ask whether the Energy Department would fund earmarks even though the legislation stated that agencies were not legally bound to fund the projects. The senators were concerned because of reports that the DOE stated it would fund the earmarks anyway.[34] Secretary Bodman responded by issuing a memorandum to the department's program secretarial officers that, while "some of your offices have begun to receive requests from some Congressional offices, asking that the Department continue to fund programs or activities that received earmarked funds in prior years," that "the funding provided by J.S. Res. 20 will not be subject to nonstatutory earmarks." The Secretary mandated an additional level of scrutiny of funding decisions, stating that, "If H.J. Res. 20 is enacted into law, I will ask each of you to submit a report containing your recommendations about which, if any, earmarks . . . should continue to receive funding" and that "no final decisions are to be made concerning those potential recipients until after you have submitted your report and received further guidance from the Secretary's office." To hold Secretary Bodman to his word, Senator McCain had the Secretary's response letter and memorandum entered into the Congressional Record during the debate prior to passage of the bill.[35] When legislators request information from agencies, they are not simply asking for the agency's expertise. These requests are strategic.

Moreover, legislators do not only request information from agencies, but they offer it as well. Legislators notify agencies of new technology they urge the agency to consider, although these requests can also serve as introductions on behalf of particular companies looking for government contracts. They also advise agencies based on the legislator's previous experiences and expertise, often acquired from former occupations. For example, Rep. Silvestre Reyes (D-TX) referenced his "26.5 years as a Border Patrol vet" in a letter to DHS Secretary Chertoff and Attorney General Gonzales about enforcing immigration laws.[36] Not surprisingly, legislators also inform agencies about the interests and concerns of groups, communities, organizations, and industries, often from within their constituencies (e.g., Lowande, Ritchie, and Lauterbach 2019). These communications are important because legislators can notify agencies about the unintended consequences of policies. For instance, several legislators alerted DHS to the potential problems the new Western Hemisphere Travel Initiative (WHTI) rules requiring passports for border crossings would raise for religious groups, such as Amish communities, who have religious objections to being photographed.[37]

The exchange of information between legislators and agencies reveals an important characteristic of separation of powers in practice. There is constant collaboration between legislators and agencies, both on legislating and on implementing law.

Enforcement

Finally, agencies can quietly shift their enforcement activities without making formal policy changes and still obtain the desired outcome. Agencies have wide discretion over the enforcement of policy, which they can use to shape outcomes in ways comparable to legislating because enforcement decisions can apply to, or exempt, broad swaths of industry, regions, occupations, people, or innumerable other categories (e.g., Barkow 2016; Scholz and Wei 1986). Indeed, agencies have long exercised enforcement discretion on a categorical basis.[38] Moreover, agencies strategically try to avoid public scrutiny of their enforcement activities (e.g., Muehlenbachs, Sinha, and Sinha 2011).[39]

This enforcement discretion, often referred to as prosecutorial discretion, describes the wide latitude agencies have in deciding when and how to prosecute violations of the law. For example, what determines a violation? How will the regulated be monitored for potential violations? What are the consequences for violations (e.g., fines, license revocation)? What classes of people, industries, occupations, products, or regions should be targeted or exempted? Should the law be enforced at all? While the public is most aware of prosecutorial discretion related to issues such as immigration and marijuana, agencies use discretion related to the enforcement of laws across a wide span of policies.[40]

In fact, agencies have significant liberty to avoid enforcing the law. Agency enforcement policy mostly escapes political oversight and judicial review, and decisions not to enforce are "presumed immune from judicial review."[41] Indeed, the Supreme Court ruled that agency decisions not to enforce are presumptively unreviewable in a case brought against the Food and Drug Administration (FDA). Death row inmates sued the FDA for refusing to take enforcement action to block the use of a drug that had not been approved for human execution. The Court ruled against the inmates and reasoned that "an agency's decision not to prosecute or enforce... is a decision generally committed to an agency's absolute discretion," and that such decisions involve a "complicated balancing of a number of factors which are peculiarly within [the agency's] expertise" such as "whether agency resources are best spent on this violation or another, whether the agency is likely to succeed if it acts, whether the particular enforcement action requested best fits the agency's overall policies, and, indeed, whether the agency has enough resources to undertake the action at all." The Court concluded, "An agency generally cannot act against each technical violation of the statute it is charged with enforcing."[42]

The consequence, some argue, is "nearly unfettered discretion":[43]

> On a typical day, Labor Department officials decide what plants to inspect for occupational safety violations with little or no external review. Prosecutors decide whom to indict. Treasury officials decide whether to freeze the assets of a charity because of alleged links to terrorism. Homeland security inspectors decide whether a Namibian woman will be turned away at a port of entry without being allowed to plead her case for asylum, and whose name is placed on a government "no-fly" list. These reservoirs of discretion persist even in settings where judicial review of executive branch action is considered a central tool, one that not only resolves individual claims but prevents systemic mistakes or abuses.[44]

On a case-by-case basis, such discretion is not paramount to public policy. When such enforcement discretion covers broad categories of people, industries, and regional characteristics, it becomes proportionate to policy. In fact, policymaking that is taken up formally in the rulemaking process sometimes begins as guidance or enforcement decisions.

Prosecutorial discretion is broad but not unlimited. There are two potential limitations on prosecutorial discretion. First, selective prosecution based on race, religion, or other unjustifiable factors—such as exercising one's constitutional rights—is prohibited.[45] However, there is a high bar for claims of selective prosecution as defendants must show "clear evidence," including that the agency action was motivated by a discriminatory intent.[46] Second, it could be argued that an agency is violating the Take Care Clause, based on Article II, Section 3 of the US Constitution, by abdicating its duty to implement statute if the agency established a policy of non-enforcement. However, in practice, no court has invalidated a policy of non-enforcement based on the Take Care Clause.[47] Thus, while prosecutorial discretion is not unlimited, it is extremely broad, particularly in practice.

Often agencies do not even have the resources to fully enforce statute, and so they make decisions about how to prioritize cases and targets. For example, DHS only has resources to deport less than 4% of an unauthorized population each year, and so it must decide how to prioritize deportations. These decisions on prioritizing deportations are based on broad classifications including age, health, and behavior, even while being made on a case-by-case basis.[48]

An agency's enforcement discretion offers opportunities for legislators to influence policy outcomes through administrative enforcement practices. In fact, some research suggests that regional agency enforcement decisions are tied to the preferences of legislators. Regional differences in enforcement are associated with the political leanings of congressional delegations and linkages facilitated by interest groups.[49] Of course, legislators also urge agencies to enforce the law, although it is often not clear whether a single legislator's interpretation of how the law should be enforced is representative of congressional intent. Whether urging agencies to enforce the law or requesting delays or limits to the enforcement of law, legislators' communications with agencies indicate a constant effort to shape the priorities, resources, and outcomes of administrative policymaking.

Even before President Obama issued the executive order known as Deferred Action for Childhood Arrivals (DACA), legislators contacted DHS to influence how the agency prioritized deportations. As I will revisit in Chapter 6, dozens of House members and senators specifically requested deferred action for childhood arrivals. Over two years before President Obama's executive order, Senators Richard Durbin (D-IL) and Richard Lugar (R-IN) wrote to Secretary Janet Napolitano asking that she halt the deportations of undocumented immigrants who would be eligible for cancellation of removal or a stay of removal under the Dream Act, legislation that had been introduced but not passed. While the Dream Act continued to languish in Congress, 24 Senate Democrats asked DHS to implement the pending legislation and publicize an application process for Dream Act cases.[50] Secretary Napolitano responded to the senators letting them know that a few weeks after the department had received their letter, the Director of ICE, John Morton, had issued a memorandum outlining the immigration enforcement priorities of ICE, how prosecutorial discretion should be used, and stating that "individuals present in the United States since childhood" should be considered a positive factor when exercising prosecutorial discretion.[51]

Enforcement discretion has also played a visible role in the regulation (or lack thereof) of marijuana, particularly in states that have legalized the drug. Several members of Congress intervened to take advantage of agency enforcement discretion on behalf of their states. For example, in 2018, Attorney General Jeff Sessions rescinded an Obama-era DOJ policy, known as the Cole Memo, that sanctioned non-interference with states that had legalized marijuana.[52] The DOJ statement announcing the move characterized it as a "return to the rule of law" and stated that "Attorney General Sessions directs all U.S. Attorneys to enforce the laws enacted by Congress."[53] Sessions's action panicked members of Congress representing states where marijuana was legal because of the impact on the states' now thriving marijuana industries.[54]

Several lawmakers asked the Attorney General to uphold the Cole memo. These efforts included a group of eleven senators led by Senators Elizabeth Warren (D-MA) and Lisa Murkowski (R-AK) who wrote to Sessions in 2017. Later, the Colorado congressional delegation sent a letter requesting that the Attorney General reconsider the new guidance rescinding the Cole memo.[55] One member of the Colorado delegation, Senator Cory Gardner (R-CO), reinforced the letter by placing holds on DOJ nominees, arguing that the Attorney General had promised Gardner he would uphold the previous DOJ policy prior to his own nomination.[56] Despite Attorney General Sessions's assertion that the new guidance would be a return to "the rule of law," enforcement practices did not seem to change in the year following Sessions's memorandum, which some industry observers attributed, in part, to significant push back from members of Congress.[57]

Legislators' attempts to influence enforcement go well beyond prosecutorial discretion on immigration and marijuana, and legislators pair their efforts with the agency as a part of a broader strategy to complement legislative action. For example, Rep. Bob Inglis (R-SC) wrote in a letter to Energy Secretary Steven Chu asking, "Could the DOE exercise its discretion to forestall enforcement of the 2010 commercial refrigerator/freezer standards against self-contained SOC Display Merchandisers while work is progressing on a legislative resolution that would establish credible, reasonable achievable standards for those products[?]"[58] As I discuss further in the subsequent section, savvy legislators use their influence with agencies to complement legislation in some cases and to substitute for legislation in others.

Back-Channel Policymaking in Practice

Why do members of Congress contact agencies? I have thus far described how legislators take advantage of administrative policymaking tools of regulation, information, and enforcement to pursue their goals of requesting action, blocking action, coordinating with agencies, and securing agency intervention with other political actors. However, describing each tool separately does not capture the implications of these constant communications from nearly every member of Congress and the savvy ways legislators use the bureaucracy's discretion as part of a larger strategy to accomplish their policy goals. I offer a brief depiction of the broader patterns of these informal interactions.

Are Policy Contacts Substitutes for or Complements to Legislation?

Legislators do not perform policymaking activities in isolation; they construct comprehensive, long-term strategies built from various policy outlets and venues at their disposal. Thus, the legislative and bureaucratic venues are interconnected. Often legislators' policy contacts with agencies are a complement to legislation, as when a lawmaker follows up with an agency to ensure her law is being enforced. This would, at least on its surface, seem like a clear example of action in the bureaucratic venue complementing legislative action. Likewise, a legislator might continue fighting a law he failed to block in the legislative process after passage by urging an agency not to implement it, delay implementation, or by requesting loopholes. In this example, too, communication with agencies acts as a complement to a legislator's votes, floor speeches, and other behavior within the formal legislative process.

However, informal policy appeals to agencies also serve as a substitute for formal legislative action. Substitutes are distinguishable from complements when two courses of action are focused on the same goal but are not interchangeable. When pursuing a policy change, a legislator has a choice between at least two courses of action. She can introduce a bill, or she can try to pursue the change through agency policymaking. In the opening example of this book, Senator Klobuchar chose to pressure the US Fish and Wildlife Service to take administrative action rather than introduce legislation to delist the gray wolf. She substituted back-channel policymaking for legislative action.

Members of Congress will even go so far as to use agency policymaking as a substitute for statute by asking agencies to implement bills that were introduced but failed to become law. For example, Rep. Lynn Woolsey (D-CA) requested that "DHS implement the provisions of the Humane Enforcement and Legal Protections for Separated Childern [sic] Act," a bill that offered protections for children and families in immigration deten-tion.[59] Rep. Woolsey introduced the bill, but it died in committee.[60]

However, the distinction between complements and substitutes may be hazier than it seems at first pass. Even the example I described as a clear case of complementary action, when a legislator follows up on legislation, may be broken down to demonstrate substitution. Are there legislative alternatives to informally following up with bureaucrats to ensure they are implementing a law? In fact, there are. Legislation can be drafted to include incentives and penalties, such as "hammers," to hold agencies on a tighter leash (e.g., Lauterbach 2020). Legislators can use formal means of oversight, including dragging the agency in for a committee hearing. However, drafting legislative hammers can be challenging and resource intensive, and including them may make the legislation less likely to pass. Of course, it's also difficult to pass new legislation. Committee hearings are a possibility, but only if the legislator is on the right committees, and scheduling the hearing is less feasible if she is not the committee chair or is in the chamber minority. It seems, then, that the bureaucratic venue is more akin to a substitute for legislative action.

What if, however, we focus on action in the legislative and bureaucratic venues, not in isolation, but as complementary components of an overar-ching strategy? Consider, for example, a letter from then House member, Rep. Ed Markey (D-MA) to HHS Secretary Tommy Thompson. In the letter, dated January 14, 2002, Rep. Markey refers to a bill that did not become public law until June 12, 2002:

> As you know, H.R. 3448 was passed by the House of Representatives on December 12, 2001 and I anticipate that this legislation will be signed into law early this year. It would require the HHS to establish stockpiles of potassium iodide within 20 miles of every nuclear power plant, to establish guidelines for its stockpiling, distribution, and utilization, and to

inform States and local governments of the program. Your willingness to adopt a pro-active policy in this area to complement the legislation is very welcome.[61]

Rep. Markey is asking the agency to implement legislation before it is passed by Congress. Now, if the legislation was not likely to pass, Rep. Markey's request could be viewed as a substitution for legislation. In this case, however, when the legislation was very likely to pass (and did), backchanneling appears to be a complement for the slowness of the legislative process on an issue that required some immediate action (preparedness for a nuclear disaster).

However, legislators also seek administrative collaboration to assist their legislation toward passage. They might, for instance, ask the agency to proactively implement a policy or delay policy changes until public opinion is more favorable for legislative action. Consider the following example of how Senator Bob Packwood (R-OR) described his strategy for achieving one of his early policy accomplishments using a combination of administrative and legislative action.

French Pete[62]

Newly elected, Senator Packwood was frustrated with how little power he had as a freshman senator in January of 1969 when, as he put it, "the seniority system ruled everything." He was "99th out of 100 and had no pick of anything worthwhile including committee assignments." As such, he "would be appointed to committees of no use to Oregon and barely of use to the nation." To make matters worse, he and the senior senator from Oregon, Mark Hatfield (R-OR), were in opposition on some of Oregon's top priorities, despite their shared party affiliation.[63]

This led to a political battle that required not only a legislative strategy but concerted efforts in both the legislative and bureaucratic venues. In fact, low-ranking legislators can team up with like-minded bureaucrats to pursue shared policy preferences even when such preferences are at odds with those of the agency and Congress.

This unlikely inter-branch teamwork saved an old-growth forest in Oregon called French Pete. In early 1969, the timber industry was eager to begin logging in French Pete, which would destroy it as a wilderness area. Perhaps surprising to some, the Forest Service joined the timber industry in its efforts to log the forest. The Forest Service relented to environmentalists' demands by agreeing to not allow logging until their appeals were adjudicated.

Despite that promise, on November 5, 1969, the headline of the Oregon newspaper, *The Register-Guard*, read "Forest Service seeks bids for logging in French Pete." The newspaper reported that the Forest Service would begin seeking bids for logging 16.5 million board feet of timber in French Pete. Fortunately for the environmentalists, they had found an advocate in Oregon's freshman senator, Bob Packwood, who recounted the situation:

> The environmentalists had been double-crossed. My first thought was this: How stupid is the Forest Service to say that it doesn't plan to cut until the appeals are done, yet put out bids to cut? In essence, the Forest Service was saying that it didn't really care about the appeals. The agency seemed confident that it would win eventually. What game was being played?[64]

The senator "immediately insisted on meeting with the secretary of agriculture, which has jurisdiction over the Forest Service."[65] He asked that Secretary Clifford Hardin "intervene so that more time could be provided for public discussion. Hardin relented, placing a 60-day delay on the timber sales."[66] The Senator described the meeting in a diary entry dated November 19, 1969:

> We met. It was most revealing. The Forest Service's position was that asking for bids to cut was not the same as cutting. My response was, "If you don't know whether or not you're going to cut, why are you asking for bids now?" The Forest Service chief really didn't argue the point. He simply said, "The Forest Service has a national obligation to provide wood for the housing needs of the country. . . ." I responded, ". . . the people in Oregon no longer wanted their forests used principally for commercial timber, but instead preferred that they be used for recreation and wilderness."[67]

The senator later recounted, "The secretary saw the folly of pretending that in good faith you would wait until all the appeals are exhausted, and then, while the appeals are going on, put out a bid to cut. He reversed that decision. However, it was clear to me that the Forest Service and the timber industry were going to dig in."[68] In fact, the senator mused, "ironically, the Forest Service was so confident that French Pete would eventually be cut that it chose not to irritate even a junior senator, and publicly kept quiet about the delay."[69] But he knew he "had to start moving swiftly and develop a strategy and form a team if we were to delay the Forest Service's decision to cut, and eventually rescue French Pete."[70]

Moreover, the House member representing the district where French Pete was located, Rep. John Dellenback (R-OR), and the senior senator from Oregon, Mark Hatfield (R-OR), "openly supported Forest Service plans for logging in the area."[71] In short, Senator Packwood and the environmentalists were on their own.

The senator introduced a bill to delay the Forest Service's efforts to begin logging on December 19, 1969, but the freshman senator made little progress in Congress: "I tried for a year to get a hearing to no avail. It was now going to become a long slog. We would have to use every tactic possible and every available delay in hopes that public opinion would finally sway the Forest Service to our position."[72]

The role of administrative delay was critical, as legislative progress was still an uphill battle. Senator Packwood reintroduced his bill to protect French Pete at the start of the new Congress in 1971, but he described a grim outlook for the legislation:

> I was up against ... almost impossible odds in the Congress. French Pete was entirely within the State of Oregon. Under the practices of the Congress if a bill affects only one state the decision is left with that state's Members of Congress. In Oregon that was just Senator Hatfield, Congressman John Dellenback and me, and both Dellenback and Hatfield were opposed to my bill.[73]

Moreover, the senior senator from Oregon was actively fighting the bill. Under the headline "Hatfield stands pat on French Pete bill," a local Oregon newspaper reported a pathetic outlook: "Unless Hatfield supports the bill, its prospects are poor in [Chairman] Bible's subcommittee, of which he is a member. Packwood is not a member of that subcommittee nor the parent Interior Committee, hence has decidedly less influence on legislation of this nature."[74] The September 18, 1972, headline of the Roseburg *News-Review* made it official: "Hatfield Kills Packwood Bill on French Pete." The paper went on to report, "Sen. Bob Packwood's bill to preserve French Pete Creek Valle is dead, a casualty of Sen. Mark Hatfield's negative attitude toward it."[75]

Senator Packwood knew he needed help: "Delaying tactics now became all the more critical as my bill had no hope in Congress. And we had to use the time wisely to activate the environmentalists, rally grass roots and get public opinion on our side to change the attitude of the Forest Service."[76]

Then, in November of 1970, the senator and environmentalists found a valuable partner in the Forest Service. The senator read an interview published in the local newspaper with the US Forest Service's new chief of the Willamette National Forest, Zane Grey Smith, one of the youngest supervisors in the United States and "a star in the U.S. Forest Service." One statement from Smith got the senator's attention:

" 'Oh, I guess if you would take a poll of all the supervisors in the Oregon and Washington national forests, I would be the only one . . . '

'One what?' the interviewer asked.

' . . . who is a member of the Sierra Club,' Smith said."

The senator was impressed with Smith, "a very wise career bureaucrat—and I use that term in the best sense," and saw a pathway to permanently protecting French Pete through a strategy combining legislative action with administrative delay:

Forest supervisors have immense power. The secretary of agriculture and the Forest Service may have plans to cut this forest. In carrying out those plans, Smith initiates a long, long process of planning. This was not a plan for cutting. This was a plan for studying, for public input, for delay. And hopefully, at the end of that planning and all of those hearings, public opinion will win—French Pete will not be cut.

Looking for administrative delay, Senator Packwood turned to his like-minded ally in the Forest Service, Zane Smith. He described his meeting with Smith in a diary entry on Tuesday, December 18, 1973, at 3:30 p.m.:

Met with Ted Schlapfer and Zane Smith. Schlapfer is the new Regional Forester in Portland and Smith heads the Willamette National Forest in Eugene. They both agreed the best thing to do with French Pete was to put it into the overall land-use study for the entire Willamette Valley. I agreed. I asked how Hatfield and Dellenback had taken it. They indicated they weren't sure they were all that enthusiastic.

They then both smiled. No words were needed. It was a smile of mutual understanding. The Regional Forester and more importantly Zane Smith, the Willamette National Forest Supervisor, had made the decision that there would be no cutting in French Pete. Now it simply became a question of how to string out any decision until the public opinion was so over-whelming that the decision had to be to preserve French Pete. All I'm looking for is another way to delay any planned cutting of French Pete and if another study will do it for awhile then so much for the study.[77]

The strategy of legislative action and administrative delay proved effective. The senator described the continued fight:

The strategy of delay, delay was working. The tactics of winning the issue at the local level was working. The original small band of local environmentalists who had organized around French Pete was growing. Brock Evans, as the Northwest Director of the Sierra Club, was beginning to prioritize areas that were threatened and exposing those threatened area. Grass roots support was increasing. Public opinion and the environmental power to influence was growing. It was now only a matter of time.[78]

Moreover, the collaboration between senator and bureaucrat proved invaluable for the end goal:

We had the "breaks" and we seized them. And how fortunate we were in the hero, Forest Supervisor Zane Grey Smith—the right ally at the right time in the right place. Politics is indeed and so often—preparation, organization and luck.

In 1978, almost nine years after I introduced the first bill, French Pete was made a wilderness.

The senator's policy accomplishment, protecting French Pete from logging, was the product of the collaboration between the senator and bureaucrats and required both legislative and administrative efforts. While previous work on legislative effectiveness often focuses on the legislative process alone, it neglects the strategic approaches of savvy legislators reaching outside of the legislative venue. Indeed, studying this form of strategic, interconnected venue-shopping is challenging absent qualitative accounts. My intention for the qualitative accounts described in this chapter is to offer a broader, more detailed depiction of the ways legislators use their back-channel interactions with the bureaucracy beyond what is feasible in large-scale analyses in this book. In the next chapter, I begin examining these inter-branch interactions quantitatively.

Conclusion

Policies on a wide range of issues—from immigration to environmental regulations to contraceptive coverage—are the subject of lawmakers' interactions with federal agencies. Understanding the nature of these interactions is important because agencies make policy with the full force of law, and they have tools—including instruments of regulation, information, and enforcement—to accomplish their objectives. Previous literature has documented the strategies agencies develop to advance their interests and evade scrutiny and challenges by other political actors (e.g., Carpenter 2001; Potter 2019). I build on this important work by showing how legislators exploit these administrative strategies as well.

In this chapter, I offered qualitative accounts of these back-channel, inter-branch negotiations. Members of Congress regularly collaborate with agencies on public policy. Lawmakers pressure agencies to advance favored policies and to block or delay a policy they oppose. Individual members of Congress and agencies coordinate legislative and administrative action to accomplish a shared goal by strategically sidestepping opposition from others in Congress and the administration. Legislators ask agencies to intervene with other political actors, whether state governments, other nations, or even the other chamber of Congress.

Are these qualitative accounts representative of lawmakers' policy interactions with agencies? In case readers are not yet convinced of the importance of these inter-branch interactions for public policy, I make the case empirically in Chapter 5. Some skeptics, for instance, will no doubt question whether these policy appeals are merely symbolic. Are lawmakers' appeals to agencies cheap talk? When legislators reach out to agencies, is it to advance their policy preferences and priorities, or is it purely electorally motivated, as some scholars have suggested?

5

Misconceptions about Inter-Branch Relations

If members of Congress are using the bureaucracy as a backdoor for policymaking, why has it largely escaped scholarly attention? One reason for this oversight is that scholars have largely misunderstood the informal relationship between Congress and the bureaucracy, focusing, instead, on formal channels of control. Beyond the formal tools of congressional oversight, scholars have generally assumed that legislators are engaging in little more than smoke and mirrors, that these communications are not sincere efforts to influence policy.

At the foundation of this book is the assertion that legislators pressure agencies to influence policy. Yet, even this straightforward claim is at odds with long-standing assumptions made in the literature. In this chapter, I confront and systematically dispel several misconceptions in our conventional understanding of the relationship between members of Congress and the bureaucracy.

Skeptical readers, for instance, might dismiss lawmakers' policy appeals as cheap talk rather than a meaningful reflection of legislators' policy interests. Instead, it is argued, legislators use their communication with agencies to deceptively take credit for benefits accrued to their constituencies by giving "the impression of influence" over agency decisions in press releases (Grimmer, Westwood, and Messing 2014). Following Fiorina's seminal book (Fiorina 1977), it was commonly believed that these communications are primarily constituency service or requests for grants, and that legislators did not engage with agencies on policy matters to any meaningful degree outside of their committees. It is important to address these misconceptions because they are tied to the validity of my measure and the groundwork of my argument.

This chapter makes the case that lawmakers' informal appeals to agencies are purposeful efforts to influence public policy. I present evidence demonstrating that these policy communications are not cheap talk or campaign

Backdoor Lawmaking: Evading Obstacles in the US Congress. Melinda N. Ritchie, Oxford University Press.
© Melinda N. Ritchie 2023. DOI: 10.1093/oso/9780197670491.003.0005

fodder. Instead, these appeals reflect legislators' policy preferences and priorities and are related to their efforts at advancing policy within the legislative process. Moreover, the results of a placebo test establish that policy appeals are distinct from constituency service and grant requests. These quantitative findings complement the qualitative accounts from the previous chapter.

The findings of this chapter are important because they reveal that members of Congress view the bureaucracy as an alternative venue for pursuing their policy objectives. The prevalence of inter-branch policy communication indicates that this behavior has value for members of Congress given that they devote their limited time and resources to it. It also suggests that this behavior warrants greater attention from congressional scholars.

In this chapter, I lay the foundation for my examination of my theory using the dataset described in Chapter 3. First, I show that legislators contact the bureaucracy about policy issues and that this activity is widespread across Congress. Second, I offer evidence that legislators' policy appeals to the bureaucracy are a valid measure of their policy priorities. Third, I dispel several myths that have occupied the scholarly literature for decades. It is important that I establish this point of departure for testing the hypotheses described in Chapter 2 in subsequent chapters (Chapters 6, 7, and 8).

The Prevalence of Policy Appeals

Nearly all members of Congress make policy appeals to the bureaucracy. Every senator and all but nine House members contacted an agency about policy at least once during the eight-year period of my sample. Of course, even the legislators who never contacted the Departments of Labor, Homeland Security, or Energy may have contacted one of the other dozen departments not included in my sample, and they may have made contact before or after the time period covered by the dataset.

Moreover, members of Congress regularly communicate with agencies about policy. As reported in Table 5.1, senators contacted agencies about policy issues an average of 22 times during a congress, with Senator Robert Byrd contacting agencies about policy 137 times during the 110th Congress. House members averaged seven policy contacts, with Rep. Bennie Thompson (D-MS) contacting the most frequently with a total of 192 policy contacts during the 110th Congress. Table 5.2 breaks down policy contacts by

Table 5.1 Summary of Communication by Chamber and Type

	Senate				House			
	N	mean	min	max	N	mean	min	max
Policy		22	0	137		7	0	192
Casework		42	0	424		14	0	334
Grant		15	0	323		4	0	34
N	406					1765		

Table 5.2 Summary of Policy Communication by Chamber and Agency

	Senate				House			
	N	mean	min	max	N	mean	min	max
DOL		9	0	56		2	0	51
DOE		5	0	37		2	0	37
DHS		8	0	85		3	0	186
Total		22	0	137		7	0	192
N	406					1765		

agency, revealing that the averages are relatively consistent across the three departments, ranging between five through nine contacts for the Senate and two to three contacts per agency in the House.[1]

Which members of Congress reach out to agencies most frequently offers some insight into the validity of my measure of policy contact, as nearly all of them are the chair of the committee with primary jurisdiction over the agency. The most frequent policy contact (56) with the Labor Department came from Senator Ted Kennedy (D-MA) during the 110th Congress, while he was chair of the Labor Committee. Senator Jeff Bingaman (D-NM) contacted the Energy Department about policy most frequently (37 times, 110th) while he was chair of the Energy Committee and also had the second highest number of contacts during the 109th Congress while he was ranking minority member (30 times). Senator Pete Domenici (R-NM) contacted the DOE 29 times both during the 109th Congress while he was chair of the Energy Committee, and during the 110th while he was ranking minority member. Senator Robert Byrd had the most frequent contact with the Department of Homeland Security (85 times, 110th) while he was chair of the Appropriations Committee. Coming in a close second, Senator Susan Collins (R-ME) contacted DHS about policy 81 times during the

109th Congress while she was chair of the Senate Committee on Homeland Security and Government Affairs. Turning to the House, Labor Committee chair, Rep. John Kline (R-MN), contacted DOL about policy most frequently (51 times, 112th). Rep. Darrell Issa (R-CA) had the most policy contacts with DOE (37 times, 112th), notably as the Republican Oversight Committee chairman during the Obama administration. Homeland Security Committee chair, Rep. Bennie Thompson (D-MS), contacted DHS the most (186 times, 110th). These frequent correspondents offer some validity to the measure of policy contact, as we would expect chairs and ranking members of the committees with jurisdiction to have the most reason to contact agencies about policy, but not necessarily regarding grant requests and casework. Indeed, the members of Congress who most frequently contact agencies for casework and grants are a different set of legislators from those who contact about policy.[2]

These statistics align with the response of one Capitol Hill veteran—a legislative director who worked for three congressional offices over a decade. When asked how frequently his office communicated with agencies about policy, he reported that his office communicated with federal agencies about policy matters "weekly if not daily" (Ritchie 2018, 241). Considering the dataset includes three of fifteen cabinet departments, if we assume that legislators contact the other dozen cabinet departments at similar frequency, the average congressional office communicates with the bureaucracy about policy at least once or twice a week.[3] This suggests that members of Congress engage with agencies on policy matters as a regular component of their policymaking activities, and yet we know very little about it.

Taken together, nearly all members of Congress contact agencies about policy and do so fairly frequently. While the frequency of committee chairs' contact contributes validity to my measure of policy communication, these statistics reveal that policy appeals are not exclusively from committees. To the contrary, this behavior is widespread across Congress. Most legislators contacted each department in my sample at least once about policy. This prevalence conflicts with enduring assumptions in the literature that legislators' policy interactions with the bureaucracy are confined to committees and iron triangles.[4]

Can this inter-branch communication really be characterized as policymaking? The next section serves three purposes. First, I address and dispel several common misconceptions in the literature. Second, the empirical findings provide the foundation for the central argument of this book.

Finally, I validate my measure of policy appeals by presenting evidence that inter-branch policy communication represents meaningful efforts to influence policy.

Is This Policymaking? Measurement Validation and Misconceptions about Inter-Branch Communication

Are lawmakers' policy appeals to the bureaucracy a valid measure of policy-making?[5] It is possible, for instance, that legislators are merely forwarding along the letters of constituents in order to gain their favor and that policy appeals are cheap talk. It is also possible, as scholars have assumed, that these communications are deceptive credit claiming rather than deliber-ate policymaking efforts. Other common approaches subsume these inter-branch interactions under a nebulous definition of congressional oversight or conceive of them as parochial concerns detached from matters of the nation and statute. Indeed, if policy appeals are more closely related to campaigning than lawmaking, we should be suspect of this measure as well as my theoretical argument.

To assess the validity of my measure, I consider whether there is a rela-tionship between previously studied measures of legislators' policy priorities, roles, and policymaking efforts within the legislative arena and lawmaker's policy appeals to agencies. If legislators' policy contact is a valid indication of their policy priorities and policymaking efforts, we should observe a positive relationship between their policy appeals to the bureaucracy and their policymaking behavior and roles within the legislative process.[6]

As this section reveals, policy appeals are related to lawmaking, not elections. This finding breaks with conventional wisdom and contributes to our understanding of the informal relationship between Congress and the bureaucracy by overturning long-standing misconceptions. In the sections below, I systemically address several misconceptions using the novel data described in Chapter 3.[7]

Is This Cheap Talk?

Is policy communication cheap talk or a meaningful reflection of law-makers' policy priorities? If members of Congress are using inter-branch communication as a low-cost way to win favor from various interests, their policy appeals may not be sincere signals of their policy priorities.

First, these policy appeals are not as low-cost as readers might assume. Legislators are increasingly strapped for time and resources, particularly when it comes to policymaking (see Curry 2015; Hall 1996; Kingdon 1973). While legislators often rely on staff to engage with agencies, staff are also delegated costly policymaking activities including drafting legislation, maintaining relationships with interest groups, and making voting recommendations. Moreover, a growing line of research shows that staff have considerable influence over policymaking (Malbin 1980; Montgomery and Nyhan 2017). In short, staff do everything; engaging with the bureaucracy is not the exception.[8] Second, as demonstrated in Chapter 4, policy appeals can be quite technical in nature and require a substantial degree of policy expertise. While administrative staff in the district offices—known as caseworkers— manage constituency service, policy appeals require specialized expertise that is expected of policy or legislative staff—including legislative assistants, legislative directors, and the chiefs of staff.

I address this question empirically in two ways. I compare lawmakers' policy appeals to their legislative agendas. Legislative agendas are the set of policy issues that are the focus of legislators' participation in Congress and reflect their individual policy priorities. If policy appeals are directed by a lawmaker's policy priorities, we would expect the issues about which the lawmaker contacts the bureaucracy to reflect their legislative agendas. While legislative agendas are built from a range of policymaking activities, the bills lawmakers introduce or sponsor provide the foundation. Bill sponsorship is not costless but is less constrained by party leadership than roll-call votes. Instead, lawmakers can draft bills that reflect their own priorities and interests. Thus, bill introductions provide a useful reflection of lawmakers' legislative agendas (see Schiller 1995, 2000; Sulkin 2005, 2011).[9]

The data allow me to classify policy contact by the issues managed by an agency (policies managed by the DOL, DHS, and DOE). I compare the frequency of a legislator's policy contact with a particular agency (the DOL, DHS, or DOE) to the number of bills she introduces related to the corresponding issue area (labor, homeland security, or energy, respectively) during the same time period (2005–2012).[10] If policy contact is a valid measure of policy priorities, we should expect it to be significantly and positively correlated with bill introductions related to the same issue area. In other words, members of Congress contact the bureaucracy more frequently on issues that are on their legislative agendas. This result would indicate that a lawmaker's policy appeals are a credible signal of her policy priorities.

Second, I examine policy appeals by members of committees with jurisdiction. While legislators have limited control over their committee assignments, committee membership can also provide a measure of legislators' policy priorities. I have already shown that policy appeals are not exclusive to committees, but we would still expect lawmakers to have more frequent policy interactions with agencies under their committee's jurisdiction because of the additional attention legislators give to the issues under their committee's authority.[11] If policy appeals are positively related to bill introductions and committee membership, it suggests that they are a credible signal of legislators' policy priorities. In short, policy appeals are not cheap talk.

Is This Deceptive Credit Claiming or Earnest Policymaking?

Are legislators' policy appeals just fodder for press releases?[12] Some scholars argue that legislators contact agencies to generate a belief that they are responsible for benefits accrued to their constituencies, focusing on how such communications are a feature of legislators' presentational styles for their constituents rather than earnest policymaking efforts (Fiorina 1977; Grimmer 2013; Grimmer, Westwood, and Messing 2014). Legislators create the impression of influence by deceptively taking credit for agency decisions (Grimmer, Westwood, and Messing 2014 but see Ritchie and You 2019).[13] In short, legislators' requests to the bureaucracy are merely a theatrical prop.

Other depictions have characterized legislators' policy appeals to agencies as position-taking—strategically taking a popular, public position on an issue without necessarily intending to affect policy. Like deceptive credit claiming, this characterization assumes that the value of policy appeals is dependent on the public attention they bring to a lawmaker. In other words, these inter-branch communications are little more than smoke and mirrors.

In fact, formal participation in the legislative process faced similar skepticism as congressional scholars were reluctant to move beyond roll-call votes. Scholars questioned the credibility of legislative activities—such as bill sponsorship—as policymaking efforts, suggesting that they are motivated by position-taking rather than policy influence. It was assumed these activities were not intended to actually influence policy; but instead, they were used for their symbolic value. Indeed, Sulkin describes how these assumptions are "typically based on the (correct) observation that most introduced measures do not progress very far in the legislative process and hence have little direct effect on policy outputs. Thus, the arguments goes, it seems plausible that legislators undertake them not out of sincere desire to affect policy, but simply to reap the electoral benefits of position taking" (Sulkin 2011, 30). Yet, Sulkin points out that such assumptions fail to recognize how the policymaking process really works and that legislator behavior can influence policy beyond the direct effects described in civic textbooks:

> Kingdon (1984) argues that the agenda-setting process often takes place over an extended period of time, with support for a policy alternative "built gradually through a process of constant discussion, speeches, hearings, and bill introductions" (18). A particular introduction may be crucial to this "softening up" process, but it could be almost impossible to link it directly to a downstream policy outcome. Along the same lines, Koger (2003) contends that legislative success should be defined broadly because measures that fail to become law may still fulfill their sponsor's and cosponsors' goals in a variety of other ways. For example, the measures may "[be] incorporated into subsequent legislative proposals[,] ... stop another bill or class of bills[,] ... [or] send a signal of congressional interest to the executive branch on some regulatory issue" (230). Under all of these scenarios, a legislator's behavior can leave a legacy in policy that could not be predicted by simply tracking the fates of his or her introductions or cosponsorships.

Aligning with this reasoning, legislators' policy appeals to agencies— while external to the formal legislative process and often without a direct, identifiable effect—can have an impact on policy similar to formal legislative participation.

Moreover, Sulkin (2011) makes the point that any activity could be symbolic:[14] "If we also rule out roll call voting, which Mayhew explicitly called out as position taking (1974, 61), there is not much left ... So, unless we are prepared to say that every legislative activity is symbolic, or that legislators simply do not care about policy, categorizing whole classes of activities as symbolic offers us little analytical leverage" (Sulkin 2011, 32–3). In short, formal legislative participation also can be used for credit claiming or position-taking, whether or not it influences policy outcomes.[15]

My argument is not that policy appeals are never used for position-taking, credit-claiming, or for any other objective. Like bill introductions and votes, policy appeals are driven by a wide variety of motivations. My objective, rather, is to show that they are used, to a degree comparable to formal legislative participation, to influence policy.

As such, I take up the question of whether legislators' policy appeals to agencies are deliberate efforts at policymaking. If legislators' policy communication with agencies represents earnest policymaking, we would expect it to be positively associated with their efforts to advance policies within the legislative process. Volden and Wiseman's legislative effectiveness scores (LES) offer an appropriate measure of legislators' efforts to advance policies, especially as they capture the amorphous skills and efforts required through the various stages of legislating (e.g., negotiating, gaining support for cosponsors, navigating committees and floor procedures, etc.) (Volden and Wiseman 2014). These informal and even unorthodox efforts also characterize back-channel policymaking, as legislators are motivated to move outside the legislative venue to advance policy. If lawmakers' policymaking efforts in the backchannel and the legislative process are linked, it suggests legislators' individual capacity for and focus on advancing policy is not isolated to the traditional venue for legislating. In short, a positive association between LES and policy appeals indicates that lawmakers' appeals to the bureaucracy are motivated by the same objective as when they advance policy in Congress. Lawmakers' efforts in either venue may vary based on conditions of institutional constraint and opportunity, as I examine in Chapter 6, but their individual capacity and intent for policymaking straddles the separate branches.

An alternative way to assess whether policy communication is intended for campaign fodder is to examine electoral incentives. While the connection between electoral incentives and legislator behavior can be complex (see Sulkin 2005, 2011), if policy communication is a campaign-driven activity, we might see it become more frequent as an election approaches. We would likely see this relationship primarily for senators since House members are in a constant campaign due to their short, two-year terms. We might also observe vulnerable legislators contacting agencies more frequently in order to increase their press release counts. Again, these electoral associations can be complicated, but robust associations might bring the validity of the measure into question.

Is This Oversight?

It is common practice to characterize the interactions between Congress and the bureaucracy as congressional oversight. In Chapters 1 and 2, I explain why characterizing these informal interactions between individual legislators and agencies as oversight lacks conceptual clarity and precision. In short, given that "Congress is a 'they' not an 'it,'" we should not assume that legislators are engaging with agencies to ensure legislative intent rather than evade it themselves (Shepsle 1992).

However, I consider this conventional wisdom empirically by accounting for membership on the Oversight Committee. In fact, it would be surprising if committees tasked with overseeing agencies did not account for policy communication at all, and a positive association between oversight committees and my measure offers some validation of the nature of policy communication, particularly if we do not observe the same relationships with casework and grant requests. A relationship between Oversight Committee membership and policy appeals is also not inconsistent with my theory. First, policy appeals from individual members of the Oversight Committee, or any other committee, do not indicate they are probing abuse, waste, or violations of the intent of Congress (i.e., traditional portrayals of oversight). Moreover, Oversight Committee membership may offer legislators additional leverage over agencies given the threat of hearings and investigations, which could increase members' incentive for making policy appeals (see Chapters 6 and 8 for further discussion and analysis on this point). Second, the purpose of accounting for oversight is to show the robustness of the relationships with the measures of policy priorities (e.g., bill sponsorship) while controlling for committees with oversight. Of course, legislators contact agencies for many reasons, including oversight. However, the expected results would offer evidence that we paint with too broad a brush when suggesting that inter-branch policy interactions are solely to investigate abuse and waste and to ensure the implementation of statute—setting aside conceptual issues of collective intent addressed in previous chapters.[16]

Placebo Test: Is This Constituency Service by Another Name?

In his seminal book, Fiorina offered the cynic's view of the relationship between Congress and the bureaucracy:

Public policy emerges from the system almost as an afterthought. The shape of policy is a by-product of the way the system operates, rather than a consciously directed effort to deal with social and economic problems. Congressmen know that the specific impact of broad national policies on their districts is difficult to see, that the effects are hidden, so to speak. They know too that individual congressmen are not held responsible for the collective outcome produced by 535 members of Congress. Thus, in order to attain reelection, congressmen focus on things that are both more recognizable in their impact and more credible indicators of the individual congressman's power—federal projects and individual favors for constituents. In order to purchase a steady flow of the latter, congressmen trade away less valuable currency—their views on public policy.

Fiorina's portrait of members of Congress as "monopoly suppliers of bureaucratic 'unsticking' services" has become the prominent view on the relationship between individual legislators and agencies (Fiorina 1977, 179–180).

While Fiorina revealed an important and enduring feature of Congress, the ensuing perception may be overstated and oversimplified. As I have shown in previous chapters, members of Congress regularly engage with the bureaucracy on matters of policy, even complex, technical issues that would be challenging to present to their constituents. I also address the myth that individual legislators' interactions with the bureaucracy are merely casework and grant requests empirically using the classification scheme and resulting dataset described in Chapter 3.

I employ a placebo test using casework and grant requests as substitutes for policy communication to examine whether the results I find are unique to my measure. The results underscore the distinctiveness of policy communication and offer further validation of the measure. We might expect some of the associations predicted for policy appeals to extend to these other two types of communication, particularly since grant requests could be viewed as distributive policy. For example, legislators who prioritize energy issues are also likely to request grants from the DOE. Moreover, it bears restating that the category labeled "casework" also includes non-policy contacts, such as event invitations to be the keynote speaker at an energy-themed conference, that could be related to legislative priorities and committee membership. However, these factors would work against my expectations, offering a conservative test of the validity of the measure. Strong results consistent with my predictions for policy communication paired with conflicting, relatively weak results for grant requests and casework bolster the validity of my measure as distinctly reflecting policymaking efforts.

Evaluating Inter-Branch Communication

I use the dataset described in Chapter 3 to address each question described in the previous sections and to offer validation of my measure of policy appeals. The dependent variable is the count of policy contacts from a legislator to an agency during a Congress.[17] To assess whether policy appeals are cheap talk, I examine the relationship between the number of times a legislator contacted each department about policy with the number of bills the legislator introduced during the same Congress on labor, energy, or homeland security issues (corresponding to the issues under the department's jurisdiction) and with the legislator's committee membership. If policy appeals are a meaningful reflection of a lawmaker's policy priorities, we would expect policy contacts to be positively associated with the corresponding bill introductions and higher for members of the committee with primary jurisdiction over the agency.

To consider whether policy appeals are motivated by deceptive credit claiming or position-taking, I examine the relationship between the number of times a legislator contacts the bureaucracy about policy and her legislative effectiveness scores (LES), vote share in the previous election, and, for senators, a variable indicating if the senator is within two years of her next election. If policy appeals are motivated by earnest policymaking, we would expect to observe a positive relationship between the frequency of policy communication and LES, which would suggest that lawmakers who are focused on advancing policy through the legislative process are also driven to advance policy in the bureaucratic venue. If, contrary to my argument, policy appeals are electorally driven fodder for the campaign trail, we would observe a negative relationship between frequency of policy appeals and vote share (a measure of electoral safety) and a positive relationship with an approaching election, suggesting that electorally vulnerable legislators contact agencies more as an election draws near. I expect to find the opposite or a null relationship between policy appeals and these measures of electoral incentives.

Finally, I account for a legislator's membership on the Oversight Committee.[18] I expect that Oversight Committee members may contact agencies about policy more. However, accounting for Oversight Committee membership, as well as membership on committees with jurisdiction over the agencies, allows me to examine whether the relationship between policy appeals and measures of policy priorities (e.g., bill introductions) and policymaking efforts (e.g., LES) remain robust when accounting for traditional sources of oversight.

The results presented in Table 5.3 also account for the legislators' party affiliation, the population of the legislators' district or state, and, for senators, whether the senator did not serve the entirety of her term. But substantive

Table 5.3 Legislative Determinants of Policy Contact

	Senate			House		
	DOL	DOE	DHS	DOL	DOE	DHS
Labor bills	0.746* (1.97)			0.210** (2.27)		
Labor Committee	1.665 (1.41)			1.059** (2.08)		
Energy bills		0.856*** (6.15)			0.466*** (3.94)	
Energy Committee		1.414 (1.60)			1.133*** (3.67)	
Homeland security bills			0.975** (2.08)			1.423* (1.83)
Homeland Security/ Oversight Committee	0.517 (0.38)	1.730* (1.84)	3.047 (1.58)			4.234*** (3.13)
Oversight Committee				0.704* (1.89)	0.382 (0.96)	0.712* (1.89)
LES	0.696 (1.23)	0.658** (2.07)	1.176* (1.88)	0.284** (2.30)	0.155** (2.34)	0.368** (2.19)
Vote share	4.758 (0.78)	7.041** (2.37)	6.429 (1.42)	−0.639 (−1.35)	−1.147*** (−2.74)	−1.052 (−0.69)
Election within 2 yrs.	−0.480 (−0.75)	−0.252 (−0.69)	−0.613 (−0.91)			
Republican	0.921 (0.74)	0.107 (0.18)	−0.328 (−0.21)	0.165 (0.92)	−0.022 (−0.13)	−1.104* (−1.79)
Constant	3.785 (0.99)	−2.277 (−1.05)	2.473 (0.88)	2.002** (2.31)	1.050 (1.41)	−0.016 (−0.01)
Congress FE	Y	Y	Y	Y	Y	Y
N	403	403	403	1765	1765	1765
adj. R^2	0.073	0.295	0.199	0.063	0.099	0.180

t statistics in parentheses. Robust standard errors are clustered by legislator.
$^*p < 0.1$, $^{**}p < 0.05$, $^{***}p < 0.01$

findings are consistent when these variables are excluded. I also account for a wide-range of time invariant characteristics, including unobservable factors, particular to each Congress. For instance, the 2009 economic stimulus may have contributed to higher or lower levels of policy appeals during the 111th Congress. I use a Congress fixed effect, which accounts for such events by examining variation within each Congress. Table 5.3 displays the results for the Senate in the first three columns and results for the House in the last three columns. The first and fourth columns present the results for the DOL, the second and fifth columns present the DOE results, and the results for DHS are displayed in the third and sixth columns.[19]

First, consistent across both the House and Senate and all three departments, we observe a positive and significant association between policy communication and bill introductions within an issue area. This offers the first strong, empirical evidence that policy communication is, in fact, measuring a legislator's policy priorities.

Second, across both chambers and all three departments, we observe a positive relationship between policy communication and membership on the committee with jurisdiction, with all three models showing statistically significant relationships in the House. In the Senate, the association between policy communication with DHS and membership on the Committee on Homeland Security and Governmental Affairs is statistically significant, although it is important to note that the Senate's Homeland Security Committee also serves as its chief oversight committee. Why might we observe a stronger relationship between policy communication and committee membership in the House than the Senate? This result is consistent with what we know about chamber differences in the committee system. Committees play a larger role in the House, with its larger membership and incentives for House members to specialize if they want to have any influence. In the Senate, individual senators have more power and are on more committees, and thus they spend less time and resources working through their committees (e.g., Volden and Wiseman 2018).

Third, I find that policy communication is positively and significantly related to measures of legislative effectiveness (LES) across all three departments in the House models and two of the three departments in the Senate models. The relationship is positive across all models. Lawmakers who are focused on advancing policy through the legislative process are also driven to advance policy through the bureaucracy. These results suggest that policy appeals to agencies are meaningful efforts at policymaking.

Fourth, there does not appear to be a strong relationship between policy communication and electoral factors. In fact, senators' policy communication is positively associated with vote share (significantly so in the DOE model) and negatively associated with an approaching election. In the House models, policy communication is negatively associated with vote share, but only significant in the DOE model. These chamber differences could suggest that senators and House members use policy communication in distinct ways, with a closer tie to electoral considerations in the House. I explore these chamber differences further in subsequent chapters. Overall, though, the results do not offer evidence of a strong relationship between policy communication and electoral status.

Fifth, I find some evidence of a relationship between oversight and policy communication. There appears to be a consistently positive relationship between membership on the oversight committees and policy communication. This relationship is significant in the House for the DOL and DHS models. The Senate models are more challenging to interpret given that the Senate Oversight Committee also has jurisdiction over the DHS. However, these models show a positive relationship that is significant only for the DOE. Of course, committees with jurisdiction also play an oversight role. More importantly, however, even when accounting for these oversight venues, we still observe strong relationships with measures of legislative policymaking, such as bill introductions and LES. The robustness of the relationships with policymaking measures suggests that policy communication with agencies is not solely, or even primarily, consumed by oversight functions.

Placebo Test

Are these patterns particular to policy communication? If we observe the same patterns for constituency service, readers would have reason to doubt the validity of the measure of policy appeals. How do the results for policy communication compare to grants and casework? I address this question by substituting the number of grant- and casework-related contacts as the dependent variables in place of policy communication. Next, I compare results for policy, grants, and casework when the agencies are aggregated in Table 5.4.

To be clear, it would not be surprising to observe some of the same relationships for grants and casework as for policy communication. As noted

Table 5.4 Placebo Test: Policy Contact, Grant Requests, and Casework

	Senate			House		
	Policy	Grant	Casework	Policy	Grant	Casework
LES	2.352**	−1.568	−0.119	0.883***	0.066	0.157
	(2.53)	(−0.83)	(−0.04)	(3.88)	(0.95)	(0.75)
Oversight Committee	5.367*	0.622	−3.481	1.810**	0.247	−0.994
	(1.71)	(0.35)	(−0.49)	(2.08)	(0.68)	(−0.68)
Election within 2 yrs.	−1.269	−0.193	0.042			
	(−1.17)	(−0.17)	(0.01)			
Vote share	13.130	30.330	−0.056	−2.928	−1.196	−7.314**
	(1.29)	(1.11)	(−0.00)	(−1.63)	(−1.53)	(−2.11)
Republican	1.019	−4.671*	2.124	−0.998	−0.538**	−0.795
	(0.37)	(−1.84)	(0.27)	(−1.39)	(−2.53)	(−0.63)
Constant	7.910	−16.370	38.150	3.286*	6.598***	1.933
	(1.16)	(−0.80)	(1.32)	(1.69)	(6.61)	(0.28)
Congress FE	Y	Y	Y	Y	Y	Y
N	403	403	403	1765	1765	1765
adj. R^2	0.220	0.210	0.132	0.138	0.270	0.020

t statistics in parentheses. Robust standard errors are clustered by legislator. All models include contacts to the DOE, DOL, and DHS.
$^*p < 0.1$, $^{**}p < 0.05$, $^{***}p < 0.01$

above, grants are a type of distributive policy. Moreover, the casework category includes event invitations that could be related to a legislator's policy interests, and constituency requests often reflect district or state characteristics that are tied to a legislator's priorities. Thus, this placebo test offers a conservative assessment of the measure.

Critically, the positive, significant relationship with LES appears to be exclusive to policy communications. Lawmakers who are focused on advancing policy through the legislative process make more policy appeals to the bureaucracy. None of the models presented in Table 5.4 show a significant relationship between LES and grants or casework, and the coefficients are negative in the Senate models. This comparison of the results across policy, grants, and casework offers strong evidence that policy communication measures meaningful efforts at policymaking and is clearly distinct from grants and casework.

The results for Oversight Committee membership offer further confirmation. Oversight Committee membership is positively and significantly associated with policy communication but is not robust for grant requests and is negatively associated with casework. The results for Oversight Committee membership offer further confirmation that policy communication is distinct from casework.

The electoral variables, too, offer additional evidence of this distinction between policy communication and constituency service. Contrary to the belief that policy appeals are mere campaign fodder, senators contact agencies about policy less often as their next election approaches. While the relationship is not statistically significant, it is notable that it is in the opposite direction of what electoral arguments would expect. Moreover, the results show that senators do engage in more casework as an election approaches, consistent with assumptions about the electoral value of casework. Likewise, senators contact agencies about policy more frequently when they hold safe seats, a relationship that is the reverse of what we would expect to observe if policy appeals were electoral fodder. The results for House members present a similar story. Policy communication from House members is negatively, but not significantly, associated with vote share. But electorally vulnerable House members engage in significantly more casework than their safe seat colleagues. Beyond the validation of my measure, these results confirm legislators' perception that casework has electoral value, consistent with Fiorina's (1977) classic argument.

Taken together, these results suggest that policy communication is, in fact, a policymaking behavior. Legislators' policy appeals to the bureaucracy mirror their policy efforts in the House and Senate chambers. Lawmakers use the bureaucracy as an alternative venue for policymaking.

Conclusion

The objective of this chapter is to convince skeptical readers that inter-branch policy contacts reflect lawmakers' earnest policymaking efforts and are sincere signals of their policy priorities. This chapter offers quantitative evidence to complement the qualitative accounts in Chapter 4. The findings of this chapter show consistent and robust associations between lawmakers' policy appeals to agencies and measures of their policy priorities and policymaking efforts within the legislative process. Policy communication is positively and significantly associated with bill introductions and

LES across both chambers and all three departments, indicating that the backchannel serves as an alternative policymaking venue for members of Congress. Moreover, these results are robust when I include membership on the committee with jurisdiction over an agency and on the Oversight Committee, suggesting that inter-branch policymaking cannot be subsumed under textbook notions of oversight. I do not find evidence that legislators' contact with agencies is related to electoral contexts. Finally, I use casework and grant-related contacts in a placebo test to further validate and establish my measure as a distinct form of inter-branch communication and policy-making.

Additionally, I show that members of Congress regularly contact agencies about policy issues and that this behavior is widespread throughout Congress. All of the senators and nearly all of the House members in my sample contacted an agency about policy issues. Moreover, the estimates of the frequency of inter-branch policy communication presented in this chapter are conservative as the sample includes three out of fifteen cabinet departments.

These findings counter several misconceptions in the literature. First, individual lawmakers' communication with agencies is not confined to case-work and grant requests. Legislators regularly communicate with agencies about policy. Second, these policy interactions are not limited to committees and oversight. Third, policy communications are not merely empty position-taking, fodder for press releases, or deceptive credit claiming. These inter-branch interactions represent meaningful policymaking efforts.

In conjunction, Chapters 3 and 5 provide the foundation for the remainder of the book by validating my measure of policy communication and establishing inter-branch communication as a form of policymaking. Chapter 6 tests my theoretical argument that members of Congress use backchannels of communication with the bureaucracy to evade constraints of the legislative process. Chapter 7 shows how legislators take advantage of the discreet nature of the backchannel on controversial issues. In Chapter 8, I examine agency responsiveness to legislators' policy requests. This chapter and the remaining empirical chapters support the central argument of this book: Members of Congress strategically use back-channel communications with the bureaucracy to influence policy outside of the lawmaking process and beyond the public eye.

Appendix

Table 5A.1 Descriptive Statistics of Policy Contacts by Chamber, Committee, and Party

	Senate				House			
	N	mean	min	max	N	mean	min	max
Labor Committee	84	10	1	56	231	3	0	51
Not on Labor Committee	323	8	0	40	1534	2	0	19
Homeland Security Committee	66	11	0	81	154	9	0	186
Not on Homeland Security Committee	340	7	0	85	1611	3	0	101
Energy Committee	95	7	0	37	240	3	0	21
Not on Energy Committee	312	5	0	25	1525	1	0	37
Democrats	209	23	2	137	900	7	0	192
Republicans	198	20	0	118	865	7	0	72
N	406				1765			

Note: Statistics by committee membership include only policy contacts to the agency under the committee's jurisdiction. Partisanship is determined by caucus participation.

Table 5A.2 Descriptive Statistics of Sample by Chamber

	Senate				House			
	No.	mean	min	max	No.	mean	min	max
No. of unique members	148				665			
Republicans	77				361			
Democrats	71				304			
Majority leader	14				34			
Minority leader	14				29			
Labor Committee	36				115			
Energy Committee	46				90			
Homeland Security Committee	31				75			
Oversight Committee (House)					67			
Election within 2 yrs. (Senate)	120							
Seniority (Yrs. in Office)		6.88	1	26		5.90	1	29
LES		1.01	0.01	5.97		1	0	18.69
Vote share		.61	.39	1		.67	.30	1
Labor Bill Introductions		1.58	0	11		1.13	0	21
Energy Bill Introductions		2.07	0	15		.76	0	18
Homeland Security Bill Introductions		1.55	0	19		.72	0	18

Note: Entries for dichotomous variables represent the number of unique members. Partisanship is determined by caucus participation.

6

The Bureaucracy: Congress's Backdoor to Policy Influence

The 111th Congress (2009–2011) was a fruitful time for the Democratic agenda. Democrats took advantage of the party's unified control with a flurry of legislative productivity on several fronts including the passage of the Affordable Care Act, pay equity protections for women, and the repeal of "don't ask, don't tell." In fact, the 111th Congress is considered one of the most productive in history.[1]

One objective on the Democrats' agenda lagged, however. Despite promising negotiations with key Republicans, the Democratic majority failed to pass the Dream Act, legislation that would have created a path for citizenship for immigrants who arrived in the US as children, referred to as Dreamers.[2] The favorable conditions of the 111th Congress moved the Dream Act within striking distance of passage, but it was not enough to push the legislation over the finish line.

The window of opportunity for the Dream Act closed with the end of the 111th Congress. After a crushing defeat in the 2010 election, Democrats faced divided government at the start of the 112th Congress after enjoying two years of unified control. With Republicans capturing the House and six additional Senate seats in the new year, the Dream Act was a legislative dead end in the 112th Congress.[3]

Yet, the lawmakers did not stop their efforts on behalf of Dreamers. Instead, they changed venues. Several members of Congress wrote to DHS Secretary Janet Napolitano asking her to implement the Dream Act, despite Congress's failure to pass the legislation.[4] Secretary Napolitano responded to the lawmakers notifying them that a memorandum had been issued directing the agency to use its discretion to protect childhood arrivals.[5] It would still be another year before President Obama issued his executive order commonly known as DACA.[6]

Legislators' efforts to lobby agencies are not recognized in the extant literature on Congress. Lawmakers' tenacity to secure policy change following

Backdoor Lawmaking: Evading Obstacles in the US Congress. Melinda N. Ritchie, Oxford University Press.
© Melinda N. Ritchie 2023. DOI: 10.1093/oso/9780197670491.003.0006

failure in the legislative process is not captured in studies of participation or legislative effectiveness. Yet, as I have shown in previous chapters, these policymaking efforts are not unusual. Legislators do not limit themselves to the legislative branch. Obstacles in the legislative process drive them to shift their efforts to the bureaucratic venue. Members of Congress are, first and foremost, not legislators, but policymakers; legislation is but one avenue through which they achieve their goals.

This chapter tests a central argument of the theory of back-channel policymaking. In the previous chapter, I provided the foundation for the analyses that follow by establishing that legislators' policy appeals to agencies are earnest policymaking efforts and a valid measure of their policy interests. I employ the dataset described in Chapter 3 to connect the theoretical arguments of Chapter 2 with quantitative analyses. In this chapter, I focus on one of the two ways constraints in Congress motivate lawmakers to exploit the bureaucracy.

This chapter examines how obstacles in Congress drive legislators to pursue agency policymaking as a substitute for legislative action. While agency discretion may be useful in the face of legislative hurdles, there are also limits to agency policymaking. Administrative action can be overturned or reversed and has less permanence than statute. Moreover, while a legislator's ability to influence policy in Congress is limited, administrative policymaking can be constrained by statute and presidential preferences and priorities. How do members of Congress weigh the trade-offs?

There are costs to policymaking in both the legislative and bureaucratic venues. The balance of these costs across venues determines a legislator's strategy. While legislators may be constrained from achieving policy change in Congress, they may not have the capability or opportunity to advance their objectives through the bureaucracy. In the sections that follow, I test a series of hypotheses derived from my theory that reflect these strategic considerations.

The purpose of this chapter is to consider how constraints, capacity, and opportunity interact to influence a lawmaker's strategy for advancing her policy objectives. First, I consider the trade-off between constraints and capacity by examining the relationship between legislators' experiences and institutional positions on how frequently they appeal to agencies. I show how constraints in Congress may motivate lawmakers to take advantage of the bureaucracy, but the costs of inter-branch negotiations limit their ability to exploit it.

Second, I then consider how a legislator's strategy accounts for the broader political environment and the opportunity to achieve her policy objectives within the executive branch. I examine the conditions under which lawmakers appeal to agencies and show that legislators exploit the bureaucracy when they face obstacles in Congress but also see opportunity in the executive branch.

Finally, I consider how these three factors—constraints in the legislative process, opportunity in the executive branch, and capacity—interact to affect a lawmaker's strategy for advancing policy and how the effect differs across chambers. In other words, I ask: Who uses the backchannel and under what conditions do they use it? These two questions are important for understanding how the separation of powers is exploited and the broader implications for policymaking and power in the United States.

Who Uses the Backchannel?

Some members of Congress are more powerful than others. The unequal distribution of power in Congress can be explained largely by the resources, skills, and advantages accrued from a legislator's institutional position and how many years she has spent walking the halls of the Capitol Building. In this section, I consider whether the bureaucracy's discretion offers an opportunity for low-ranking legislators to balance the scales, or if it serves as a second pathway for already powerful members of Congress. The answer to this question is important for determining whether back-channel policymaking mitigates or exacerbates the unequal distribution of power in Congress.

While all legislators face constraints in Congress, some are more limited than others. Institutional positions and experience (and the lack thereof) shape legislative productivity and effectiveness (Volden and Wiseman 2014, 2018). The average legislator's efforts to make policy change are often frustrated because they do not have a seat at the table. If legislators exploit the bureaucracy as an alternative policymaking venue, we would expect the members of Congress who are most constrained from influencing policy in the legislative process to appeal to the bureaucracy more frequently than their powerful colleagues. In Chapter 2, I introduced this expectation as the *legislative constraint hypothesis.*

However, there are also costs to bureaucratic policymaking. Like legislating, it requires expertise and awareness of the often obscure workings of administrative policymaking. This knowledge includes a familiarity with the agencies and individuals responsible for areas and stages of policymaking. Thus, the constraints that hinder lawmakers' participation in the legislative process may also deter their efforts to advance policies through the bureaucracy.

In other words, the constraints of the legislative process motivate lawmakers to exploit agency policymaking, but power, influence, and resources within Congress facilitate legislators' capacity to take advantage of it. A senior committee chair, for instance, has experience, policy expertise, and prior relationships with administrators that could facilitate further communication with an agency. Senator Ted Kennedy's decades of experience on the Labor Committee undoubtedly lowered the cost of his efforts with the Labor Department.

While I do not measure the agency's response to policy appeals in this chapter (but see Chapter 8), the potential for reciprocity has implications for how often legislators contact agencies. Agencies are more likely to give a member of Congress what she wants if they have reason to believe she can pay the agency back—or punish the agency for unresponsiveness—in the future. Previous work suggests that the more influence a lawmaker has in the legislative process, the more influence she will have over an agency (e.g., Arnold 1979, Bang and Hollibaugh 2022).[7] The perception of having an advantage incentivizes legislators to contact the bureaucracy if they expect the agency will respond favorably. Legislators who expect to carry more weight with an agency—such as leadership and committee chairs—members of the committees with jurisdiction, and White House co-partisans, may view the backchannel as more worthwhile.[8]

Taken together, members of Congress who are in the most need of an alternative way to influence policy may be the least capable of taking advantage of it. If this is the case, we should expect legislators in positions of power and influence in Congress to exploit their advantages with the bureaucracy more frequently than legislators who lack resources and experience within the legislative process. In Chapter 2, I refer to this expectation as the *capacity hypothesis*.

At the level of individual legislators, there is a direct trade-off between legislative constraint and capacity when operationalizing the two concepts. For example, a junior lawmaker is more constrained in her ability to influence policy in Congress but also lacks the capacity of her more senior colleagues to intervene in agency policymaking. Thus, when using the same individual-level measures for both legislative constraint and capacity, the hypotheses generally offer competing predictions for each variable. Junior legislators face higher hurdles in the legislative process, and so the legislative constraint hypothesis predicts junior members make policy appeals more frequently than their senior colleagues. However, senior lawmakers have greater capacity to work with agencies, reflected in the capacity hypothesis's prediction that senior lawmakers make policy appeals more frequently than junior legislators. While these hypotheses generally offer competing predictions, they are not mutually exclusive. Both relationships could be occurring simultaneously. Constraints in Congress motivate legislators to turn to the bureaucracy as an alternative venue for advancing their policy objectives, but capacity facilitates their ability to participate in agency policymaking. Examining constraints and capacity will help us understand who uses the backchannel and under what circumstances they use it.

Indeed, all members of Congress face constraints of some sort, whether due to freshman status or the powers maintained by the minority in the Senate. Even the Senate Majority Leader cannot push through whatever law he prefers. As I explore in subsequent analyses, back-channel policymaking may be most effectively leveraged by otherwise powerful lawmakers who run up against legislative hurdles.

Table 6.1 displays the hypotheses' predicted relationships between several measures of capacity and the frequency of policy appeals. While the capacity hypothesis predicts a positive relationship between lawmakers' policy appeals to agencies and the measures of capacity, the legislative constraint hypothesis predicts a negative relationship with the measures of capacity (the reverse of which operationalizes constraints; e.g., a position on leadership captures capacity, and rank-and-file status indicates a lawmaker is constrained). Since the hypotheses' predicted relationships may be occurring simultaneously, they could cancel out any clear associations in the results. Relatedly, this test does not serve to rule out one hypothesis or the other if the relationships are conditional (i.e., if legislative constraints primarily impact the behavior of high-capacity lawmakers). Instead, the results can offer insight into which relationship has a greater direct impact on the behavior of lawmakers.

Several of these measures of capacity are associated with participation in policymaking and legislative effectiveness in previous literature. Prior experience and institutional positions can lower costs and raise expectations

Table 6.1 Expectations for Legislative Constraint and Capacity Hypotheses

Variable	Expected Relationship to the Frequency of Policy Appeals	
	Legislative constraint hypothesis	Capacity hypothesis
Bill sponsorship	No prediction	Bill sponsorship demonstrates expertise that **increases** capacity to make policy appeals within the issue area.
Committee with jurisdiction	Committee influence over policies under its jurisdiction **decreases** incentive to make policy appeals.	Committee expertise and ability to reciprocate **increase** capacity for policy appeals on issues under its jurisdiction.
Seniority	Senior lawmakers' influence in Congress **decreases** their incentive to make policy appeals.	Senior lamakers' experience, expertise, and networks **increase** capacity for policy appeals.
Leadership	Leaders' influence in Congress **decreases** their incentive to make policy appeals.	Leaders' resources and ability to reciprocate **increase** capacity for policy appeals.
Committee/subcommittee chair	Chairs' influence in Congress **decreases** their incentive to make policy appeals.	Chairs' resources, expertise, and ability to reciprocate **increase** capacity for policy appeals.
Power committee	Power committees' influence in Congress **decreases** incentive for policy appeals.	Power committees' ability to reciprocate **increases** capacity for policy appeals.
Majority	Majority influence in Congress **decreases** incentive for policy appeals.	Majority ability to reciprocate **increases** capacity for policy appeals.
White House co-partisan	Co-partisans' influence in the legislative process **decreases** their incentive to make policy appeals.	Co-partisans' shared preferences with administration **increases** capacity for policy appeals.
Ranking minority member	Ranking members' minority status in Congress **increases** their incentive for policy appeals.	Ranking members' experience and expertise **increase** capacity to make policy appeals.

Note: There is generally a trade-off between constraint and capacity (see text), but the legislative constraint hypothesis does not offer a prediction for bill sponsorship. Ranking membership operationalizes capacity (ranking) and constraint (minority), so both hypotheses predict a positive relationship.

of successful participation, thus increasing a legislator's capacity for productivity (Hall 1996; Volden and Wiseman 2014, 2018; Woon 2009).

First, a legislator's experience and expertise facilitates policymaking. As previously described, lawmakers' seniority provides a measure of their experience, professional networks, and expertise, all of which would facilitate any type of policymaking activity. Bill sponsorship measures a legislator's expertise within an issue area (Hall 1996; Sulkin 2005, 2011; Woon 2009). While the legislative constraint hypothesis does not offer clear expectations regarding the relationship between bill sponsorship and policy appeals, a positive relationship would offer support for the capacity hypothesis. I expect a positive relationship, consistent with the results from Chapter 5. If a legislator introduces bills within a particular issue area, it suggests she has knowledge and familiarity with the issue that could be used to spur or block agency action.

The other measures of capacity account for advantages afforded from institutional positions. Previous work finds that institutional roles— including majority party status (Volden and Wiseman 2014), committee membership (Schiller 1995; Woon 2009), committee and subcommittee chairmanships (Hall 1996; Volden and Wiseman 2014), leadership positions (Hall 1996), and membership on powerful committees—can all contribute to capacity for participation in policymaking and productivity. Majority party status offers an advantage over legislating (Volden and Wiseman 2014), information from leadership (Curry 2015), and control over formal means of oversight. While minority party members may need an alternative policymaking venue, members of the majority can leverage their formal powers to negotiate with the executive branch and exploit agency policymaking.

Committee membership can offer an edge to legislators pursuing policy objectives within the committee's jurisdiction through legislative means, such as bill sponsorship, by lowering costs for committee members (Schiller 1995; Sinclair 1989; Woon 2009; Wilson and Young 1997) with an established background and expertise on the issue area (Gilligan and Krehbiel 1997; Krehbiel 1991) and through political information from their colleagues and staff attending to the issue (Hall 1996). Moreover, members can influence issues that come before their committee by participating in committee hearings and markups (Hall 1996). According to the legislative constraint hypothesis, legislators who are not on a committee may be shut out of influencing the policies under the committee's jurisdiction and, thus, may try to pursue policy influence through the bureaucratic venue instead. In the previous chapter, however, committee membership is shown to be positively associated with policy appeals to the agency under its jurisdiction suggesting that it facilitates informal interactions with agencies. I consider the robustness of these results in the analyses of this chapter.

Beyond the additional staff and resources available to leaders, leadership's agenda-setting powers also provide advantages over the legislative process, which extend to the bureaucratic venue. Leaders are more aware of the details of bills that pass (Curry 2015) and, thus, have a better sense of how the bureaucracy could make modifications to policies that leaders were not able to get in the actual legislation. Some of these advantages are also shared by members of powerful committees (e.g., Appropriations, Ways and Means) who, along with leadership, carry more weight with agencies, which could lead them to exploit agency policymaking if they think it will be worthwhile. On the other hand, leaders and powerful committee members may be more invested in the collective needs of the institution and less focused on personal policymaking objectives (Volden and Wiseman 2014, 2018).

Conventional wisdom and previous research suggest that Congress engages in more frequent oversight of an administration controlled by the opposing party (Kriner and Schickler 2016). Yet, if lawmakers' requests to agencies are driven by pursuit of their individual policy objectives, as I have argued, White House co-partisans may anticipate having an advantage with the administration that could make agency policymaking an appealing option (Lowande 2019, but see Ritchie and You 2019). The expectations are less clear, though, since White House co-partisans could also have an advantage in the formal legislative process depending on which party controls Congress; they may not wish to divert resources from the legislative to the bureaucratic venue.

Finally, as the minority party's committee leaders, ranking minority members are unique since both hypotheses predict the same relationship with policy communication. This convergence stems from these ranking members' capacity—in the form of knowledge, experience, networks, and resources—to exploit agency policymaking. Yet, as minority members, they are without institutional power or clear legislative advantage.[9]

Tables 6.2 and 6.3 present the results for regression analyses predicting how frequently lawmakers make policy appeals to the bureaucracy.[10] Table 6.2 displays the results for the Senate, and Table 6.3 presents the House results. I use the count of the number of policy contacts from a legislator to an agency during a Congress as the dependent variable, and I include

Table 6.2 Legislative Constraints and Capacity as Determinants of Policy Contact, US Senate

	DOL	DOE	DHS	Total
Labor bills	1.072***			1.576***
	(3.37)			(3.19)
Labor Committee	1.312			0.693
	(1.13)			(0.33)
Energy bills		0.907***		1.352***
		(6.98)		(3.81)
Energy Committee		1.471*		−3.253**
		(1.57)		(−1.98)
Homeland security bills			1.347**	1.033*
			(2.59)	(1.65)
Homeland Security Committee			2.199	4.182
			(1.22)	(1.49)
Committee chair	−0.381	−0.914	1.074	0.747
	(−0.25)	(−0.88)	(0.55)	(0.24)
Ranking minority member	1.194	−0.500	−0.992	0.477
	(0.80)	(−0.72)	(−0.54)	(0.15)
Power committee	−1.381	−0.880*	−1.192	−2.939
	(−1.11)	(−1.76)	(−1.09)	(−1.24)
Seniority	0.297	0.216***	0.548	0.975*
	(1.55)	(2.86)	(1.63)	(1.78)
Leadership	−1.808*	0.179	0.706	−1.174
	(−1.73)	(0.25)	(0.54)	(−0.51)
Minority	−2.208**	0.737	0.322	−1.078
	(−2.04)	(1.24)	(0.21)	(−0.44)
White House co-partisan	−0.037	−0.299	−1.287	−1.276
	(−0.05)	(−0.56)	(−1.44)	(−0.83)
Constant	12.360***	1.038	9.216**	26.490***
	(3.65)	(0.58)	(2.35)	(3.78)
Congress FE	N	N	N	Y
Controls	Y	Y	Y	Y
N	403	403	403	403
adj. R^2	0.153	0.282	0.219	0.284

t statistics in parentheses. Robust standard errors are clustered by legislator.
*$p < 0.1$, **$p < 0.05$, ***$p < 0.01$

Table 6.3 Legislative Constraints and Capacity as Determinants of Policy Contact, US House of Representatives

	DOL	DOE	DHS	Total
Labor bills	0.226**			0.099
	(2.48)			(0.62)
Labor Committee	1.097**			0.942
	(2.22)			(1.52)
Energy bills		0.478***		0.353**
		(4.42)		(2.12)
Energy Committee		1.149***		1.059**
		(4.15)		(2.01)
Homeland security bills			1.472*	1.324*
			(1.92)	(1.69)
Homeland Security Committee			4.163***	4.069***
			(3.21)	(3.07)
Committee chair	1.952**	2.087***	4.959	8.808**
	(2.15)	(2.80)	(1.38)	(2.30)
Ranking minority member	1.045**	0.756**	2.654*	4.524***
	(2.18)	(2.01)	(1.78)	(2.69)
Subcommittee chair	0.381	0.395**	0.697**	1.476***
	(1.62)	(1.97)	(2.12)	(3.09)
Power committee	0.061	0.045	0.138	0.193
	(0.33)	(0.28)	(0.45)	(0.36)
Seniority	0.044	0.054**	0.057	0.163**
	(1.50)	(2.02)	(1.54)	(2.46)
Leadership	0.069	−0.147	−0.306	−0.291
	(0.25)	(−0.77)	(−0.57)	(−0.48)
Minority	−0.039	−0.071	0.584*	0.379
	(−0.34)	(−0.54)	(1.87)	(1.03)
White House co-partisan	−0.179	0.041	−0.506	−0.583
	(−1.31)	(0.32)	(−1.50)	(−1.51)
Constant	2.052***	2.147***	2.497	8.610***
	(4.53)	(5.90)	(1.53)	(4.28)
Congress FE	N	N	N	Y
Controls	Y	Y	Y	Y
N	1765	1765	1765	1765
adj. R^2	0.085	0.128	0.180	0.189

t statistics in parentheses. Robust standard errors are clustered by legislator.
*$p < 0.1$, **$p < 0.05$, ***$p < 0.01$

models that separate out each agency (in the first through third columns) in addition to a model using an aggregated measure of policy contacts (the fourth column). The independent variables include the number of bills the legislator introduced during a Congress on labor (in the DOL model), energy (in the DOE model), or homeland security issues (in the DHS model),[11] membership on the committee with jurisdiction over the agency, seniority (the number of years in Congress), and dummy variables for committee chairs, subcommittee chairs, ranking minority members, power committee members, minority party membership, and leadership.[12] The models include the controls used in Chapter 5. These variables, some of which are not shown, include party affiliation, oversight committee membership (which is also Homeland Security Committee membership in the Senate), Legislative Effectiveness Scores (LES), ideological extremity, population of the legislator's district or state, vote share, and indicator variables for approaching election and serving a partial term (in the Senate models).[13] The first three models control for divided government. The aggregate model includes a Congress fixed effect to account for time-invariant characteristics specific to each Congress. The substantive results are consistent without the Congress fixed effect.

The results largely support the capacity hypothesis, strongly so in the House. The results for bill sponsorship and committee membership from Chapter 5 are positive with a largely consistent robustness. Seniority is significantly and positively associated with policy contact across both chambers. Committee chairs contact agencies more often across both chambers, significantly more in the House. Subcommittee chairs also contact significantly more often in the House.[14] Members of powerful committees make more contacts in the House models but fewer in the Senate models. Other results are in line with the constraint hypothesis but are not robust.[15]

The chamber differences are consistent with previous depictions of the egalitarian and individualistic nature of the US Senate in contrast with the hierarchical structure of the House. While institutional positions are important for participation in the House, there is less variation in capacity among individual senators based on institutional roles. However, the results for noninstitutional characteristics of senators' experiences and behaviors (bill sponsorship and seniority) are robust and in line with previous literature (Volden and Wiseman 2018). These chamber differences could suggest that inter-branch policy communication is filtered through committees and leadership in the House, while senators use back-channel policymaking to advance their own policy objectives and individual agendas.

Consistent with both hypotheses, ranking minority members in the House contact agencies significantly more. This could suggest that capacity acts through knowledge, experience, and networks—which lower the costs of back-channel policymaking—rather than through institutional power. This may support my argument that otherwise experienced legislators pursue the bureaucratic venue when they face obstacles in the legislative process, which I consider in the sections to come.

The results thus far, however, suggest that power in Congress extends to the bureaucracy. Rather than serving as a means for balancing the unequal distribution of power, the bureaucracy provides yet another venue for influence for powerful lawmakers. In short, the rich get richer.

Do Legislators Strategically Shift Venues?

Even the most powerful members of Congress are not unlimited in their ability to accomplish their goals within the legislative process. What do these lawmakers do when their efforts are stymied in Congress? Given their capacity for back-channel policymaking, under what conditions does the bureaucracy offer an advantage over the legislative process? How do lawmakers assess the trade-offs of the broader political context when deciding whether to pursue a policy goal through the bureaucracy?

Even powerful lawmakers, for instance, confront the limitations of minority status when their party has a poor showing in an election. While there are numerous other institutional contexts that can stymie otherwise effective lawmakers, minority party membership sidelines legislators from advancing their priorities.[16] If lawmakers who are usually effective at advancing legislation find themselves in the minority, do they confront their limited status in Congress by shifting their efforts to the bureaucracy?

We can observe, for instance, cases of lawmakers' policy appeals dropping when their party gains control of the chamber. Senator Richard Durbin (D-IL), the senior senator from Illinois and Senate Democratic Whip, was in the minority during the 109th Congress and reached out to the agencies with 47 policy appeals. When the Democrats won back the Senate, Senator Durbin's policy appeals fell to 28 contacts. For comparison, the number of bills Senator Durbin introduced climbed from 68 to 87 when he went from the chamber minority to majority.

In the next section, I probe this possibility further. Having answered the question of *who* makes policy appeals to the bureaucracy, I proceed with the question of *under what conditions* lawmakers exploit the bureaucratic venue. Like other channels of policymaking, back-channel policymaking is dependent on a lawmaker's capacity—the same resources, experience, and skills required in the legislative process. Among high-capacity lawmakers, when does the bureaucracy offer a strategic advantage over the legislative process? How does the political context shape lawmakers' decisions to work through the bureaucracy?

Exploiting the Separation of Powers

Agency policymaking is not without obstacles. The broader institutional context contributes to the costs of doing business with the bureaucracy. While expending resources in the legislative venue might not be worthwhile under some conditions, the bureaucratic venue might not be much better. For example, a minority party member may need an alternative policymaking venue as she is shut out of the legislative process. But if the executive branch is also controlled by the opposing party, that may not be worthwhile either. Yet, if lawmakers see they have an advantage in the bureaucratic venue, do they exploit it?

Consider the opening example of this chapter describing the efforts by Democratic lawmakers to protect immigrants who arrived in the United States as children. These efforts started legislatively, while the political context was favorable for passing statute. The Democrats introduced the Dream Act more than ten times during the 111th Congress, when they controlled both branches of government.[17] Once the political context changed, the lawmakers shifted their efforts to the more promising venue, the Democratically-controlled executive branch. Having lost the House in the 112th Congress, they only introduced the Dream Act four times and, instead, worked through administrative policymaking under the Obama administration. The executive branch offered the clear advantage given the political context of the 112th Congress. Members of Congress strategically divert resources when the bureaucratic venue appears more promising than the legislative arena.

This leads me to the third hypothesis described in Chapter 2, which I refer to as the *bureaucratic advantage hypothesis*. I argue that members of Congress engage in back-channel policymaking when they face constraints in the legislative process *and have the advantage in the bureaucratic venue*. For example, if a legislator is in the chamber minority but shares party affiliation with the administration, it would be more efficient for the legislator to pursue her policy objectives through administrative policymaking than the legislative process. This argument assumes that legislators perceive the bureaucracy as a more promising venue when their party controls the administration and when a legislator's policy requests are unlikely to conflict with the White House's positions and priorities.

There is an alternative way the bureaucracy might provide lawmakers with a second venue to the lawmaking process. Legislators may primarily turn to this informal means of participation as a last resort when their party is completely shut out of the formal venues of lawmaking—when the opposing party controls both Congress and the White House.[18] If lawmakers are powerless in their committees and chambers and lack a party advocate in the White House, they must watch from the sidelines without formal means of recourse as the opposing party advances policy. Under such conditions, informal, inter-branch communication may be one of their few tools for pushing back. I refer to this as the *obstruction hypothesis*.

There are reasons to expect these competing hypotheses describe one chamber more aptly than the other. As the chamber differences in the earlier results highlight, House members are more firmly tethered to their party and the formal institutions within the House, particularly when their party controls the chamber or presidency. Senators are more individualistic and have greater capacity to pursue their own policy priorities—apart from the party's agenda. In contrast, even high-capacity House members are limited by short two-year terms, the constant need to campaign, and the strength of rules and procedures in the House. Thus, the bureaucratic advantage hypothesis may be more predictive of senators' behavior and the obstruction hypothesis more reflective of the House.

These competing hypotheses offer two different, nuanced explanations for why and how legislators exploit the backchannel to circumvent constraints in formal lawmaking. The bureaucratic advantage hypothesis suggests lawmakers are motivated by advancing their individual policy priorities. Moreover, this hypothesis implies that lawmakers are focused on policy outcomes rather than position-taking. Otherwise, why would it matter if the executive branch offered a more promising venue for policymaking? The obstruction hypothesis points to a more partisan motivation if legislators are using inter-branch channels to push back on the opposition's policy advances.[19]

To test these hypotheses, I interact a measure of legislative constraint (i.e., minority party status) with a measure of bureaucratic advantage (i.e., sharing party affiliation with the administration). The expectations for the relative frequency of policy appeals across conditions are displayed in Table 6.4. I focus first on the Senate. Consistent with the bureaucratic advantage hypothesis, I expect that senators contact agencies about policy more frequently when they are in the minority and share party affiliation with the president compared to when they are in the minority and are White House out-partisans—and have no advantage—and when their party controls both branches of government—in which case, they have the advantage in the formal lawmaking process. My expectations for White House out-partisans in the majority are weaker, but they may leverage formal chamber powers—which increases their capacity with agencies—to negotiate with the administration when passing a statute is limited by divided government. It is also possible, however, that these lawmakers would focus their resources on formal institutions of oversight. Alternatively, the obstruction hypothesis predicts White House out-partisans in the minority will contact most frequently.

The first and second columns of Table 6.5 display the results for the Senate analyses, which include this interaction term as well as the variables used in Table 6.2. The dependent variable is the total number of policy appeals from a senator during a Congress aggregated across agencies. The second column includes state fixed effects to account for unobserved time-invariant characteristics particular to each state.[20] Across both models, the coefficient for the interaction term is in the predicted direction (positive) and significant $(p < 0.01)$.[21]

Figures 6.1 and 6.2 show how constraints and opportunity interact to affect lawmakers' policymaking strategies.[22] Figure 6.1 presents marginal effects, indicating that the results are statistically significant across majority and minority party membership. According to Figure 6.2, senators who are in the chamber minority but share party affiliation with the adminis-tration contact the bureaucracy about policy significantly more (26 con-tacts) than when they do not share party affiliation with the administra-tion (21 contacts) and more than majority party members who are White House co-partisans (20 contacts) and who have the advantage in the formal

Table 6.4 Expectations for Bureaucratic Advantage and Obstruction Hypotheses

	Comparative Frequency of Policy Appeals	
Bureaucratic Advantage Hypothesis	Majority	Minority
White House co-partisan	Party control of formal legislative process **decreases** incentive to make policy appeals.	Legislative constraint and bureaucratic advantage **increase** incentive and opportunity to make policy appeals.
White House out-partisan	Legislating limited by divided government and majority party bargaining power with the bureaucracy **increase** both incentive and capacity for policy appeals.	Constraints in both venues **decrease** capacity and opportunity to make policy appeals.
Obstruction Hypothesis	Majority	Minority
White House co-partisan	Party control of formal legislative process **decreases** the incentive to make policy appeals.	President's co-partisans must devote effort to supporting the White House's initiatives in Congress and **decrease** efforts toward policy appeals.
White House out-partisan	Party control of Congress (and thus, formal means of oversight) **decreases** incentive to make policy appeals through informal channels.	Lack of party control over institutions **increases** incentive to make informal policy appeals as a last resort in the absence of formal power.

Note: Previous theories of oversight expect a higher frequency of oversight directed at the opposing party's administration.

Table 6.5 Constraints, Opportunity, and Capacity as Determinants of Policy Contact

	Senate			House		
	(1)	(2)	(3)	(4)	(5)	(6)
Minority x White House co-partisan	11.230*** (3.77)	12.360*** (3.65)	14.010*** (3.35)	−1.798*** (−3.23)	−1.039* (−1.92)	−1.380 (−1.56)
Minority	−6.782** (−2.10)	−5.733* (−1.98)	−5.872* (−1.68)	1.610*** (3.07)	1.562*** (2.73)	1.563** (2.01)
White House co-partisan	−6.983*** (−2.84)	−7.219*** (−2.93)	−6.368** (−2.10)	0.285 (0.71)	0.051 (0.10)	0.617 (0.85)
Constant	29.520*** (3.91)	16.750* (1.94)	26.810*** (2.87)	1.138 (0.50)	5.718* (1.81)	2.636 (0.73)
High-Capacity subset	N	N	Y	N	N	Y
State FE	N	Y	Y	Y	N	N
District FE	-	-	-	N	Y	Y
Controls	Y	Y	Y	Y	Y	Y
N	403	403	249	1765	1765	1046
adj. R^2	0.277	0.489	0.491	0.227	0.513	0.450

t statistics in parentheses. Robust standard errors are clustered by member. The third and sixth columns use a subset of the sample that includes MCs who have lagged LES above the median.
$^*p < 0.1, ^{**}p < 0.05, ^{***}p < 0.01$

lawmaking process.[23] Majority party members who are White House out-partisans contacted agencies at levels similar to minority party members who are White House co-partisans (27 contacts), suggesting legislators are also driven to contact agencies when they face opposition in the executive branch and have control in Congress. Chamber majorities can leverage formal means of oversight against agencies and use its bargaining power to negotiate with the president. Moreover, Figure 6A.3 in the Appendix shows that this relationship is particular to policy appeals. Substituting the number of bills a senator sponsored for policy appeals produces a different set of results.

Critically, the impact of minority party status and White House co-partisanship is stronger for high-capacity senators. I have argued, consistent with my empirical findings thus far, that back-channel policymaking is a strategy used by savvy policymakers and facilitated by a legislator's institutional power, experience and expertise, and innate policymaking skills. Chapter 5, for instance, presented results indicating that policy communication with agencies is more frequent among effective lawmakers, using

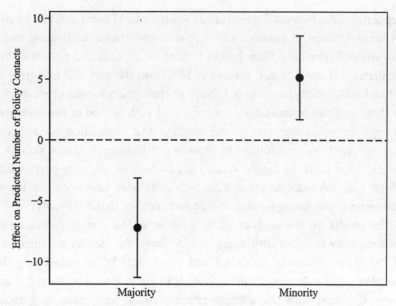

Figure 6.1 Effect of White House co-partisanship on number of policy contacts from senators by chamber status

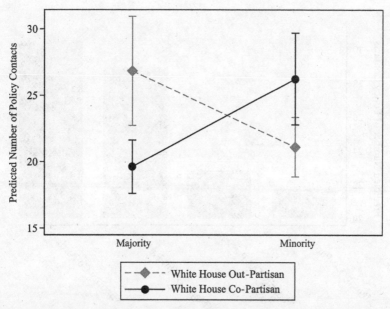

Figure 6.2 Predicted number of policy contacts from senators by White House co-partisanship and chamber status

Legislative Effectiveness Scores (LES) (Volden and Wiseman 2014). I build on these findings to untangle the legislative constraints motivating back-channel policymaking from how a legislator's capacity for policymaking facilitates it. I use a lagged version of LES from the previous Congress to subset high-capacity lawmakers. LES are an appropriate measure for capacity in these analyses because they are correlated with several of the measures of capacity, including institutional position and experience, used in the previous analyses in addition to capturing a legislator's innate skill as a policymaker. I use the lagged version of LES because minority party status affects LES. We want to know what legislators who have been previously successful at advancing legislation do when they are in the minority.

The results for the analysis using a subset of the sample consisting of high-capacity senators with a lagged LES above the median are displayed in the third column of Table 6.5 and Figure 6.3. When sub-setting the sample to high-capacity senators, those who are in the minority and share party affiliation with the administration contact the bureaucracy about policy significantly more (31 contacts) than when they do not share party affiliation with the administration (23 contacts) and more than majority party members who are White House co-partisans (22 contacts) and in

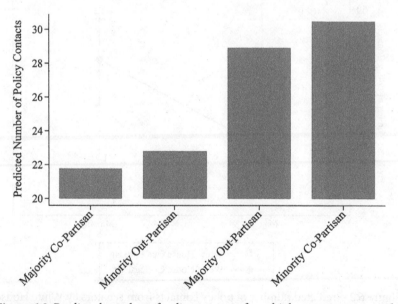

Figure 6.3 Predicted number of policy contacts from high-capacity senators by White House co-partisanship and chamber status

comparison to majority party members who are White House out-partisans (29 contacts).[24] These results suggest that legislative constraints, opportunity in the executive branch, and a lawmaker's capacity all play a role in back-channel policymaking.

These results suggest that senators try to exploit agency policymaking when the executive branch offers a more promising policymaking venue than Congress. While legislators' capacity facilitates their ability to engage with agency policymaking, institutional context factors into their choice of policymaking venue in a way that reflects the strategic advantages and disadvantages of either venue. In short, savvy senators strategically choose venues. As I describe in the next section, however, this calculation looks different in the House of Representatives.

Confronting the Administration in the US House of Representatives

The results for House members reflects chamber differences in capacity and hierarchy described earlier. Unlike their colleagues in the Senate, House members are more limited in their ability to advance their own policy agendas in the formal legislative process. The constant need to campaign, limited staff and resources, and the hierarchy of the House motivate legislators to work through their committees and party structure and to depend on position-taking, messaging strategies, and credit claiming for their party's accomplishments.

Consequently, House members are dependent on the accomplishments and reputations of party leaders, both in Congress and the White House. This tether to party means that, even when in the minority, White House allies still face pressure to participate in the formal lawmaking process in order to provide legislative support to the president (Lee 2016, 63). Since the party can leverage presidential power and shares responsibility for government operations and responding to crises, minority members are expected to collaborate with the majority on legislation. The president's shared responsibility for outcomes is important for legislators' behavior because their electoral fortunes are tied to their party leaders, whether in Congress or in the White House (Lee 2016).

When the opposing party controls both the legislative and executive branches, House members cannot depend on their party's accomplishments and must resort to strategies of confrontation outside formal channels of authority (Lee 2016). House members in the minority are limited in their ability to influence policy through their committees and lack formal oversight powers. Moreover, as White House out-partisans, they are unable to credit claim for their party's accomplishments. Consequently, they resort to attacking the opposition in power.

I find chamber differences consistent with these limitations and incentives of House members. House members are already very limited in their ability to influence policy in Congress. Thus, when House members' opportunities for influence are further reduced because their party is out of power, they resort to attacking the opposition. We observe this strategic behavior in how House members use informal inter-branch communication to attack the opposing party's administration when they are shut out of the legislative process.

Table 6.5 presents results consistent with this argument and distinct from the Senate findings. The fourth and fifth columns show a negative and significant coefficient for the interaction of minority party status and White House co-partisanship. Figures 6.4 and 6.5 show that while there is not a statistically significant difference for majority members based on

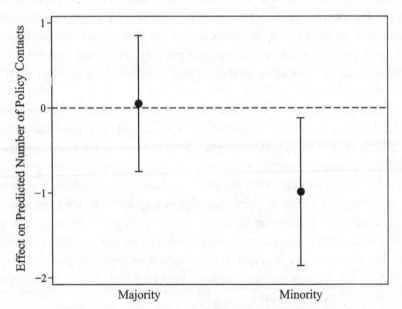

Figure 6.4 Effect of White House co-partisanship on number of policy contacts from House members by chamber status

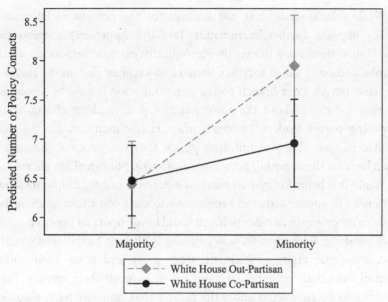

Figure 6.5 Predicted number of policy contacts from House members by White House co-partisanship and chamber status

shared party affiliation with the White House, minority party members contact the administration more frequently when it is controlled by the opposing party.[25] This difference of about one contact between minority party members who are White House out-partisans in comparison with minority party members who share party affiliation with the administration is statistically significant.[26] The effect is not significant when the analysis is conducted on a subset of high-capacity lawmakers, as shown in the sixth column. This could be due to the smaller sample size. Although rather weak, these results are more in line with the obstruction hypothesis and suggest that there are clear differences between how senators and House members engage with the bureaucracy.

Majority party members in the House are focused on working through the legislative process governed by their party. Unlike the Senate results, we do not observe majority party members engaging with the opposing party administration at higher levels, an indication of the importance of the formal power of House committees and hierarchy. When in the majority, House members work through formal channels and through party leadership in contrast to the individualistic Senate. When in the minority, House members use their informal communications with the administration to confront the opposing party's agencies.

While this analysis does not account for the content of lawmakers' policy appeals, further examination (see the Appendix) suggests that the House results are driven by ideologically extreme opposition to the administration.[27] Taken together, these results suggest that, in the House of Representatives, inter-branch policy communication is used by ideologues to raise concerns about the administrative policymaking efforts by the opposing party's leaders. In short, when House members are the most limited in their ability to influence policy, they use informal channels to push back on the opposing party's administrative policymaking efforts.

While this behavior may be more of a political one for House members who need to appear active and responsive to their constituency when they have no other way to advance policy, it could have important implications for policymaking. Back-channel policymaking is likely to be the most effective and, some may argue, problematic, when party leaders use their unified control over both branches of government to push their agenda. These efforts may be conducted under the radar unless minority party members bring attention to and raise concerns about how the controlling party is circumventing the legislative process and abusing the separation of powers. This informal channel may be one of the few tools House members have to resist the policy actions of the controlling party when they are shut out of the legislative process.

Conclusion

Does Congress control the bureaucracy? This question has dominated the literature and overshadowed the strategic ways individual legislators take advantage of bureaucratic discretion to bypass the collective authority of Congress. My results suggest that members of Congress use informal backchannels with the bureaucracy to circumvent institutional hurdles in Congress when they are shut out of the formal lawmaking process. These results are critical for two reasons. First, individual legislators, even powerful ones, are often limited in their ability to advance policy in the legislative process. Second, agencies have a great deal of influence over policy and have developed policymaking strategies of their own that skirt the scrutiny of Congress, interest groups, and the OMB (Potter 2019, 2017).

Savvy legislators do not limit themselves to the formal powers granted to them as lawmakers. Instead, members of Congress take advantage of agencies' influence to advance policies in the bureaucratic venue that would be difficult to accomplish through the legislative process.

Moreover, senators and House members use this informal backchannel differently. Senators engage with agencies more frequently when the bureaucracy offers a more promising policymaking venue than the legislative process. House members appear to use this informal platform to confront and resist administrative policymaking when they are shut out of the formal lawmaking process and without options in Congress. In both chambers, the bureaucracy presents an alternative venue for policy influence.

These findings might offer a promising outlook for how a determined low-ranking legislator could use the bureaucratic venue to effectively represent her constituency even in the midst of gridlock and polarization. However, this backdoor policymaking venue may further exacerbate the unequal power distribution in Congress. The legislators who have the most need for an alternative policymaking venue are the least capable of taking advantage of it. Instead, the bureaucratic backdoor allows powerful members of Congress to further expand their influence through informal channels spanning branches of government, thus undermining the separation of powers and the institutional authority of Congress.

One remaining question that could shed further insight into these normative issues is how agencies respond to requests from legislators. In Chapter 8, I examine agency responsiveness to legislators' policy appeals and variation across members of Congress. Do agencies prioritize these powerful lawmakers?

First, though, I examine another type of constraint legislators face within their own constituencies and parties. While this chapter focused on how back-channel policymaking can be exploited because it occurs beyond the bounds of the formal institutions of Congress, another advantage of agency policymaking is its discreet quality. Do lawmakers take advantage of this less visible policymaking venue? Under what conditions is it strategic for lawmakers to choose to act through opaque administrative processes over the limelight of the legislative process? In the next chapter, I examine how lawmakers strategically use back-channel policymaking to avoid drawing attention to their actions on controversial issues.

Appendix

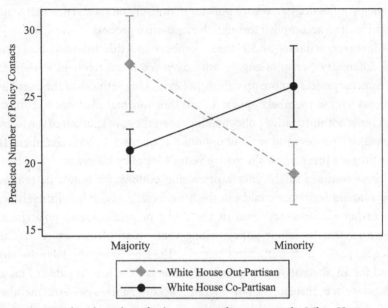

Figure 6A.1 Predicted number of policy contacts from senators by White House co-partisanship and chamber status (senator fixed effect)

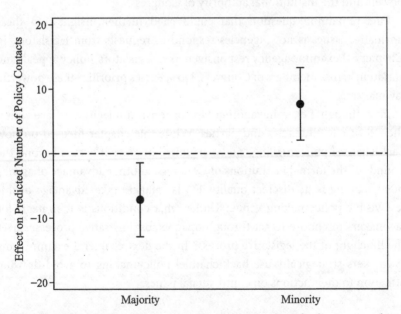

Figure 6A.2 Effect of White House co-partisanship on number of policy contacts from high-capacity senators by chamber status

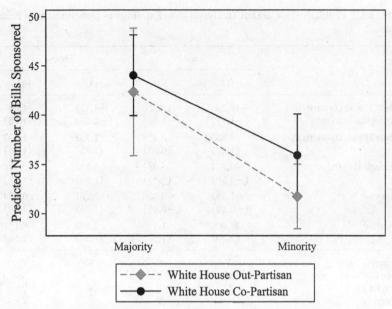

Figure 6A.3 Predicted number of bills sponsored by senators by White House co-partisanship and chamber status

Analysis Examining Ideological Extremity and Inter-Branch Communication

Table 6A.1 show results for models that include an interaction between White House co-partisanship and ideological extremity. Robust across both specifications for the House, the interaction term's coefficient shows a negative and significant relationship, suggesting that ideologically extreme White House out-partisans engage more frequently with agencies. Figure 6A.4 indicates that this relationship is significant for the most extreme House members, which includes about 10% of the sample.[28] Figure 6A.5 shows White House out-partisans' predicted number of policy appeals increases across ideological extremity and decreases slightly for White House co-partisans, with moderate White House co-partisans contacting more than moderate out-partisans. In comparison, while the interaction term's coefficient is significant in one of the Senate models, the effect is not robust across a meaningful portion of the sample, and it is not clear whether the effect is driven by ideologically extreme White House out-partisans or moderate White House co-partisans.

Table 6A.1 Legislative Constraints and Ideological Extremity as Determinants of Policy Contact

	Senate		House	
	(1)	(2)	(3)	(4)
White House co-partisan x Ideological extremity	−19.360* (−1.73)	−12.260 (−1.00)	−4.552* (−1.86)	−4.087* (−1.75)
White House co-partisan	5.885 (1.17)	3.434 (0.63)	1.532 (1.45)	1.452 (1.49)
Ideological extremity	−6.881 (−0.96)	5.951 (0.66)	5.532* (1.68)	2.990 (1.27)
Minority	−1.533 (−0.62)	−0.050 (−0.02)	0.661* (1.73)	0.804** (2.09)
Constant	23.300*** (3.30)	11.990 (1.37)	2.889 (1.24)	8.151*** (2.68)
Congress FE	Y	Y	Y	Y
State FE	N	Y	Y	N
District FE	N	Y	N	Y
Controls	Y	Y	Y	Y
N	403	403	1765	1765
adj. R^2	0.289	0.496	0.237	0.525

t statistics in parentheses. Robust standard errors are clustered by member.
*$p < 0.1$, **$p < 0.05$, ***$p < 0.01$

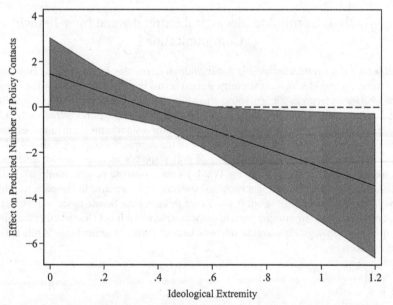

Figure 6A.4 Effect of White House co-partisanship on number of policy contacts from House members across ideological extremity

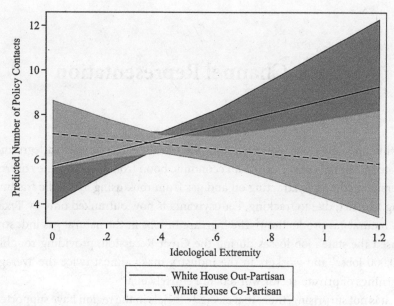

Figure 6A.5 Predicted number of policy contacts from House members across ideological extremity

7

Back-Channel Representation

While the nation struggled through the Great Recession, the battleground state of Pennsylvania enjoyed an economic boon from fracking, the controversial method of extracting oil and gas from rock using hydraulic fracturing.[1] In fact, due to fracking, Pennsylvania is now outranked only by Texas in natural gas production.[2] The increase in jobs in the natural gas industry eased the state's job losses during the Great Recession, providing roughly 30,000 jobs,[3] and workers in the industry make almost twice the average earnings of private-sector workers in Pennsylvania.[4]

It is not surprising, then, that elected officials in the region have supported increases in fracking and fought regulation of the industry. Pennsylvania's politicians featured their strong support for fracking as a prominent element of their campaigns and press conferences.[5] Fracking became a high-profile issue in recent presidential races, too. In fact, the Trump campaign believed that fracking in Pennsylvania was the key to winning the presidency. News headlines summed up President Trump's last blitz of rallies in the state for the 2020 campaign: "Trump's final pitch to Pennsylvania: I love fracking."[6]

Yet, fracking has become a divisive issue for the Democratic Party, pitting environmental concerns against the economic interests of its traditional base of organized labor. Fracking bears environmental costs including potential contamination to the water supply. In fact, after years of rumination, Democratic Governor Andrew Cuomo banned fracking in neighboring New York State over health concerns despite the potential economic gains.[7] This trade-off has created challenges for Democratic candidates campaigning in states that have become economically dependent on fracking. During the 2020 presidential election, Pennsylvania's union leaders were concerned that Biden's position on fracking was "nuanced, and he hasn't always explained it clearly." Unlike Trump's rallies, the Biden campaign avoided emphasizing fracking and, instead, chose to focus on other issues while campaigning in the state.[8]

Backdoor Lawmaking: Evading Obstacles in the US Congress. Melinda N. Ritchie, Oxford University Press.
© Melinda N. Ritchie 2023. DOI: 10.1093/oso/9780197670491.003.0007

Indeed, scholarly research on the political consequences of fracking finds that it is a win-win situation for Republicans (Cooper, Kim, and Urpelainen 2018; Fedaseyeu, Gilje, and Strahan 2015; Sances and You 2022), but the issue is more challenging for Democrats, particularly those representing oil and natural gas producing states. While Republicans have heartedly supported fracking, consistent with the party's traditional anti-regulation platform, Democrats walk a tightrope between their party's environmental priorities and the economic welfare of their states.[9]

These partisan differences are reflected in the strategies elected officials pursue. For example, Pennsylvania is currently represented by both a Republican and a Democrat in the Senate. Republican Senator Pat Toomey's position on fracking is clear. The senator has been very public about his support for fracking and his opposition to regulation of the industry, even using the issue to attack Democrats for favoring a ban on fracking at press conferences he hosted with industry leaders. He has also introduced a resolution asserting that the president does not have the authority to ban fracking.[10]

In contrast, Democratic Senator Bob Casey's position on fracking is more nuanced. He has expressed a desire to promote fracking jobs but also to protect the environment and public health. He has tried to distinguish himself from Democrats calling for a fracking ban. Instead, he supports keeping fracking jobs in the state but argues for greater regulation of the industry to ensure safety for the environment and public health.[11] This circuitous support for fracking leaves observers unclear on details and how his position may evolve with additional pressure from party, constituency, or interest groups.

Despite his arguably ambiguous position on fracking, Senator Casey has been quite active on the issue. During the 112th Congress, the senator contacted the Energy Department several times, often about fracking and the oil and gas industry.[12] In an email he wrote to Secretary Steven Chu, he offered his input for the Secretary of Energy Advisory Board (SEAB) Natural Gas Subcommittee, which was tasked with assessing the economic role of natural gas and providing recommendations to improve the environmental safety of fracking.[13] He also contacted Secretary Chu "urging the Secretary to coordinate with local, state, and other federal entities to ensure that appropriate actions to protect public health from oil and gas drilling activities are implemented" and asked for "updates on efforts the Department is conducting in this arena, and how its coordinating efforts and sharing information is proceeding."[14] In another letter coauthored with his similarly conflicted Democratic colleagues in West Virginia, Senators Jay Rockefeller and Joe Manchin, he asked for increased funding for research on oil and natural gas extraction as well as expressing opposition to a structural change to a related energy program within the department.[15] In another letter he asked Secretary Chu "to become personally involved" with reduced refining capacity out of concern for economic losses.[16] For comparison, his Republican same-state colleague, Senator Toomey, only contacted the DOE twice during the same time period, once about a loan application and a second time about high gas prices.

Senator Casey's decision to pursue a contentious issue through informal communication with the bureaucracy illustrates the central argument of this chapter: Members of Congress strategically use back-channel communication with the bureaucracy because it allows them to represent interests that are costly to represent publicly. This chapter builds on my argument that savvy legislators pursue alternative policymaking venues when they face constraints in the legislative process. In this chapter, I show how legislators choose the inconspicuous bureaucratic venue—rather than the exposed legislative process—when they face constraints within their constituencies due to conflicting pressures from their party and interest groups.

Why might legislators view the bureaucracy as useful for representing controversial interests? Beyond the strategic advantages examined in the previous chapter, back-channel policymaking offers another benefit over the legislative process. Informal communication between legislators and agencies is unique from previously studied policymaking activities because it does not occur within the legislative arena and is a less visible vehicle for representation. The discreet nature of this behavior is advantageous for lawmakers managing controversial issues or cross-pressured members of Congress who receive conflicting demands from their party, interest groups, and constituencies (Glazer et al. 1995).

The public nature of the legislative arena can be costly for cross-pressured lawmakers because they do not have control over the visibility of their participation and risk alienating groups of supporters. The risks associated with widespread visibility influences legislators' decisions about policymaking in Congress. Research shows that the costs of visibility drive members of Congress to pursue less visible strategies when they face cross-pressures (e.g., Box-Steffensmeier, Arnold, and Zorn 1997; Cohen and Noll 1991; Glazer et al. 1995; Covington 1987; Miller and Overby 2010; Koger 2003) and that they prefer less visible channels of representation that allow them control over which groups or factions are made aware of their efforts (e.g., Crespin 2010, and see Russell 2021).

Building on this research, I argue that members of Congress use their communication with the bureaucracy as a less visible way of representing conflicting interests. Unlike previously considered policymaking activities, such as roll-call voting, bill introductions, and co-sponsorship, inter-branch correspondence is not readily public. As described in Chapter 3, accessing the information for this research required submitting FOIA requests, which took many months for the agencies to complete. I then examined thousands of pages of documents. Voting and bill sponsorship records, on the other hand, are easily accessible on the internet, and some information is even regularly published in local newspapers and other media outlets.

Members of Congress are clearly under the impression that their communication with agencies is, or should be, withheld from the public. In Chapter 3, I described news coverage of legislators' reaction upon learning that agencies were releasing such communication records in response to FOIA requests. The lawmakers reacted with anger and demands that agencies desist in this practice. Clearly, members of Congress believed that their communications with the bureaucracy were, and wanted them to be, discreet.

Back-channel policymaking is useful for representing contentious issues because it allows lawmakers control over how they publicize their efforts. Members of Congress can choose to advertise their policy appeals widely in a press release circulated to all the media outlets on their distribution list, or they can make their efforts known only to targeted beneficiaries by emailing their supporters, making a speech in front of a local organization, or raising their efforts in meetings with lobbyists. Lawmakers often receive targeted publicity for their policy appeals in industry newsletters. Legislators can take credit from select interests while avoiding attention from the general public, media, election challengers, and disapproving sub-constituencies and groups. Moreover, unlike most legislative activities, the bureaucratic venue allows lawmakers to evade the attention of their colleagues in Congress. Thus, legislators can use the bureaucracy as a way of quietly representing one interest without the knowledge of other groups and principals.

Lawmakers also have control over when their policy appeals are publicized. A legislator can choose to contact an agency about an issue but delay publicizing it until, and if, the issue is raised during the next election.

While visible legislative activities force members of Congress to go on the record, legislators have more control over when and if their policy communication with agencies becomes public.

Moreover, representation via back-channel interactions offers lawmakers control over how they communicate the content of their position. In Congress, legislators must vote yea or nay, and their influence over the content of legislation is limited. Of course, legislators can introduce amendments and legislation of their own. Yet, the ability to control both the dissemination and the content of their back-channel communication allows them flexibility in constructing and publicizing their positions. This control is particularly useful for contentious issues.

In fact, policy appeals to agencies can be a helpful fix for difficult votes. If a legislator is forced into a decision requiring her to vote for two policies—one she favors and one she is against—in the same piece of legislation, she can pursue her true policy preferences by engaging with the bureaucracy regardless of her vote. When party and regional interests clash, legislators can vote with their party but then represent regional preferences with back-channel policymaking. Thus, members of Congress use their policy contacts to help explain "wrong" votes to disgruntled constituents.

This strategic integration of venues was demonstrated by the Republican senators of North Carolina, Elizabeth Dole and Richard Burr, when they were pressured by their party to vote for the US-Central American Free Trade Agreement (CAFTA), despite the potential damage to the state's textile industry. The vote was particularly contentious in North Carolina because the decline of the state's manufacturing industry in previous years had been blamed on the North American Free Trade Agreement and was a heated issue during Dole and Burr's previous campaigns.[17] The conflict of partisan pressure versus state interests was sharp in the swing state, where a large segment of the constituency did not share their party affiliation. Fast-track rules for trade agreements limited the senators' ability to influence CAFTA and stuck them with a dichotomous choice. The senators ended up voting for CAFTA. However, they later contacted the Department of Labor (DOL) to request protection for the textile industry and asked that the DOL increase the duty on socks imported from Honduras. About three months after the senators sent the letter, the administration announced it would be increasing the duty on Honduran socks. The senators strategically used the bureaucratic venue to supplement a roll-call vote in order to dodge the constraints of legislative action. Back-channel representation can be used as a substitute for legislative action if a legislator wishes to pursue a matter quietly rather than in the public venue of Congress, or it can be a supplement for other legislative activities.

Drawing on these arguments, I hypothesize that legislators contact the bureaucracy about their policy concerns more frequently when they face cross-pressures. While members of Congress have several legislative means for representing interests (e.g., introducing a bill, making a floor speech, participating in a committee hearing), the bureaucratic backchannel offers a less visible way for them to quietly represent interests that are at odds. As described in Chapter 2, I refer to this expectation as the *constituency constraint hypothesis*.

Of course, I am not suggesting that members of Congress only contact the bureaucracy to take advantage of this quiet means of policymaking. In previous chapters, I have shown that back-channel policymaking is also tied to legislators' policy priorities (Chapter 5), legislative roles, expertise, capacity, and constraints within the legislative process (Chapter 6). As with any form of participation in Congress, legislators utilize various outlets and venues for different reasons.

The findings presented in this chapter are important because they suggest that the bureaucracy provides lawmakers with a means for evading accountability. Informal communication with the bureaucracy escapes the public scrutiny of the legislative process. The public is largely unaware of legislators' policy appeals to agencies and what interests are being represented through this communication. This lack of transparency has substantial implications for accountability, but it is also an important strategic consideration for legislators who wish to represent interests quietly.

Measuring Cross-Pressures

To test the constituency constraint hypothesis, I use three measures of cross-pressures to consider conflict in terms of constituency interest, partisanship, and ideology. I define cross-pressures based on conflicts between a legislator's constituency and party, conflicting partisanship within a district or state (e.g., "purple" districts/states), and ideological differences (e.g., Box-Steffensmeier, Arnold, and Zorn 1997). The measures using constituency interests are issue-specific and capture salient interests within a lawmaker's district or state.

"Vote your district, vote your conscience, just don't surprise me." Consistent with the wisdom of Rep. Kevin McCarthy's (R-CA) line to Republicans when he was Majority Whip, cross-pressures are especially problematic for lawmakers when a salient issue in the constituency conflicts with the legislator's party.[18] To consider conflicts between party and constituency interests, I focus on interests within an issue area that have varying degrees of salience across states and districts. Fracking, for example, has greater salience among states that have become economically dependent on oil and gas production. I analyze lawmakers' policy appeals to each department (DOL, DHS, DOE) separately using different models with measures specific to the issues under the department's jurisdiction. As such, I measure cross-pressures using different issue-relevant variables for each department's analysis (e.g., oil and gas production is used in the DOE model) as described in the sections below. Issue salience is measured using state or district characteristics, consistent with previous work (Box-Steffensmeier, Arnold, and Zorn 1997).

In addition to the issue-specific measures, I use two general measures of cross-pressures. First, cross-pressures on policies can be due to conflicting partisan affiliations rather than tied to a constituency interest. Accordingly, the second type of interaction I use includes the previous presidential vote share of the state or district. Democrats representing red states must walk a tightrope, especially on partisan issues. Likewise, Republicans are increasingly cross-pressured as the Democratic presidential candidate's vote share in the state or district increases. While this variable is intended to be a more general measure of cross-pressures, its impact could be dependent on the salience of an issue. Republicans representing states with a prominent Democratic presence—like Wisconsin, for example—are likely to be cross-pressured on a range of issues, but perhaps more so on labor than immigration.

Second, a moderate voting record can also be an indication of a cross-pressured member of Congress. Previous work (Caldeira and Zorn 2004; Conley 1999) makes this case, with some scholars pointing out that "conservative Republicans and liberal Democrats in harmony with their districts could take a position with little doubt about its electoral consequences," whereas moderate Republicans and Democrats are pushed and pulled by their core constituencies in primary and general elections (Caldeira and Zorn 2004, 518). Moderate legislators are often seen as persuadable and are targeted by groups and political actors trying to influence their votes. Some theories of vote buying include models in which party leaders compete for the votes of moderate legislators (Krehbiel, Meirowitz, and Wiseman 2015). Previous work has used measures based on voting records to consider the role of cross-pressures on legislative behavior, finding that legislators who are more moderate or who vote out of line with the party are more likely to behave in ways consistent with expectations for cross-pressured legislators (Box-Steffensmeier, Arnold, and Zorn 1997; Caldeira and Zorn 2004). I include ideological extremity—the absolute value of first-dimension DW-NOMINATE scores (Poole and Rosenthal 1991)—with the expectation that cross-pressured moderates will contact agencies more frequently than their extreme colleagues. Taken together, there are a total of three measures of cross-pressures in each analysis.

My theoretical argument relies on the premise that legislators engage in back-channel communications because it is a less visible means for representing interests that are costly to represent publicly. I provide additional scrutiny of my argument by testing this critical assumption regarding visibility. I include models with the number of bills a legislator introduced as the dependent variable in place of policy communication as a placebo test. My results for policy communication are less meaningful if legislators' bill sponsorship produces similar results. Instead, I expect this visible form of representation to have no relationship, or possibly even the opposite relationship, with my measures of cross-pressures. Legislators may be more publicly active when both the constituency and party support the legislator's position on an issue, although this likely depends on the issue's salience within the constituency. I incorporate bill introductions into my analysis to offer a comparison to policy communication.[19] I present the results by policy area.

Labor Policy

When it comes to labor policy, the conflict between trade liberalization and the interests of workers, particularly in blue-collar industries like manufacturing, has been politically contentious.[20] Members of Congress representing constituencies with blue-collar industries can be reluctant to vote for trade agreements, which must now be accompanied by assistance for workers harmed by trade (Trade Adjustment Assistance or TAA) in order to be politically palatable (see Ritchie and You 2021). Due to the Republican Party's customary and consistent support for free trade, Republicans from states with a substantial blue-collar population face cross-pressure on labor issues.[21] However, Democrats are not likely to become cross-pressured based on the blue-collar population in their states, since the party has an established reputation of supporting labor interests and is more open to its members voting against trade agreements.[22] In the DOL analyses, I measure cross-pressures using an interaction between party and the proportion of the blue collar population in a state or district, which allows me to consider the effect of the blue collar population conditional on the legislator's party. I expect that Republicans representing constituencies with larger blue collar populations contact the DOL about policy more frequently than Republicans representing smaller blue collar populations and in comparison to Democrats.

Table 7.1 presents results for the labor models.[23] The dependent variable in the first and third columns is the number of policy contacts from a legislator to the DOL and, in the second and third columns, the number

Table 7.1 Cross-Pressures as Determinants of Policy Contact with the US Department of Labor and Labor Bill Sponsorship

	Senate		House	
	DOL Policy	Labor Bills	DOL Policy	Labor Bills
Republican × blue-collar pop.	49.000*	−4.384	5.253**	1.693
	(1.86)	(−0.70)	(2.08)	(1.18)
Republican × Democratic vote share	28.370**	−0.023	4.275**	2.069*
	(2.53)	(−0.01)	(2.12)	(1.81)
Ideological extremity	−8.854***	2.837***	−0.077	1.751***
	(−3.04)	(4.14)	(−0.15)	(5.88)
Republican	−22.540**	0.444	−3.340**	−1.766**
	(−2.32)	(0.19)	(−2.53)	(−2.36)
Blue-collar pop.	−22.070	1.950	−0.584	−1.382
	(−1.16)	(0.43)	(−0.35)	(−1.45)
Democratic vote share	−3.839	2.373	−2.410**	−0.781
	(−0.52)	(1.37)	(−2.34)	(−1.33)
Constant	14.730**	−3.775**	2.897**	−0.213
	(2.09)	(−2.26)	(2.54)	(−0.33)
Congress FE	Y	Y	Y	Y
Controls	Y	Y	Y	Y
N	403	403	1765	1765
adj. R^2	0.2340	0.3182	0.0906	0.0881

t statistics in parentheses. Robust standard errors are clustered by member. The table displays results of seemingly unrelated regression (SUR) models.
*$p < 0.1$, **$p < 0.05$, ***$p < 0.01$

of labor-related bills a legislator sponsored. The first two columns display the results for the Senate joint seemingly unrelated regression (SUR) model and the third and fourth column display the House joint model results. In addition to the controls from Chapter 5, the models include measures of relevant constituency characteristics based on the issue area and agency's jurisdiction (and consistent with Ritchie 2018), private union membership, and the number of mines in a district or state.

The results in Table 7.1 are remarkably consistent and supportive of the constituency constraint hypothesis across the three measures of cross-pressures and both chambers. Across each of the measures of cross-pressures, the relationship with policy communication is in the expected direction and is significant for all except one measure, ideological extremity, in the House model. Moderate senators and House members contact the DOL about policy more (significantly more in the Senate model) than ideologues. Moreover, we observe the opposite relationship between ideological extremity and labor bill sponsorship, consistent with expectations for the more visible venue. Ideologues in both chambers sponsor significantly more labor bills than their moderate counterparts.

The table also displays that Republicans—in both the Senate and House models—communicate more with the DOL when they represent constituencies with a larger blue-collar population, in comparison with Republicans representing smaller blue-collar constituencies and in comparison to Democrats (who are arguably less cross-pressured on labor issues regardless of their constituencies).[24]

Figures 7.1 and 7.2 demonstrate the effects of party and blue-collar cross-pressures on senators' policy appeals, and Figures 7.3 and 7.4 illustrate the behavior of House members. These effects are significant for about half of the Senate sample, for senators with blue-collar populations equal to or greater than 23% of the constituency (see Figure 7.1). Figure 7.3 shows that the effects are significant for House members who represent districts where the percentage of the blue-collar population is under 10% and above 35%, which includes approximately 5% of the sample (about 82 observations).

The predicted number of policy appeals from Republicans and Democrats across the proportion of the blue-collar populations they represent are displayed in Figure 7.2 (Senate) and Figure 7.4 (House). Across both chambers, there is a consistent relationship in the expected direction. Republican senators representing states with the highest proportion of blue-collar workers contact the DOL about policy approximately five more times than

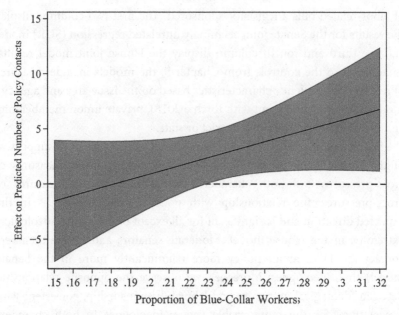

Figure 7.1 Effect of senator's party affiliation on number of policy contacts from senators to the US Department of Labor across state's blue-collar population

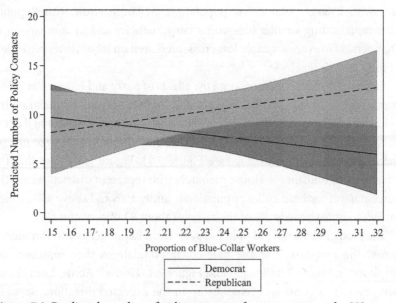

Figure 7.2 Predicted number of policy contacts from senators to the US Department of Labor across state's blue-collar population

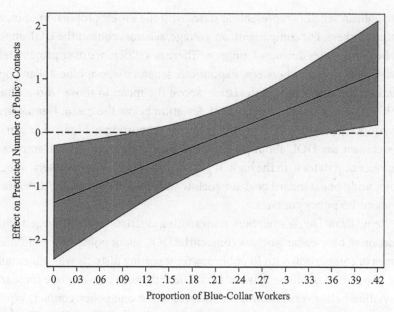

Figure 7.3 Effect of legislator's party affiliation on number of policy contacts from House members to the US Department of Labor across district's blue-collar population

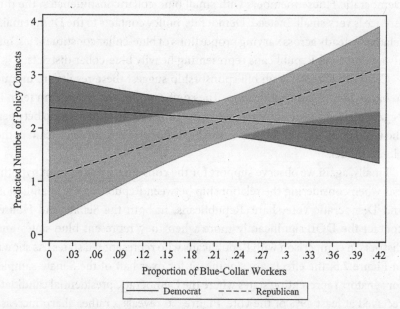

Figure 7.4 Predicted number of policy contacts from House members to the US Department of Labor across district's blue-collar population

Republican senators representing states with the lowest proportion of blue-collar workers. For comparison, on average, senators contact the DOL about policy nine times during a Congress. There is a difference of approximately two policy contacts between Republican senators whose blue-collar populations are one standard deviation above the mean to those whose blue-collar populations are one standard deviation below the mean. Democratic senators representing states with the lowest proportion of blue-collar workers contact the DOL about policy about four more times than Democrats representing states with the highest proportion of blue-collar workers. When comparing one standard deviation below and above the mean, the difference is about 1.5 policy contacts.

Republican House members representing districts with the largest proportion of blue-collar workers contact the DOL about policy two additional times in comparison with Republicans representing districts with the smallest population of blue-collar workers. The difference between one standard deviation below versus above the mean is about one policy contact. While these effects may seem small, keep in mind the average number of policy contacts to the DOL from House members is two contacts. While Democrats representing large blue-collar districts contact the DOL slightly less than Democratic House members with small blue-collar constituencies, the difference is very small. Instead, Democrats' policy contacts to the DOL remain relatively steady across varying proportions of blue-collar constituencies, but always less than Republicans representing heavily blue-collar districts.

Critically, the effects on bill sponsorship suggest these results are unique to back-channel communication. The coefficient for the interaction term is negative in the Senate, although it is not significant. The relationship between the interaction term and bill sponsorship is positive but not significant in the House model.

Finally, again we observe support for the constituency constraint hypothesis when considering the relationship between Republican Party affiliation and Democratic vote share. Republicans, in both the Senate and House, contact the DOL significantly more when they represent blue states and districts in comparison with Republicans who represent red states. As shown in Figure 7.5, the effects are significant for over half of the Senate sample, for senators representing states where the Democratic presidential candidate received at least 49% of the vote. Figure 7.6 reveals a rather sharp increase of 14 policy contacts when comparing Republican senators in the reddest of states to Republican senators representing the bluest of states. Comparing

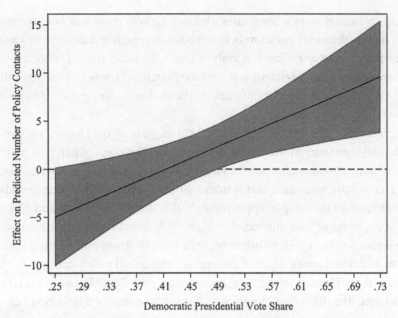

Figure 7.5 Effect of senator's party affiliation on the number of policy contacts from senators to the US Department of Labor across state's presidential vote share

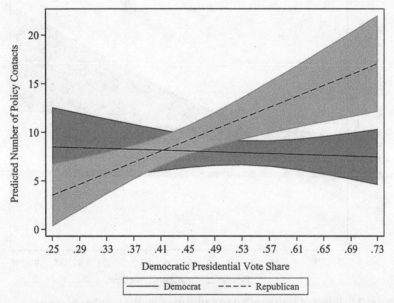

Figure 7.6 Predicted number of policy contacts from senators to the US Department of Labor across state's presidential vote share

Republican senators whose states' Democratic vote share was one standard deviation above the mean to below the mean reveals a difference of about six policy contacts. There is only a slight decrease from Democrats in increasingly blue states, which is not unexpected as Democrats are generally not cross-pressured on labor issues (particularly not during the time period covered by this dataset).

Figure 7.7 presents the marginal effects of party across Democratic presidential vote share in the House. In the House, the effect of party on policy communication is significant for House members representing districts with a Democratic vote share that is under 40% and above 70%, which includes about 35% of the sample (approximately 22% in the lower range and 12% in the upper range). As illustrated in Figure 7.8, Republican House members representing the bluest of districts contact the DOL regarding policy about two additional times, equal to the average number of policy contacts to the DOL from House members, in comparison with Republicans in very red districts. The difference in policy contacts at one standard deviation below and above the mean is about one policy contact. Democrats in very red states contact about two additional times in comparison with Democrats in very

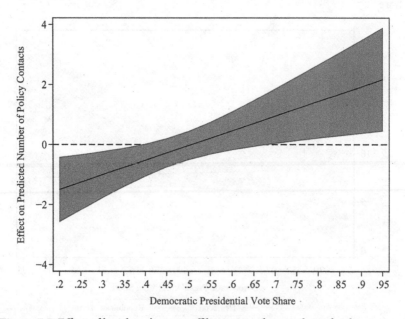

Figure 7.7 Effect of legislator's party affiliation on the number of policy contacts from House members to the US Department of Labor across district's presidential vote share

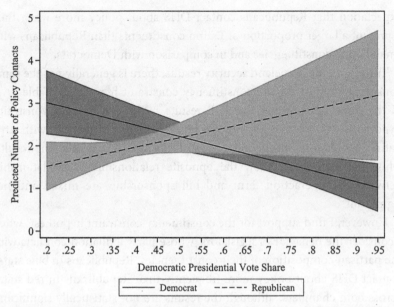

Figure 7.8 Predicted number of policy contacts from House members to the US Department of Labor across district's presidential vote share

blue states. The difference in policy communication when we examine one standard deviation below and above the mean is about one contact.

While there is also a positive and significant relationship between this interaction term and labor bill sponsorship in the House, the coefficient in the Senate model is negative. These results offer consistently strong support for the constituency constraint hypothesis.

Homeland Security Policy

Immigration has become a hot-button issue under DHS's jurisdiction. The Republican Party has developed a reputation for being tough on immigration (e.g., opposing migration based on family status, in favor of strengthening border security). The party's stance on immigration has created conflict for Republican legislators who represent constituencies with substantial Latino populations and have tried to distinguish themselves from the party on this issue. I measure cross-pressures using an interaction between party and the proportion of the Latino population with the expectation that Republicans contact DHS about policy more when they represent a larger proportion of Latino constituents than Republicans with small Latino constituencies and in comparison with Democrats.[25]

Turning to the homeland security results, there is generally not the same consistent support for the constituency constraint hypothesis. Table 7A.1 in the Appendix presents the SUR results.[26] The constituency constraint hypothesis suggests that Republicans representing constituencies with large Latino populations would engage with DHS more frequently. The results, while not significant, show the opposite relationship. The relationship between the interaction term and bill sponsorship are mixed and not significant.

However, I find support for the constituency constraint hypothesis when I consider the behavior of legislators' whose party affiliation conflicts with the partisan composition of their constituencies. Republicans in blue states contact DHS about policy more frequently than Republicans in red states across both chambers, although the results are not statistically significant. Moreover, the relationship between the interaction term and bill sponsorship is in the expected direction across both chambers.

While the results show moderate senators contacting DHS about policy more frequently than ideologues, the results are not significant. In the House model, the relationship is not in the expected direction but also not significant. Ideologically extreme House members sponsor more homeland security bills than their moderate colleagues, but the result is not significant. In the Senate, ideological extremity is negatively, but not significantly, associated with bill sponsorship.

The results offer some support for the constituency constraint hypotheses but are not as consistent and robust as the results in the labor models. There could be several reasons for the discrepancy. First, the DOL's jurisdiction is clearer and narrower (primarily related to worker protection) than the issues managed by the DHS. The DHS's jurisdiction comprises a more varied range of issues including immigration and border security, but also emergency management and disaster response (under the Federal Emergency Management Agency or FEMA), infrastructure and transportation security, cybersecurity, economic security, election security, civil rights and liberties, human trafficking, law enforcement, and terrorism prevention. DHS's wide-ranging jurisdiction creates challenges for examining how legislators engage with the agency and how to measure the effect of conflicting pressures on contact with the agency.

Second, the interaction between party and the size of the Latino constituency may not be an adequate measure of cross-pressures on homeland
security issues, particularly for the time period covered by the dataset.
Of course, public opinion on immigration can vary substantially within
Latino constituencies. Moreover, at the time, the Republican Party was
not as unified behind a hardliner immigration platform as it was in later
years. Instead, President George W. Bush and other prominent Republicans,
particularly along the southern border, were proponents of immigration
reform. A more appropriate measure might be the party affiliation of the
constituency interacted with the size of the Latino population. It could
be particularly challenging for legislators representing constituencies with
large Latino populations in red states regardless of the legislator's own party
affiliation. Figures 7.9 and 7.10 show Senate results from an OLS model
using Democratic presidential vote share in place of the party affiliation
of the legislator. The relationship shown in the figures is in the direction
expected by the constituency constraint hypothesis.

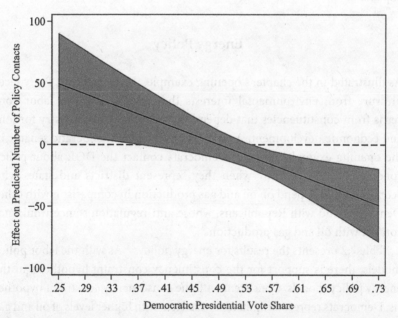

Figure 7.9 Effect of senator's party affiliation on the number of policy contacts
from senators to the US Department of Homeland Security across proportion
of state's Latino population

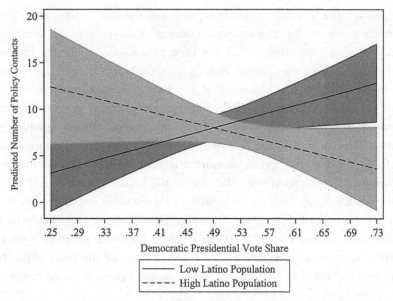

Figure 7.10 Predicted number of policy contacts from senators to the US Department of Homeland Security across proportion of state's Latino population

Energy Policy

As illustrated in the chapter's opening example, the Democratic Party faces pressure from environmental interests that often clash with labor concerns from constituencies that depend on the oil and gas industry for jobs and economic development. As with Pennsylvania's Democratic senator in the opening example, I expect Democrats contact the DOE about policy concerns more frequently when they represent districts and states with economies that depend on oil and gas production in comparison with other Democrats and with Republicans, whose anti-regulation stance would not conflict with oil and gas production.[27]

Table 7.2 presents the results for energy policy.[28] As with the labor policy models, there is support for the constituency constraint hypothesis in the energy policy models. Consistent with the constituency constraint hypothesis, Democrats representing states or districts with higher levels of oil and gas production contact the DOE more frequently than Democrats representing low oil and gas production constituencies and more than Republicans. This result is in the expected direction and significant across both the Senate and the House. Moreover, the results for energy bill sponsorship suggest that this

Table 7.2 Cross-Pressures as Determinants of Policy Contact with the US Department of Energy and Energy Bill Sponsorship

	Senate		House	
	DOE Policy	Energy Bills	DOE Policy	Energy Bills
Republican × oil and gas production	−1.789***	0.179	−2.341***	0.987***
	(−3.41)	(0.70)	(−4.12)	(3.58)
Republican × Democratic vote share	4.657	−3.312	0.691	0.883
	(0.74)	(−1.10)	(0.41)	(1.07)
Ideological extremity	0.194	−0.881	0.162	0.104
	(0.11)	(−1.06)	(0.34)	(0.45)
Oil and natural gas production	1.805***	−0.171	1.966***	−0.586**
	(3.51)	(−0.68)	(3.96)	(−2.43)
Republican	−1.168	0.998	−0.197	−0.791*
	(−0.37)	(0.66)	(−0.22)	(−1.87)
Democratic vote share	1.711	1.040	−0.879	−0.443
	(0.43)	(0.55)	(−1.00)	(−1.04)
Constant	−2.725	0.880	1.168	0.455
	(−1.13)	(0.76)	(1.34)	(1.08)
Congress FE	Y	Y	Y	Y
Controls	Y	Y	Y	Y
N	403	403	1756	1756
adj. R^2	0.3039	0.2520	0.1082	0.1103

t statistics in parentheses. Oil and gas production in quadrillion Btu. Robust standard errors are clustered by member. Table displays results of seemingly unrelated regression (SUR) models.
*$p < 0.1$, **$p < 0.05$, ***$p < 0.01$

result is unique to the bureaucratic venue. The interaction term is positively related to bill sponsorship across both chambers and significant in the House model.

The distinction between policy contact and bill introductions is particularly striking in the House, as shown in Figures 7.11 and 7.12. Figure 7.12 illustrates a clear increase in policy contacts from Democrats as oil and gas production increases while Republicans' contacts stay relatively stable. Democrats in high oil and gas production districts contacted the DOE about six additional times—nearly four times the average number of policy contacts the agency receives—compared to Democrats in districts with no oil and gas production. Figure 7.11 shows that the effect is significant for oil and gas production over approximately 275 trillion Btu, which is about 8% of the sample, suggesting that the cross-pressures primarily have an impact in districts where oil and gas production play a major role in the economy. The results for cross-pressured Democrats offer consistent and

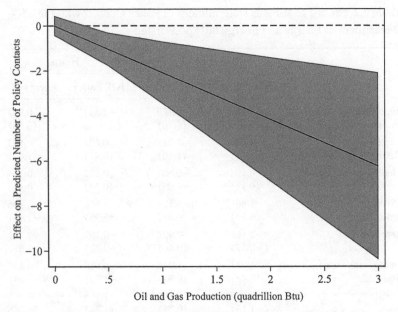

Figure 7.11 Effect of legislator's party affiliation on the number of policy contacts from House members to the US Department of Energy across district's oil and gas production

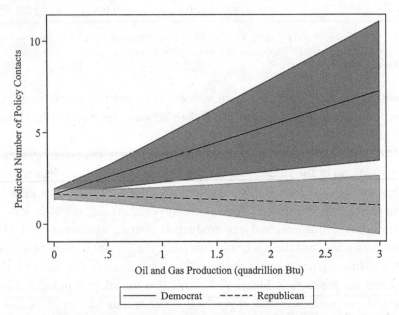

Figure 7.12 Predicted number of policy contacts from House members to the US Department of Energy across district's oil and gas production

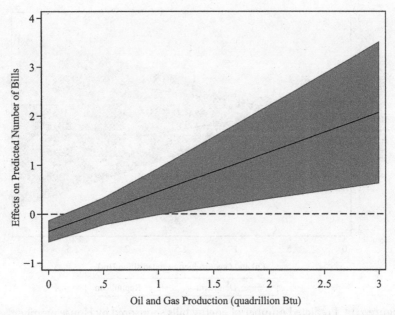

Figure 7.13 Effect of legislator's party affiliation on the number of energy bills House members sponsor across district's oil and gas production

strong support for the constituency constraint hypothesis, which mirror the results for cross-pressured Republicans in the labor policy models.

Moreover, Figures 7.13 and 7.14 display the relationship between the interaction of party and oil and gas production and energy bill sponsorship which is consistent with expectations. In fact, Republicans sponsor more energy bills as oil and gas production in their district increases while Democrats sponsor fewer bills when their districts depend on this controversial type of energy production. Taken together, these relationships correspond to what we would expect if bill sponsorship is used for visible representation and back-channel communications with agencies is strategically used to represent interests that are costly to represent publicly.

The results for the two general measures of cross-pressures are not statistically significant. Moderate senators and House members contact the DOE about policy less than ideologues, although the results are not significant. Ideologically extreme House members sponsor more energy bills, but the results are not significant and do not extend to the Senate. Finally, the relationship for the interaction term between legislator party affiliation and Democratic vote share and policy communication is in the expected direction but not significant across both chambers. The results for this interaction with energy bill sponsorship are mixed and not significant.

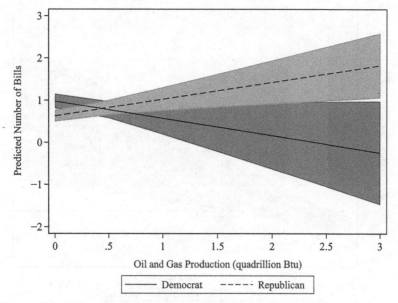

Figure 7.14 Predicted number of energy bills sponsored by House members across district's oil and gas production

The results for the issue-specific measure demonstrate strong support for the constituency constraint hypothesis and suggest that issue salience within the constituency plays an important role in how cross-pressures affect legislators' behaviors. The results for the two general measures may occur because these measures do not account for the salience of energy issues within the district or state. In short, there may be conflicting interests within the constituency, but a lack of attention or stake in energy issues means the legislator is unlikely to take heat.

Conclusion

This chapter presents empirical evidence that members of Congress use back-channel communication with the bureaucracy to represent interests that are costly to represent publicly. This theory of inter-branch representation departs from conventional wisdom that legislators use contact with the bureaucracy solely for credit claiming and press release fodder. Instead, savvy legislators use the bureaucratic backdoor to quietly represent interests on contentious issues.

The results presented in this chapter offer consistent support across two departments, the DOL and DOE, and in both the Senate and House. The inconsistent results for the DHS could be due to the wide-range of issues under the agency's jurisdiction and the challenges of measuring cross-pressures. However, the DOL and DOE results suggest that conflicted senators and House members engage more with agencies on policy matters across several measures of cross-pressures, particularly measures that account for issue salience within the constituency. Moreover, examining the effect of these same measures on participation in a visible policymaking venue suggests that this finding is particular to back-channel communication. I even find that legislators who are not cross-pressured represent interests more often through public means of participation in some cases. These findings have important implications for representation and accountability across venues.

In the next chapter, I offer the last analysis of the book by considering agency responsiveness to legislators' policy appeals. Are these contacts effective means for influencing policy? Do agencies privilege communications from some legislators more than others?

Appendix

Table 7A.1 Cross-Pressures as Determinants of Policy Contact with the US Department of Homeland Security and Homeland Security Bill Sponsorship

	Senate		House	
	DHS Policy Contacts	Homeland Security Bills	DHS Policy Contacts	Homeland Security Bills
Republican x Latino population prop.	−8.933 (−0.95)	−1.108 (−0.47)	−0.606 (−0.28)	0.286 (0.69)
Republican x Democratic vote share	19.920 (1.64)	−2.431 (−0.79)	2.864 (0.63)	−0.619 (−0.71)
Ideological extremity	−1.073 (−0.32)	−0.115 (−0.13)	1.702 (1.41)	0.117 (0.51)
Latino population prop.	0.540 (0.08)	0.381 (0.21)	−1.008 (−0.87)	0.516** (2.33)
Republican	−7.888 (−1.33)	1.103 (0.74)	−2.667 (−1.16)	0.446 (1.01)
Democratic vote share	−0.113 (−0.02)	−0.208 (−0.11)	0.347 (0.15)	0.181 (0.41)
Constant	4.810 (1.07)	0.626 (0.55)	−2.153 (−0.96)	0.656 (1.53)
Congress FE	Y	Y	Y	Y
Controls	Y	Y	Y	Y
N	403	403	1765	1765
adj. R^2	0.2746	0.2430	0.1574	0.2037

t statistics in parentheses. Robust standard errors are clustered by member. The table displays results of seemingly unrelated regression (SUR) models.
*$p < 0.1$, **$p < 0.05$, ***$p < 0.01$

8

Congressional Access and Influence
in the Bureaucracy

Legislators are not the only targets of lobbying. Federal agencies are lobbied by interest and industry groups, American states and municipalities, and foreign nations (e.g., Carpenter 2010; Ban and You 2019; Goldstein and You 2017; You 2020; Haeder and Yackee 2015). Hundreds of lobbyists descend on agencies like the Departments of Energy and Labor every year on behalf of clients ranging from the American Hotel and Lodging Association and Cornell University to Koch Industries, Chevron, and Facebook. Nearly two thousand lobbyists filed reports listing the Department of Homeland Security as a target of their lobbying in 2020 alone.[1]

Members of Congress lobby agencies, too. They are not required to register as lobbyists, nor do they hire outside lobbying firms. Yet, members of Congress receive unrivaled access to some of the most powerful policy-makers in the United States government.

Why do legislators lobby agencies? I answer this question in the previous chapters by showing how legislators use agency policymaking as a substitute for legislative action. Members of Congress pressure agencies in order to evade the constraints of the legislative process and to inconspicuously influence policy through quiet backchannels. However, the implicit answer underlying the previous chapters is that legislators lobby agencies because they believe these interactions allow them to influence policymaking. This is the same reason interest groups lobby legislators after a law has already passed; interest groups believe that legislators can influence administrative policymaking on their behalf (You 2017). Setting aside the beliefs and expectations of legislators and interest groups, the question remains: Is lobbying agencies an effective way to influence policy?

There are, of course, limitations on an agency's ability to fulfill a law-maker's request. In the opening example of the book, for instance, I described how the Fish and Wildlife Service managed to delist the gray wolf, as Senator Klobuchar requested, only to have the delisting overturned by the

Backdoor Lawmaking: Evading Obstacles in the US Congress. Melinda N. Ritchie, Oxford University Press.
© Melinda N. Ritchie 2023. DOI: 10.1093/oso/9780197670491.003.0008

courts. As I explain in Chapter 4, agencies can be responsive to lawmakers' policy appeals by proposing a rule or delaying enforcement, but they cannot guarantee outcomes.

Moreover, if a legislator's request runs counter to the president's priorities, the interests of a critical mass of other members of Congress, or even a single powerful lawmaker, the agency may need to weigh the competing interests.[2] This chapter focuses on how agencies weigh these competing concerns and when lawmakers' efforts to lobby agencies are most effective. While agencies have the incentive to be responsive to every legislator's request given unlimited resources (Ritchie and You 2019), that may not always be possible. How, then, do agencies prioritize lawmakers' policy appeals?

In Chapter 2, I argue that agencies are motivated to be responsive to lawmakers in order to build coalitions of support in Congress and to avoid angering lawmakers who might retaliate. The *retaliation hypothesis* proposes that agencies prioritize lawmakers who have the capacity and the motivation to retaliate against the agency. While any lawmaker can vote against an agency's priorities, one legislator, particularly in the House, cannot derail a bill. Moreover, spending limited resources to retaliate against an agency generally is not a priority for the average lawmaker. Bureaucrats, for their part, are risk-averse and want to avoid making enemies with any legislator. However, prioritizing lawmakers with the most ability and motivation to create challenges for the agency is an efficient strategy. Who in Congress has the greatest capacity and motivation to create problems for agencies?

First, we must consider how lawmakers retaliate against agencies. What tools do legislators have to use as leverage against agencies? What costs do agencies want to avoid?

Inter-Branch Retaliation

Members of Congress use threats and coercion to pressure agencies to do their bidding. Legislators drag bureaucrats in front of committee hearings, interrogate them, and even brutally attack their character on national television. They demand investigations, audits, and reviews of agency procedures, ethics, and budgetary decisions. Lawmakers vote against the agency's budget and priorities, and senators hold up nominees the administration appointed to the agency. They pursue legislation that is costly for the agency or force the agency to re-structure itself. They attack the agency and its principals in the press. Members of Congress have a wide range of tools of retaliation, both formal and informal, at their disposal.

Even casual observers of Congress recall the marathon committee hearing on the 2012 attack on the US compound in Benghazi when former Secretary of State Hillary Clinton was grilled for over eight hours. Yet, less prominent agency officials are often the targets of committee hearings and other demands of congressional oversight that can be costly to agencies even when they are not televised. Committee hearings and congressional investigations are often used to pursue policy change as well as impose costs on an administration. Although generally led by party leaders, rank-and-file legislators will use their time to air grievances and attack the witness, the agency, and the president. For example, what was supposed to be a House Intelligence Committee hearing in 2021 on global threats to the United States was, instead, waylaid by House members attacking intelligence officials for perceived wrongs committed by the FBI during the previous administration and venting about political and personal grievances.[3] Congressional investigations are often driven by partisan antagonism when the opposition controls the White House, particularly during times of intense polarization (Kriner and Schickler 2016, 66).[4]

In fact, research suggests even the threat of oversight hearings and investigations can be an effective tool for legislators. Hearings and investigations have been shown to spur legislation, but even anticipation of a hearing can yield preemptive policy change by the administration and unilateral agency action. Ironically, congressional hearings may allow legislators to achieve policy change through agency action when support for legislation is lacking (Kriner and Schickler 2016).

Committee hearings are not the only way lawmakers retaliate against the executive branch. There is a history of senators obstructing nominees' confirmation over policy disagreements with the administration. While, in the end, the Senate generally confirms the president's nominees, senators can delay a nomination by placing a hold, which signals the senator's concerns with the nominee and prolongs the process. Committees can also be a source of delays if committee members raise concerns about the nominee's qualifications or especially if the committee chair wants to block a nominee by refusing to hold a hearing. These dilatory tactics may have little to do with the nominee and, instead, can be used as leverage over a policy disagreement with the administration.[5] For example, in 2006, Senator Wyden (D-OR) placed a hold on the Bush administration's nominee for Solicitor for the Department of the Interior and pledged to block future nominees over funding for rural schools and roads.[6] Likewise, Senator Cory Gardner (R-CO) held up nominees to the DOJ over Attorney General Jeff Sessions's move to reverse the Cole Memo policy, which deferred to state authorities, and begin enforcing federal marijuana laws (Foster 2022). These types of ultimatums may not keep the nominee from being confirmed, but they can lead to costly publicity and raise doubts about the reputation of the nominee. Moreover, while the nominee might ultimately be confirmed, a senator's dilatory tactics can drag out the already burdensome process for several months and demand additional effort from the administration (McCarty and Razaghian 1999).

Introducing legislation, or merely threatening to introduce a bill, can be enough to spur agency action even if the bill has little chance of ever becoming law. Senator Amy Klobuchar demonstrated this tactic in the opening example of Chapter 1 when she told the Fish and Wildlife Administration that she would be introducing legislation to delist the gray wolf if the agency did not move forward with rulemaking. Bureaucrats are risk-averse and would prefer to take an action voluntarily than to face the prospect of new legislation and statutory obligations.[7]

Bills—even bills that are unlikely to ever become law—can trigger agency responsiveness. A congressional fellow described how his House office reached out to an agency on an issue of importance to the congressman but received no response. However, the legislator then introduced a bill on the matter, prompting agency officials to show up at the legislator's office.[8]

The power that a bill introduction carries with agencies is an important strategic tool for legislators. As discussed previously, the average bill has less than a 5% chance of becoming law due to the obstacles of the legislative process. The possibility that introducing legislation may carry more weight in the bureaucratic venue than in the legislative process means that legislators' formal authority and power may be used in other venues more effectively than in Congress. In short, a legislator's power exceeds their Article I authority and spills over the institutional partitions of the separation of powers.

Lawmakers even negotiate informal agreements with agencies prior to a vote. This inter-branch logrolling is illustrated by the example described in Chapter 4 when Senators John McCain (R-AZ) and Tom Coburn (R-OK) asked the Secretary of Energy how he intended to implement ambiguous language in a bill and demanded a response before voting on the legislation.

Members of Congress hold bills, budgets, and nominees hostage in order to extract policy concessions from agencies.

Members of Congress do not even need to rely on their formal powers as lawmakers for retaliation. Legislators can use the clout of their congressional seat as a platform or congressional bully pulpit by attacking an agency in the press or on social media. Immigration and Customs Enforcement (ICE) has been a frequent target, with some legislators, including Reps. Ilhan Omar (D-MN) and Alexandria Ocasio-Cortez (D-NY), even tweeting support for calls to abolish the agency. Rep. Ilhan Omar tweeted, "The negligence we've seen from ICE detention centers is unacceptable. We can't let this dehumanizing and irresponsible agency continue. We must #AbolishICE."[9] One can imagine that ICE officials would not want to give the congresswomen additional ammunition by appearing unresponsive to their policy appeals.

Often the public attacks on an agency are directed at the administration. Senator Michael Bennet (D-CO), for instance, used his congressional bully pulpit to criticize an action by the Trump administration's EPA: "Just when you think the Trump Administration's attacks on the environment can't get any worse, today the @EPA announced it's gutting the #CleanPowerPlan— essentially giving a huge handout to big polluters at the expense of public health and our planet."[10] However, members of Congress can also be critical of an agency across administrations. Rep. Brian Higgins (D-NY), for example, has regularly criticized FEMA in the press since his early years in Congress.[11]

Legislators' influence over agencies need not be so direct. Retaliatory action can have an indirect influence over agency behavior across a wide range of policy issues. If a lawmaker targets an agency with costly oversight demands or attacks the agency in the press, the agency will be motivated to be more sensitive to the lawmaker's policy appeals across the board. In other words, the subject of legislators' retaliation need not be the same as their policy appeals. A legislator might not raise an agency's unresponsiveness on a particular policy appeal during a hearing or in a press release. However, if an agency is repeatedly unresponsive to a lawmaker's requests, the agency can expect her to attack as issues arise in the future.[12]

In fact, a lawmaker's attack on an agency is generally not an isolated incident. Members of Congress have been known to develop long-standing feuds with a particular agency. In some cases, a lawmaker has gone to war with a particular appointee, even calling for the appointee to be impeached. Rep. Jim Jordan (R-OH), for example, called for the impeachment of IRS

Commissioner John Koskinen over his crusade to ensure the Tea Party was not targeted.[13] This type of long-term antagonistic relationship with a lawmaker can be a thorn in an agency's side. It's worth an agency's effort to not make enemies in Congress.

In short, lawmakers' threats are credible. Legislators have a range of formal and informal tools of retaliation at their disposal, and they can create costly challenges for agencies, appointees, and the administration. While legislators are unlikely to pursue further action for every appeal, agencies are risk-averse and will use their discretion and available resources to try to satisfy a legislator's request (Ritchie and You 2019). Agencies view lawmakers' policy appeals as credible signals of their preferences, preference intensity, and of further consequences if the agency is unresponsive. However, this argument runs counter to arguments and empirical results in previous literature examining agency responsiveness. Instead, previous work has largely concluded that agencies reward friends of the administration rather than prioritize its enemies.

Rewarding Friends or Appeasing Enemies?

Much of the previous literature concludes that friends of the administration are the likely recipients of agency benefits and attention (e.g., Anagnoson 1982; Bertelli and Grose 2009; Berry, Burden, and Howell 2010; Lowande 2019; Mills and Kalaf-Hughes 2015; Neiheisel and Brady 2017).[14] Agencies deliver more federal grants to senators who are ideologically close to the agency's leadership (Bertelli and Grose 2009) and support grant requests from legislators who are likely to be supportive of the agency's goals (Neiheisel and Brady 2017). Regions represented by presidential co-partisans receive more federal funds, an indication "that members of Congress who belong to the president's party are advantaged in the budgetary process" (Berry, Burden, and Howell 2010, 783). Agencies also respond more quickly to requests from members of the president's party (Lowande 2019) and give them a heads up about grants coming to their districts (Anagnoson 1982). In fact, agencies favor legislators who share the administration's party affiliation by accelerating grants for incumbent co-partisans coming up for reelection and by notifying them about a grant their district or state is receiving first, as one Republican administrator (for HUD and EDA) described:

The procedure generally is that within a day or two after the assistant secretary's signature, the public affairs people write a release. Then we look at the congressional district and the senators. If there is one Republican and two Democrats, the Republican gets it at 10 a.m., the Democrats at 1:30 to 3 p.m. That's a three- to five-hour time lag. It's different in the West, delayed a bit just in time for the local weeklies. Tuesday noon was their deadline generally. For Democrats on the agency's authorizing committee—with one Republican congressman—we'd try to give the committee guy a break. He'd get the announcement at the same time as the Republican or one half to one hour later. (Anagnoson 1982, 554)

Yet, much of this literature focuses on distributive benefits where the legislators' preferences can be assumed. Legislators presumably want more grants and speedy notifications and responses. On matters of policy, the legislators' preferences and priorities are less clear, so direct signals from lawmakers take on greater importance.

Rather than rewarding friends of the administration, I argue that—particularly when responding to policy signals—agencies have an incentive to prioritize legislators who are most likely, and most driven, to retaliate. Agencies are risk-averse, especially when dealing with uncertainty over the actions and reactions of elected officials (Krause 2003). Moreover, members of Congress are known to retaliate against political actors who betray their interests. In fact, threats and retaliation are a standard tool for legislators in their dealings with a wide range of political actors, including their colleagues. For instance, legislators are less likely to cosponsor the bills of colleagues who renege on support for their legislation (Bernhard and Sulkin 2013). Thus, agencies have an incentive to tread lightly with legislators who are already inclined to pick a fight. They have less to worry about from friends of the administration, who have other incentives to support the agency and administration—including shared party and ideological goals and reputational costs and rewards—regardless of how the agency treats them.

This is not without support from previous empirical findings. While Ritchie and You (2019) find that agencies are generally responsive to any legislator's request regardless of status, party, or ideology, the authors find that the liberal-leaning Labor Department was significantly more inclined to give Republican senators what they requested. The authors' conclude that:

this result could suggest the agency is [trying to] appease the members of Congress who are most likely to retaliate (i.e., Republicans are more likely to have preferences that are at odds with the DOL) and have the greatest capacity to impose costs on the agency (e.g., senators attract more press attention, have greater leverage in the chamber, and confirmation authority). (Ritchie and You 2019, 91, n. 25)

In short, agencies are motivated to appease their powerful enemies.

Retaliatory Power

Motivation for retaliation is not the only factor driving agency responsiveness. Lawmakers' power and capacity for retaliation also carries weight with agencies. Lawmakers' institutional positions, roles, and rank can make them a greater threat to an agency. The findings from Ritchie and You (2019) described above highlight an example of this argument: Republican senators are particularly influential with the DOL because of their ideological differences with the liberal agency, but also because they are senators with control over appointee confirmation. A senator is going to have more influence over an agency's fortunes than the average House member. Thus, it is in the agency's interest to prioritize requests from senators over House members.

Agencies are also more likely to be swayed if a critical mass of lawmakers organize to pressure an agency on behalf of the policy appeal. Like the logic underlying interest group lobbying, if lawmakers are able to mobilize their colleagues, it is a signal of greater capacity for retaliation. Presumably aware of this advantage, legislators collaborate on policy appeals by urging their colleagues to sign onto a letter, similar to cosponsorship of legislation. If an agency is unresponsive to a letter co-signed by hundreds of lawmakers, the risk is greater that the agency will anger one or more of the legislators and face retaliation. Moreover, a critical mass of cosignatories could signal capacity for passing legislation if the agency does not act voluntarily. It also could be viewed as neglectful of legislative intent if the agency ignores a collective body of legislators, even if the request breaks with statute and the number of cosignatories is less than what is required to pass legislation (e.g., policy appeals supporting the Dream Act). Thus, agencies are motivated to prioritize a collaborative appeal from a band of lawmakers over an appeal from a single lawmaker.[15]

In fact, the argument that agencies are more responsive to lawmakers in positions of influence is not inconsistent with the literature or even new. Agencies have been shown to be more responsive to members of the committee with jurisdiction over the agency (Arnold 1979; Ferejohn 1974) and the majority party (Kernell and McDonald 1999; Levitt and Snyder 1995), for instance. Likewise, it is often assumed that members of the oversight committee, congressional leadership, and committee leadership carry more weight with agencies due to their power within Congress, their influence over the agency's budgets and programs, and the ability to make oversight demands. Indeed, the formal power of these positions are likely an important consideration for agencies in deciding how much attention, time, and effort to devote to them. Agencies have a strong incentive to prioritize appeals from legislators with formal power and oversight authority over the agency— particularly members of the committee with jurisdiction. In fact, it would be surprising if we did not observe that agencies prioritize the committee with jurisdiction; it could be reason for skepticism of the validity of the measure of prioritization.

However, previous work has focused on institutional mechanisms of control and collective institutions within the body of Congress along the lines of the *structure and process* arguments (McCubbins, Noll, and Weingast 1987, 1989) rather than considering the variety of both formal and informal means of retaliation across individual lawmakers. I depart from this literature by arguing that agencies are strategic about responding to lawmakers' signals of their preferences and priorities and the likelihood of retaliation from any lawmaker (Ritchie and You 2019). Moreover, there has been very little work examining agency responsiveness to lawmakers' informal signals. In fact, there are but four studies of which I am aware at the writing of this book that empirically examine the impact of legislator requests on the actual outcomes of agency decisions (Mills and Kalaf-Hughes 2015; Mills, Kalaf-Hughes, and MacDonald 2016; Neiheisel and Brady 2017; Ritchie and You 2019). Why are there so few studies of the impact of legislator contacts on agency decisions?

As I describe in Chapter 3, data on congressional communications to agencies are difficult to obtain and labor-intensive to code. The other challenge for studies of agency responsiveness, however, is mirrored in the literature on interest group lobbying. In short, measuring influence is challenging.

The Approaches and Challenges for Measuring Influence

The challenges for measuring agency responsiveness to Congress are similar to the challenges of testing theories of interest group influence. In fact, the literature on interest groups finds little evidence of the effects of lobbying on policy outcomes like floor votes, likely because influence occurs at earlier stages of the policymaking process and in ways that are more difficult to observe (Baumgartner and Leech 1998; Baumgartner et al. 2009; Burstein and Linton 2002). Instead, scholars have examined and found indirect evidence of interest group influence by focusing on committee participation (Hall and Miler 2008; Hall and Wayman 1990), information subsidizing (Hall and Deardorff 2006; Esterling 2004), and the attention of and access to decision makers (Kalla and Broockman 2016; Miler 2007, 2010).

Similar to studies on interest group lobbying (Kalla and Broockman 2016, also see Balla 2000), I conceptualize influence in terms of legislators' access to agency policymakers, particularly those with the greatest power to make decisions. Considering influence in terms of access to policymakers builds on previous work on interest group success at lobbying Congress (Hansen 1991) and the power of campaign contributions for lobbyists (Kalla and Broockman 2016). Another advantage of this approach is that it allows me to consider variation in access across a wide range of policy requests that may differ in how challenging they are to actually accomplish, thus offering a standardized metric for comparison. Moreover, using a measure of access offers a way to compare and assess previous measures of responsiveness, such as speed of response (Balla 2000; Lowande 2019). My measure of access offers a unique standard by which to assess this previous measure of responsiveness.

Thus far, the few studies that have tested agency responsiveness to legislator requests have relied on a measure of the outcome of an agency decision (i.e., Mills and Kalaf-Hughes 2015; Mills, Kalaf-Hughes, and MacDonald 2016; Neiheisel and Brady 2017; Ritchie and You 2019), the amount of time it took for an agency to respond to a request (i.e., Balla 2000; Lowande 2019), the signature level, or the length of the response (Balla 2000). While studies using outcome measures are ideal for testing legislator influence on agency decisions, they generally depend on a more limited focus on a particular program or agency. Alternatively, measuring agency responsiveness with the amount of time lapsed between legislator contact and agency response allows for comparison across many issues and agencies. However, using time lapsed as a measure of responsiveness or prioritization is also limited because it does not capture the content or quality of the response.

Moreover, time lapsed may not appropriately measure agency prioritization at all. Intuitively, the requests made by legislators will vary in terms of time and effort demanded by the task. In fact, typical, routine constituency service—such as expediting a visa or passport renewal—would undoubtedly take less time to complete than responding to a grant application. Moreover, casework or even grant allocations would certainly take less time for an agency than responding to a request for promulgating a rule or issuing agency guidelines. However, we would never assume that a quicker response to casework was an indication of the importance of casework in relation to policy. We would not interpret an agency's speedier response to casework as an indication that the agency prioritized constituency service over policy-related communications from lawmakers.

Fortunately, we do not need to rely on intuition alone. I use a novel measure of agency prioritization, as categorized and recorded by the agency itself, to assess how agencies prioritize communications from Congress. The records are included in the congressional correspondence logs I obtained under the Freedom of Information Act (FOIA), as described in Chapter 3. In addition to other information about its communication with members of Congress—such as the name of the legislators, a summary of the subject of the contact, and dates of contact—the US Department of Energy includes an indication of the priority level of the contact. This internal record of prioritization is used to determine who at the agency sees the request. Communications prioritized at the highest level are given to the Secretary of Energy. The levels of prioritization and instructions for how each category of communication should be handled are described in detail in the US Department of Energy guide for the management of correspondence.[16] As displayed in Table 8.1, communication to the DOE is assigned to one of five levels of priority (in order of highest to lowest priority): Essential Critical, Essential, Important Critical, Important, Routine. Items assigned to the top three categories (designated "critical items") are sent via electronic mail to the Secretary, Deputy Secretary, and Under Secretaries every

Table 8.1 Agency Correspondence Management, US Department of Energy

		Agency Prioritization of Communication		
Priority Level	Critical Item	Recipient	Due Date	Originator
Essential Critical	Y	Secretary, Deputy and Under Secretaries	8 work days	President, VP, WH senior staff/advisors, cabinet, governors, mayors of major cities, heads of state, chairs and ranking minority members, congressional delegations, true congressionals (addressed to Secretary (S), Deputy (DS) and Under Secretaries (US))
Essential	Y	Secretary, Deputy and Under Secretaries	8 work days	President, VP, WH senior staff/advisors, cabinet, governors, mayors of major cities, heads of state, chairs and ranking minority members, congressional delegations, true congressionals (to S, DS, and US)
Important Critical	Y	Secretary, Deputy and Under Secretaries	8 work days	President, VP, WH senior staff/advisors, cabinet, governors, mayors of major cities, heads of state, chairs and ranking minority members, congressional delegations, true congressionals (to S, DS, and US)
Important	N	Program Officials	15 work days	Fed. independent agencies, true congressionals (to program officials), Congress–constituent referrals, fed/state officials, whistleblower correspondence, Boy/Girl Scout awards
Routine	N		30 work days	Citizen mail, write-in campaigns

afternoon. Clearly, communication receiving this "critical item" designation is prioritized and benefits from greater and immediate access to the most important policymakers and decision makers in the agency, including the cabinet member.

Table 8.1 also displays guidance about the length of time that should be allotted to communication based on the priority level and originator of the correspondence.[17] The guidance (while suggestive, as indicated by the DOE) does offer a sense of the association between response time and prioritization, as well as how communication may be prioritized based on the originator. Communication assigned to the highest priority levels (deemed "critical items") is allocated the shortest response time (8 days) consistent with arguments made in previous work (Balla 2000; Lowande 2019). These high-priority contacts originate from the White House, the cabinet, governors, international heads of states, and other important members of the political and corporate arenas. These originators also include "Chairmen and Ranking Minority Members of Congress," congressional delegations, and "True Congressionals (addressed to S, DS, & US)." The agency distinction of "True Congressionals" refers to letters or contacts that address primarily public policy issues (as opposed to contacts about casework, for instance). Communication that is not deemed "critical" is assigned 15 work days and includes communication from independent agencies and federal and state officials and, for our purposes, constituency service referrals from members of Congress (as well as "True Congressionals" that are addressed to a Program Official). Communication assigned to the lowest priority level is allotted 30 work days and includes "citizen mail" and write-in campaigns. Keep in mind that these guidelines do not account for other factors, such as the complexity or difficulty of the request, which might affect how long it would take the agency to respond. That said, these guidelines suggest that agency response time is negatively associated with prioritization, as assumed in previous work.

What Types of Contacts Are Prioritized by Agencies?

However, the data offer a different verdict. As I described in Chapter 3, the records I obtained under FOIA include the date the agency closed out the correspondence or a due date based on guidance from the handbook.[18] I use these dates to examine how long it takes an agency to respond to contacts based on the categorization described in Chapter 3. Figure 8.1 (left-hand panel) displays the agency's response time (in terms of days lapsed) by type of contact. In fact, as my earlier intuition predicted, it takes agencies longer to respond to policy communication than to constituency service and grant requests. This is consistent with my argument that it would be more challenging and require greater time, effort, and resources to respond to policy communication than a status inquiry on a worker's compensation case.[19] When combining three agencies (DOE, DOL, DHS) in Figure 8.1c, the average response time to policy communication is 30 days. The average response time is 20 days for grants and 24 days for casework. While the DOE and DHS records include only the "due date" rather than the date the agency actually closed the case, DOL records include the "close out date" and show a consistent pattern.[20] Figure 8.1a shows the DOL's response time across contact type, with the agency taking an average of 52 days to respond to policy appeals in comparison to 33 days and 25 days to respond to grant requests and constituency service, respectively. Based on previous assumptions underlying the use of response time as a measure of prioritization, Figure 8.1 (left-hand panel) would suggest that agencies prioritize grants and casework over policy. Intuitively, this interpretation seems questionable.

But perhaps the problem lies not with using response time as a measure of prioritization, but with my coding procedure and categorization of the types of communication. We can consider this possibility by using DOE's recorded priority levels. If the problem lies with response time as a measure of prioritization, rather than my categorization and coding of contact types, we would expect to observe a discrepancy between DOE's priority levels and response time based on contact type.

In fact, this is precisely what we find displayed in Figures 8.1 (right-hand panel) and 8.2. Figure 8.1b (and the identical figure displayed in Figure 8.1d) presents the average agency prioritization after converting the priority levels to a numerical scale from one to five, with lower averages associated with higher prioritization. Policy communication is clearly the highest priority with an average of 1.68, followed by grant requests at 2.19. Casework is the lowest priority, with an average of 2.71.

Figure 8.2 presents a more accessible representation by showing the number of contacts at each priority level by contact type. Policy communication dominates the highest priority level ("essential critical") and comprises a smaller proportion of the contacts in the lower priority levels. Grant

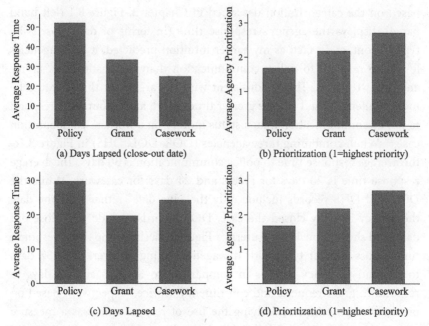

Figure 8.1 Agency responsiveness in terms of response time (left-hand panel) and prioritization (right-hand panel) across contact types

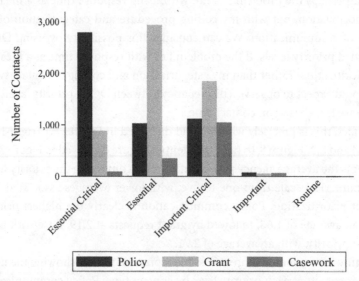

Figure 8.2 Agency prioritization across contact types, US Department of Energy

requests dominate the second highest priority level ("essential") as well as the third highest priority level ("important critical"). Most of the constituency service-related contacts are in the third highest priority level ("important critical") and comprise a small proportion of the contacts in the highest priority levels. These descriptive statistics offer additional validation of my categorization and coding of communication types and reason for skepticism of response time as a measure of agency responsiveness and prioritization.

Given these descriptive patterns, it is important to consider whether there are discrepancies between the conclusions drawn in previous work using response time and when using my novel measure of agency prioritization. The drawback of my measure of agency prioritization is that it is limited to the DOE. However, I can still compare the two measures in tests of my expectations (informed by theoretical arguments in previous work) about how agency responsiveness might vary across legislators. In the next section, I include models using response time as a comparison as I turn back to my theoretical expectations regarding agency responsiveness to policy appeals.

Agency Prioritization and Access to Agency Policymakers

There are theoretical reasons to expect different results based on whether agency responsiveness is measured using prioritization or response time. How might threat of retaliation impact these two agency responses in different ways?

In Chapter 2, I argue that agencies are motivated to be responsive to any request from any legislator (also see Ritchie and You 2019), but, given limited resources, agencies prioritize legislators who have the greatest capacity and motivation for imposing costs on the agency. My operationalization of prioritization matches the agency's characterization as described in the DOE's handbook as well as previous literature on policy influence (Kalla and Broockman 2016): High-priority communications get access to the top policymakers. Based on the retaliation hypothesis, I expect that policy appeals from lawmakers with the greatest ability and motivation to impose costs on the agency reach the desk of the cabinet member.

How might prioritization affect how quickly an agency responds to a legislator's appeal? As previous work argues, agencies are likely to be motivated to respond as quickly as possible to a lawmaker's correspondence. However, as I show above, some requests take longer to handle than others.

The content, complexity, difficulty, and nature of the request affects how long it takes an agency to respond. Moreover, if an agency prioritizes a policy appeal from a powerful lawmaker, the agency may want to expend more time, efforts, and resources fulfilling the request, which may take longer than responding to a request the agency does not prioritize and does not intend to satisfy. Relatedly, if requests that are prioritized get the attention of the top policymaker, they may take longer to receive a response due to the busier schedules of the cabinet member and other top appointees compared to low-priority requests that are handled by lower-level bureaucrats.

In fact, agencies may take *longer* to respond to high-priority requests.[21] However, if agencies are motivated to appease enemies of the administration, the timeliness of the agency's response may be strategically important in order to head off further escalation of a conflict. Based on this logic, I develop separate predictions for how agencies prioritize legislators' policy appeals and how long the agencies take to respond to the appeals based on two key characteristics: First, a lawmakers' capacity to retaliate and, second, a lawmaker's motivation to retaliate. While agencies prioritize lawmakers based on both of these factors, I expect they take longer to satisfy the requests of powerful lawmakers who are not necessarily motivated to retaliate against the administration and respond faster to perceived enemies of the agency.

Table 8.2 presents the expectations. The table includes variables intended to capture a lawmaker's capacity to impose costs and variables measuring a lawmaker's motivation to retaliate. Based on the retaliation hypothesis, I expect that agencies prioritize lawmakers' appeals based on the measures in both conceptual categories, as described by the priority expectations in the third column. As shown in the fourth column, I expect agencies to take longer to respond to appeals based on the lawmakers' capacity to retaliate but to respond more quickly to appeals from legislators who are motivated to retaliate.

First, there are several reasons to expect agencies to prioritize senators over House members. The filibuster power and confirmation authority give individual senators greater capacity for imposing costs on an agency in comparison to House members. Also, senators are able to attract press attention more easily than House members (Sellers 2010), providing them informal capacity for imposing reputational costs on the agency. Finally, senators have more resources, staff, and time between elections. Therefore, senators present a greater threat if the agency is not responsive.

Second, we should expect agencies to prioritize members of the committee with primary jurisdiction over the agency. In the tradition of iron

Table 8.2 Agency Responsiveness: Expectations

Concept	Variable	Retaliation Hypothesis Expectations	
		Priority expectation	Response time expectation
Capacity to retaliate	Senator	Agencies prioritize senators over House members.	Agencies take longer to respond to senators.
	Committee	Agencies prioritize committee members.	Agencies take longer to respond to committee members.
	Majority	Agencies prioritize majority party members.	Agencies take longer to respond to majority party members.
	Collaborative	Agencies prioritize contacts from multiple lawmakers.	Agencies take longer to respond to collaborative contacts.
	Oversight committee	Agencies prioritize oversight committee members.	Agencies take longer to respond to oversight committee members.
	Committee chair	Agencies prioritize committee chairs.	Agencies take longer to respond to committee chairs.
	Leadership	Agencies prioritize leaders.	Agencies take longer to respond to leaders.
	Seniority	Agencies prioritize lawmakers with more seniority.	Agencies take longer to respond to senior lawmakers.
Motivation to retaliate	White House out-partisan	Agencies prioritize White House out-partisans.	Agencies respond faster to White House out-partisans.
	Party affiliation	DOL prioritizes Republicans. DHS prioritizes Democrats.	DOL responds faster to Republicans. DHS responds faster to Democrats.

triangles, committees with jurisdiction have long been viewed as having utmost importance to an agency. In fact, it would be surprising to find evidence to the contrary and might suggest the need for skepticism of my measure of prioritization.

Third, agencies are likely to prioritize appeals from groups of lawmakers over a single legislator's appeal. As explained earlier, collaborative efforts involving many lawmakers indicates greater capacity for legislative action or other means of retaliation.

Fourth, research suggests majority party members carry more weight with agencies (Kernell and McDonald 1999; Lowande 2019). The majority is seen as having influence over the legislative fortunes of agencies and the ability to make costly oversight demands. As such, I would expect agencies to prioritize the majority party.

Likewise, members of leadership, committee chairs and subcommittee chairs, and oversight committees likely have leverage with agencies given their formal power over the legislative agenda and oversight. Indeed, as presented in Table 8.1, the correspondence guidelines from the agency stated that contacts from chairs and subcommittee chairs are "critical items."

Finally, I expect agencies to prioritize senior lawmakers, who are often powerful and have greater resources than their junior colleagues. Senior lawmakers may also have accumulated experience and expertise along the way that may make them more strategic in their dealings with agencies. Moreover, agencies may already have a long-standing relationship with senior lawmakers.

I now turn to lawmakers' motivation to retaliate. I expect agencies to prioritize legislators who do not share the president's party affiliation and legislators who are more likely to have ideological conflict with the agency. As described earlier, this expectation runs counter to previous literature which concludes that agencies reward friends of the administration and ideological allies (Bertelli and Grose 2009). In fact, the conventional wisdom suggests that agencies prioritize White House co-partisans for political reasons, such as patronage to its allies and as electoral support.

However, unlike the measures of capacity, I expect that agencies respond faster to these enemies of the administration in order to head off further conflict with unfriendly legislators. Risk-averse agencies have an incentive to prevent a conflict from escalating and from making long-term enemies of lawmakers. While previous work has argued that the administration would favor presidential co-partisans with the distribution of grants, particularistic favors, and speedy responses, I argue that, when responding to policy appeals, risk-averse agencies are motivated to head off conflicts with political opposition to the administration. Agencies have less to fear from like-minded legislators who have shared interests and fortunes without concern about an escalating conflict. Thus, I expect to observe shorter response times to political opposition.

These predictions are generally consistent across the agencies with the exception of party affiliation. I expect the liberal-leaning DOL to prioritize Republican lawmakers and respond more quickly to their appeals while the conservative-leaning DHS should prioritize and respond more quickly to Democrats' appeals. However, the DOE is a more ideologically neutral agency, and since I only have my measure of prioritization for DOE, there is not a clear test available for my expectations of prioritization. I do, however, test the response time expectation using the DOL and DHS.

Results

Table 8.3 provides side-by-side comparisons to contrast results of the models using my novel agency-assigned prioritization level (the first column) versus response time (in the second, third, and fourth columns) as measures of agency prioritization. These measures serve as the dependent variables in their respective models. The models are specific to each agency. As mentioned previously, the agency-assigned prioritization level could be obtained only from the DOE while all three agencies have a measure of the number of days it took the agency to respond. Keep in mind that the measure of prioritization as assigned by the agency is inversely related to prioritization, so the lower the number, the higher the appeal was prioritized by the agency. Negative coefficients for this dependent variable indicate that the DOE prioritized appeals associated with the independent variable.

First, as expected, the DOE prioritizes policy appeals from members of the Energy Committee. The coefficient is negative and significant, showing that the DOE prioritizes policy appeals from these members. The importance of the committee with jurisdiction over the agency it oversees is a long-standing and consistent conclusion drawn from the literature, and so it would be surprising to not get this result. In fact, this finding offers additional confirmation of my measure of agency prioritization. Indeed, it is implausible that the DOE would not prioritize contacts from the Energy Committee.

Table 8.3 Agency Responsiveness as Measured by Agency Prioritization of Policy Contact and Response Time by Select Agencies

	Agency Priority	Days Lapsed		
	DOE	DOE	DOL	DHS
Capacity to retaliate				
Senate	−0.083*	4.483***	5.486**	0.074
	(−1.70)	(4.01)	(1.97)	(0.14)
Committee with jurisdiction	−0.105***	0.891	0.707	0.218
	(−3.09)	(0.94)	(0.27)	(0.34)
Majority	−0.118***	−4.074***	−4.194	−1.429***
	(−2.91)	(−3.90)	(−1.33)	(−2.70)
Collaborative contact	−0.621***	−3.136***	15.450***	−0.429
	(−15.31)	(−3.47)	(5.11)	(−0.96)
Oversight committee	0.013	1.101	−2.679	−0.531
	(0.27)	(0.93)	(−0.86)	(−0.87)
Leadership	0.035	−0.340	2.881	0.239
	(0.85)	(−0.21)	(1.03)	(0.45)
Seniority	0.000	0.090	0.538***	0.065
	(0.09)	(0.86)	(2.66)	(1.42)
Motivation to retaliate				
White House out-partisan	−0.088***	−3.142***	1.696	0.006
	(3.04)	(3.45)	(−0.84)	(−0.02)
Republican	0.030	−0.691	−5.356**	0.804**
	(0.89)	(−0.86)	(−2.13)	(2.08)
Total contacts to agency	0.137***	−0.945	−0.145***	−0.000
	(3.75)	(−0.81)	(−4.38)	(−0.06)
Constant	1.895***	17.110***	62.340***	18.410***
	(26.12)	(11.23)	(11.14)	(25.63)
Congress FE	Y	Y	Y	Y
N	5013	4081	6844	8204
adj. R^2	0.160	0.027	0.026	0.011

t statistics in parentheses. Robust standard errors clustered on the legislator.

* $p < 0.1$, ** $p < 0.05$, *** $p < 0.01$

Yet, the results show that all three agencies take longer to respond to their committees with jurisdiction. The coefficient is positive, although not significant, across each agency. This is consistent with my expectations described in Table 8.2 and my argument that agencies should take longer to respond to appeals from lawmakers who have influence over the agency because the agency has an interest in investing more effort in producing a higher-quality response. In fact, other model specifications show the DOE taking significantly longer to respond to Energy Committee members (see the seemingly unrelated regression (SUR) model displayed in Table 8A.2 in the Appendix). Moreover, the relationship is consistent across all three agencies and conflicts with the assumption that agencies respond faster to priority contacts. The coefficients are in the opposite direction of what we would expect to observe if shorter response time was an appropriate measure of prioritization. These results offer further validation of my agency-assigned priority level measure and cast doubt on response time measures.

Second, as expected, the DOE prioritizes policy appeals from senators over House members. The coefficient is negative and significant and offers further support for my measure of prioritization. An individual senator has more power than a single House member, especially over confirmation of appointees, and so it is not surprising that agencies would prioritize members of the upper chamber.

All three agencies take longer to respond to senators' requests, as predicted in Table 8.2. If agencies prioritize appeals from senators, it is in their interest to expend more effort, and, thus, time, to try to satisfy the senator's request. This relationship is positive across all three agencies and significant for the DOE and the DOL, which take approximately one additional work week to respond to senators in comparison to House members. Based on previous work using response time as a measure of prioritization, this result would suggest that agencies prioritize House members over senators, which seems unlikely. Again, the results suggest we should not assume faster responses indicate higher priority responses.

Interestingly, I find that the DOE prioritizes requests from groups of lawmakers over contacts from a single legislator. This result is intuitive but important because it suggests that recruiting colleagues to join lobbying efforts is an effective strategy. While the relationship between my measure of agency prioritization and collaborative contact is positive and significant, the results are more mixed when I use response time as the dependent variable. The DOL takes significantly longer to respond to collaborative contact, in line with my expectations. In fact, the DOL takes an additional two to three weeks to respond to requests from a group of lawmakers. The DOE and DHS respond faster to group contacts, although not significantly so for DHS. The inconsistent results across agencies could be related to the composition of the group of lawmakers. Is it a bipartisan effort? Is the request from a state delegation or committee? The discrepancy across agencies could be due to differences in the characteristics of the lawmakers.

As expected, the DOE prioritizes policy appeals from members of the majority party, and the relationship is significant. We also see all three agencies respond faster to majority party members, although the results are not significant for the DOL. The results for response time are not in line with the expectations described in Table 8.2 but are generally consistent with results in previous work.

The relationship between prioritization and oversight committee membership, leadership, or seniority is not as expected, but the results are not significant. The relationship between response time and these variables is mixed and not significant except that the DOL takes significantly longer to respond to senior lawmakers, consistent with my expectations.

Critically, I find that agencies prioritize enemies of the administration. The DOE prioritizes lawmakers who do not share the president's party affiliation, and the relationship is significant. This finding is consistent with my theoretical argument and contradicts previous literature that assumes agencies reward friends of the administration.

Moreover, the DOE responds significantly faster to these White House out-partisans. Also in line with my expectations, the DOL responds significantly faster to Republicans, and the DHS responds significantly faster to Democrats. These results support my theoretical argument that agencies respond faster to enemies of the administration in order to curtail an escalating conflict. These results also contradict previous literature that assumes agencies reward friends of the administration. The relationship between response time and White House out-partisans is positive but not significant for both the DOL and DHS. As I mentioned earlier, the DOE is considered ideologically neutral, and so I did not expect there to be a significant relationship between the party affiliation and DOE prioritization or response time.

Other results show that the DOE prioritizes appeals from lawmakers it hears from infrequently, and the relationship is significant. In other words, the DOE ranks lawmakers who make frequent requests of the agency as a low priority. We also see that all three agencies respond faster to legislators who frequently contact the agency, significantly so for DOL (and negligible for DHS). Taken together, these results may suggest that agencies are familiar with these lawmakers, the types of requests they tend to make, and how to respond. Thus, they do not need to make these legislators a priority and take less time to respond.

Other results (not displayed in the table) show that the agencies take longer to respond to subcommittee chairs, and the relationship is significant for DOE and DHS. Conventional wisdom suggests agencies prioritize sub-committee chairs, so this result casts further doubt on faster response time as a measure of prioritization. The longer response time for subcommittee chairs is consistent with my argument that agencies would be motivated to spend more time and effort on responding to these powerful lawmakers. The results for the prioritization level for subcommittee chairs, however, is not significant. The results for power committee membership and com-mittee chairs are mixed and not significant, although the DOE responds significantly faster to power committee members. The DOE prioritizes and responds faster to contacts from lawmakers from large delegations. This could be due to other characteristics of the state or its delegation.

One interpretation of the set of findings produced by these two measures is that response time is not an appropriate measure of agency prioritization but that it lends insight into the motivations of agencies when confronted by legislators who are antagonistic to the administration or agency. When a legislator attacks the agency in a letter or email, speed is of the essence. The agency is motivated to respond quickly to head off an escalating conflict.

How to Effectively Lobby Federal Agencies

The findings of this chapter help answer a question posed earlier in the book: Does back-channel policymaking provide an alternative avenue for lawmak-ers who have limited influence in Congress, or does it offer lawmakers who are already powerful even more control over the policymaking process? This chapter suggests that the rich get richer in the back-channel market for public policy.

The results of this chapter dovetail with the previous findings in the book to offer a disconcerting conclusion. As I showed in Chapter 6, powerful lawmakers have greater capacity, resources, expertise, and experience to try to take advantage of agency policymaking.[22] This chapter shows that these powerful lawmakers are also more likely to get access to the top policymakers at the agency. In short, power in Congress translates into backdoor influence with the bureaucracy.

The implications of this finding are particularly concerning because back-channel policymaking evades the collective authority of Congress. Powerful lawmakers are controlling both venues of policymaking and wielding both formal and informal power to skirt the Article I authority of Congress and of each legislator sent to Capitol Hill to represent her constituents. This further exacerbates the already unequal power distribution in Congress and undermines the democratic norm of equal representation.

The covert nature of back-channel policymaking means that most legislators are in the dark about how powerful lawmakers span the branches of government to construct public policy. Powerful lawmakers control the structure of legislation, including the level of discretion granted to agencies, and they have undue influence over how agencies use their discretion. Meanwhile, the average legislator is forced to legislate in the dark (Curry 2015). While such puppetry may allow congressional leaders to advance legislative productivity in the midst of gridlock and dysfunction, it does not allow for accountability nor is it the legislative process as described in the Constitution.

However, one important finding from this chapter diverts from this cynical interpretation. Legislators are not without strategies for getting their concerns in front of agency heads. When legislators collaborate to pursue policy change through the bureaucracy, it gets the agency's attention. Collaborative policy appeals consistently received strong, robust prioritization by the DOE across both the House and Senate (see Table 8A.1 in the Appendix for a breakdown across chambers). As shown in Figure 8.3, collaborative policy appeals overwhelmingly receive the highest level of prioritization by the agency. Bands of lawmakers attract the immediate attention of the Secretary of Energy. In addition to the credible retaliatory threat of a gang of lawmakers, policy appeals from large groups of legislators may offer the pretense of legal authority even if the number of cosignatories does not meet statutory thresholds. Similar to co-sponsorship, legislators' efforts to get their colleagues on board with requests to agencies appears to be worth their time.

Thus, while powerful lawmakers may wield an inflated influence over the policymaking process, collaborative action on the part of legislators may

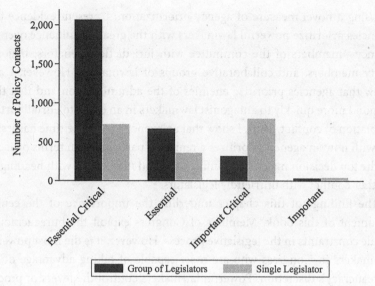

Figure 8.3 Agency prioritization of policy contacts from groups of legislators versus single legislators, US Department of Energy

even the playing field. Legislators do not have control over their committee assignment, whether their party is in the majority, or the procedures and outcomes of their chamber, but they can work with their colleagues to build support for policy change. Moreover, this book suggests such collective action may be more effective in the bureaucratic venue than through the legislative process. There is no filibuster in the bureaucracy.

Conclusion

Agencies are a target of lobbying by members of Congress because of the growing dominance of administrative lawmaking. Legislators reach out to agencies with a diverse range of policy interests and often these interests are in conflict. How do agencies weigh the competing interests?

Until this chapter, I have focused on the motivations of legislators. In this chapter, I examined the incentives and calculations of agencies. Agencies have an incentive to satisfy the requests of members of Congress, regardless of status, position, or party. However, given limited resources, agencies are motivated to prioritize lawmakers who have the capacity to impose costs on the agency and who are motivated to retaliate against the agency. Agencies are driven to appease their powerful enemies.

Using a novel measure of agency prioritization, I present evidence that agencies prioritize powerful lawmakers with the greatest influence over the agency—members of the committee with jurisdiction, senators, majority party members, and collaborative groups of lawmakers. However, I also show that agencies prioritize enemies of the administration and that they respond more quickly to antagonist lawmakers in an effort to curtail further escalation of conflict. Thus, I show that an agency's response time has less to do with how an agency prioritizes a request—particularly in terms of access to the top decision makers and influence—and more to do with heading off further conflict with unfriendly legislators.

The findings of this chapter underline the importance of the central argument of this book. Members of Congress exploit the bureaucracy to evade constraints in the legislative process. However, it is the most powerful lawmakers in Congress who are most capable of taking advantage of the bureaucracy's discretion. Powerful lawmakers control the levers of process across the branches of government, thus undermining the separation of powers. I address the implications of the findings of the book in the concluding chapter.

Appendix

Agency Prioritization by Chamber

Table 8A.1 presents the results for agency prioritization by chamber. The results for the House are in the first and third columns, and the Senate results are presented in the second and fourth columns. In the response time models (the third and fourth columns), the three agencies are combined.

The results are generally consistent with the substantive conclusions drawn from Table 8.3 and with conventional wisdom about chamber differences. Energy Committee membership is prioritized in the House—where committees take on greater importance—rather than in the Senate. The prioritization of majority party members is more salient in the House than the Senate, although the agencies respond significantly faster to Senate majority party members than senators in the minority. Agencies respond significantly faster to committee chairs in the Senate. The DOE model reveals a significant and positive relationship between prioritization and subcommittee chairs in the House, leadership in the Senate, and senior senators. Agencies take significantly longer to respond to House leadership and senior lawmakers in both chambers, consistent with my expectations.

The results for collaborative appeals from groups of lawmakers are very robust. The DOE prioritizes requests from bands of lawmakers across both chambers and the

Table 8A.1 Agency Prioritization of Policy Contact (DOE) and Response Time (DOL, DHS, DOE) by Chamber

		Priority		Days Lapsed	
		House	Senate	House	Senate
Capacity to	Energy	−0.188***	0.049		
retaliate	Committee	(−3.80)	(1.30)		
	Majority	−0.124**	−0.053	−1.155	−2.493**
		(−2.53)	(−0.57)	(−0.42)	(−2.25)
	Collaborative	−0.564***	−0.683***	4.375**	3.285***
	contact	(−10.41)	(−11.62)	(2.41)	(3.83)
	Oversight	−0.020	0.052	−2.240	0.859
	Committee	(−0.28)	(0.90)	(−1.61)	(0.40)
	Leadership	−0.105	0.088**	2.506*	−0.004
		(−1.44)	(2.03)	(1.74)	(−0.00)
	Seniority	−0.002	0.008*	0.338***	0.254**
		(−0.35)	(1.67)	(2.72)	(2.13)
Motivation	White House	−0.048	−0.150***	−3.129**	1.787*
to retaliate	out-partisan	(−1.18)	(−3.22)	(−2.13)	(1.91)
	Republican	0.019	0.031	−2.577	−1.000
		(0.45)	(0.63)	(−1.46)	(−0.89)
	Total contacts	0.164***	0.064	−0.022**	−0.004
		(3.44)	(1.26)	(−2.30)	(−0.27)
	Delegation size	−0.004***	−0.001	−0.054	0.067
		(−2.89)	(−0.49)	(−0.82)	(1.16)
	Constant	1.970***	1.900***	57.29***	56.04***
		(26.66)	(16.42)	(13.06)	(18.74)
	Congress FE	Y	Y	Y	Y
	Agency FE	-	-	Y	Y
	N	2834	2179	8237	10892
	adj. R^2	0.147	0.185	0.094	0.157

t statistics in parentheses.
*$p < 0.1$, **$p < 0.05$, ***$p < 0.01$

relationships are significant. The agencies take significantly longer to respond to these appeals across both agencies as well, as expected. In line with my theoretical argument and the findings in Ritchie and You (2019), the DOE prioritizes White House out-partisans and the relationship is significant in the Senate model. The agencies respond significantly faster to White House out-partisans in the House and slower to out-partisans in the Senate. Finally, the DOE ranks appeals from House members who frequently contact the agency as a significantly lower priority, and the agencies respond significantly faster to these frequent correspondents in the House. As in the previous table, the DOE prioritizes contacts from lawmakers with large state delegations, and the relationship is significant in the House.

Table 8A.2 Agency Responsiveness as Measured by Agency Prioritization of Policy Contact and Response Time (DOE), Seemingly Unrelated Regression (SUR)

	Agency Priority	Days Lapsed
Energy Committee	−0.072***	1.123**
	(−4.26)	(2.28)
Senate	−0.014	1.876***
	(−0.75)	(3.37)
White House co-partisan	0.067***	1.122**
	(4.28)	(2.44)
Majority	−0.080***	−1.770***
	(−4.13)	(−3.12)
Oversight Committee	−0.013	−0.206
	(−0.57)	(−0.32)
Committee chair	−0.057**	−0.138
	(−2.18)	(−0.18)
Leadership	−0.023	−0.503
	(−1.11)	(−0.83)
Power Committee	0.039**	0.586
	(2.30)	(1.18)
Seniority	−0.002	0.031
	(−1.18)	(0.69)
Delegation size	−0.002***	−0.042***
	(−3.92)	(−2.69)
Group	−0.685***	2.502***
	(−47.12)	(−5.86)
Republican	−0.047***	0.133
	(−2.61)	(0.25)
Divided government	0.466***	6.321***
	(16.44)	(7.60)
Total DOE contacts	0.062***	0.060
	(3.75)	(0.12)
Constant	1.945***	18.390***
	(56.73)	(18.25)
Congress FE	Y	Y
N	10350	10350
adj. R^2	0.2485	0.0282

A Breusch-Pagan test of independence allows me to reject the null hypothesis that the residuals from the two equations are independent ($\tilde{X}^2 = 453.579$, p=0.000).

t statistics in parentheses.

*$p < 0.1$, **$p < 0.05$, ***$p < 0.01$

9
Conclusion

This book describes what resembles a backdoor for public policy. Members of Congress exploit the bureaucracy's discretion over policy by using agency action as a substitute for legislation. Legislators pressure agencies to make policy changes they are unable to pass through legislative action. Scholarly hand-wringing over the executive's siphoning of legislative power has overlooked lawmakers' own exploitation of the separation of powers. The sole focus on Congress's constitutional authority for legislating has neglected the informal power of the congressional seat. The informal, discreet transactions between legislators and agencies has created a back-channel market for public policy.

Legislators take advantage of the bureaucracy to elude the collective authority of Congress and to evade public accountability. On its own, each piece of evidence presented in this book has important, and often concerning, implications. Stepping back, the bigger picture suggests powerful lawmakers and bureaucrats are shaping public policy in the shadow of the separation of powers.

Legislators Evading Congress

In this book I show how members of Congress use the bureaucracy to evade obstacles in the legislative process using qualitative accounts and quantitative analyses. Departing from previous literature, I demonstrate how the bureaucracy provides opportunities for advancing lawmakers' policy objectives. Legislators view the bureaucracy as an accomplice for policy gain, not only as a rogue agent in need of oversight. In Chapter 6, I find that senators make policy appeals to the bureaucracy more frequently when they are in the minority in the Senate and share party affiliation with the administration. This result runs counter to previous assumptions that lawmakers' interactions with agencies are driven by a need to rein in the opposition's administration. This antagonistic oversight is a feature of formal or institutional means of control, but informal, inter-branch interactions are

Backdoor Lawmaking: Evading Obstacles in the US Congress. Melinda N. Ritchie, Oxford University Press.
© Melinda N. Ritchie 2023. DOI: 10.1093/oso/9780197670491.003.0009

driven by legislators' calculations to determine the most promising venue for advancing their policy objectives.

This strategic shifting of venues is displayed in the qualitative accounts in Chapter 4 as well. Members of Congress collaborate with like-minded agency officials to strategically coordinate agency action with legislative opportunities. These inter-branch teams delay implementation until the lawmaker can shore up support in Congress for new legislation, create loopholes using prosecutorial discretion, and use procedural maneuvers to make changes to the status quo that would not pass Congress. This coordination across the separation of powers allows lawmakers to dodge obstacles in the formal lawmaking process.

Evading Accountability

Lawmakers use the bureaucracy as a veil for evading public scrutiny. In Chapter 7, I show that members of Congress turn to the bureaucracy to represent interests that are costly to represent publicly. Legislators make policy appeals to agencies more frequently on issues that are contentious and when they face conflicting pressures from their party and constituency. Moreover, I show that this strategic backchanneling differs from how they use visible venues of participation intended for position-taking, like bill sponsorship. While the obscurity of administrative policymaking offers lawmakers' a convenient way to influence policy and represent interests quietly, it has heavy implications for accountability and transparency.

Legislators and agencies each have their own set of informal and discreet strategies for policymaking. These strategies have been studied in isolation, with scholars examining agency policymaking (Potter 2019) or legislative maneuvers (Curry 2015). Yet, little attention has been paid to the inter-branch exchanges that govern off the headlines. My findings complement work on agencies' strategic efforts to advance their priorities and build policymaking power (Carpenter 2001).

The Rich Get Richer

Even more concerning, I find that it is the most powerful lawmakers who are in the best position to take advantage of the backdoor for public policy. My results in Chapters 6 and 8 indicate that legislators' power in Congress translates into leverage with the bureaucracy. In Chapter 6, I find that lawmakers' capacity in the legislative process facilitates their ability to engage with the bureaucracy. In Chapter 8, I find that these powerful lawmakers are also more likely to get greater access to the top policymakers at the agency.[1] In short, inter-branch policymaking could exacerbate the already unequal power distribution in Congress.[2]

The unequal advantage that powerful lawmakers have in the bureaucratic venue has important implications for democratic representation. The asymmetrical distribution of resources, information, and authority in Congress means that some lawmakers have an advantage over how legislation is drafted, what policies are considered, and how much and what information the rank-and-file receive (Curry 2015). These institutionalized inequities are amplified by the informal inequities of influence in the bureaucratic venue. These inequities break with normative assumptions that congressional control of the bureaucracy preserves democratic ideals.

Thus, not only is the democratic notion of one lawmaker one vote undermined, but many legislators may be unknowingly voting to give powerful lawmakers more authority than they realize. The implications of powerful lawmakers having a second pathway for influence and control is particularly important given that they also have outweighed authority over legislation.

Deliberate Discretion?

The findings of this book suggest that powerful lawmakers do not only delegate to the bureaucracy in order to benefit from the expertise of bureaucrats. They delegate in order to avoid conflict in Congress and pass statute that will allow them to benefit from the bureaucracy's discretion ex post. These powerful lawmakers are not relinquishing control by delegating authority to bureaucrats. To the contrary, they are delegating to bureaucrats in order to preserve their policy preferences from deterioration by the institutional obstacles, disparate interests, and discordant demands of the United States Congress.

In order to achieve passage, for instance, leadership may need to shape contentious legislative language to buy votes without losing votes. At times, such compromises may be delicate if not impossible to maintain for passage. However, leaving contentious details out of the legislation could allow leadership to build a coalition for passage while maintaining control over the controversial aspects of the law under the veil of bureaucratic implementation. In other words, if leaders and committee members think it will be difficult to get their preferred bill to pass, they can write the bill using vague language to secure passage with the intention of appealing to the bureaucracy after passage to get what they really want.

This scheme may be orchestrated in advance with the cooperation of the administration, particularly under unified government. For example, to secure votes for a bill, legislative language can be crafted to allow for future loopholes. The president can then make promises to members of Congress in order to secure their votes on pending legislation while directing the bureaucracy to be responsive to requests for exceptions from these pivotal legislators. In fact, news coverage of the Central American Free Trade Agreement (CAFTA) offers some evidence of this type of deal-making. The coverage describes how Republican members of Congress were pressured to vote for CAFTA despite considerable push-back from the textile industry of their states. During a late night meeting, a deal was struck between President George W. Bush and Republican Rep. Robert B. Aderholt, who represented Fort Payne, Alabama—the self-described "sock capital of the world." The legislator agreed to vote for CAFTA. In exchange, the White House committed to reinstate tariffs on socks from Honduras by December 19, 2007.[3] In October of 2007, Congressman Aderholt contacted the Labor Department to remind the administration of its promise.

Backdoor Policymaking or Tenacious Representation?

Back-channel policymaking need not be as nefarious as it may seem at first blush. While powerful lawmakers may have the advantage, some of my findings suggest that tenacious members of Congress use the backchannel to overcome disadvantages and that their determination is rewarded. In fact, legislators' doggedly advancing policy in both the legislative and bureaucratic venues may be a model of effective representation.

Quantitative and qualitative evidence suggest that persistent and strategic lawmakers use their relationships with the bureaucracy to overcome a lack of status and power within Congress. For instance, I show that lawmakers who are effective within the legislative process are also tenacious in pursuit of advancing policy through the bureaucracy (Chapter 5). Likewise, I demonstrate that savvy lawmakers shift their policymaking efforts to the bureaucracy when they find themselves in the Senate minority (Chapter 6). These quantitative findings complement the qualitative accounts of a rookie senator partnering with a like-minded bureaucrat to bob and weave powerful resistance from same-party, senior members of his own state and a powerful committee chair in order to pass environmental protections (Chapter 4). Thus, it is the most skilled and tenacious lawmakers, regardless of status, who strategically shift to the bureaucratic venue when they face obstacles in Congress.

Critically, lawmakers who mobilize their colleagues are able to capture the attention of agencies. In Chapter 8, I find that legislators can gain traction and attention from top appointees by recruiting their colleagues to join them in collaborative efforts to advance policies through agency action. This finding suggests that collective action by lawmakers may be able to overcome the gridlock of procedural hurdles, super-majoritarian requirements, and gate-keeping committees and leadership.

Moreover, legislators who are completely shut out of the formal mechanisms of authority in Congress can use informal inter-branch communication as a last resort for holding the party in power accountable. House members, for instance, may be spread too thin and consumed by constant campaigning to be as effective at advancing policy initiatives through the bureaucracy. Instead, my findings suggest that House members use inter-branch communication as a way to push back on an administration when they are shut out of formal means of oversight. In Chapter 6, I find that House members contact agencies about policy most frequently when they are in the minority and do not share party affiliation with the president and that these inter-branch channels are dominated by ideologues in the opposition. This finding suggests that even overwhelmed, under-resourced House members use informal appeals to the administration to provide representation when they are shut out of formal channels of influence and oversight.

Indeed, back-channel policymaking can be a last resort for legislators when leadership steamrolls controversial legislation through Congress. For example, the REAL ID Act of 2005, if implemented, would prevent citizens from boarding commercial airlines with a driver's license unless the license met new standards set by the federal government. There was substantial opposition to the REAL ID Act, particularly with concern about the potential threat to civil liberties. In fact, it was unclear whether the legislation had enough support in Congress to pass on its own. However, leadership used procedural maneuvers to shut down debate on the legislation, and the REAL

ID Act was inserted into a "must-pass" military spending bill that provided funding for troops in Iraq and tsunami relief that passed with overwhelming support and was signed into law on May 11, 2005.[4] Leadership's steamrolling maneuvers did not go unnoticed. Twelve senators had signed a letter to then-Senate Majority Leader Bill Frist urging him to leave REAL ID out of the appropriations bill.[5] Many of these senators also introduced an amendment cosponsored by senior member of the Senate Homeland Security committee, Senator Joseph Lieberman, stating that the Real ID Act language should not have been inserted in the legislation. The amendment was ruled non-germane. The bill became law, despite these protests from lawmakers.

Yet, several members of Congress, including Senator Lieberman, reached out to the Secretary of Homeland Security with their concerns about REAL ID in attempts to block or delay the legislation from being implemented. In fact, as of the writing of this book nearly 20 years after REAL ID's passage in 2005, citizens can still board commercial airlines without a REAL ID compliant driver's license. According to the Transportation and Security Administration (TSA), REAL ID-compliant driver's licenses will be required starting May 7, 2025. However, that deadline is one of a string of deadlines that have been extended over the past several years.[6]

In the meantime, lawmakers who oppose REAL ID have been working, often in conjunction with like-minded bureaucrats, to pass new legislation that would replace and water down the most controversial elements of REAL ID, potentially before the REAL ID Act could ever be fully implemented (e.g., the PASS Act, at times referred to as "REAL ID lite"). In fact, DHS Secretary Janet Napolitano supported replacing REAL ID with the PASS Act and testified in support of it during a 2009 committee hearing:

> Pass ID is a bill that I support. The Department of Homeland Security (DHS) worked with governors and other stakeholders to provide technical assistance in its drafting and—so the approach that Pass ID takes to fix REAL ID is one that I support. I think it makes sense. . . . As has already been commented upon, the first attempt to do this—the REAL ID Act—was a start that badly needs to be fixed. Pass ID is a fix for REAL ID.[7]

In short, Secretary Napolitano delayed implementation of the REAL ID Act while allies in Congress worked to replace it. Informal collaboration with the bureaucracy can serve as legislators' last protest against leadership's procedural bulldozer.

The case of the REAL ID Act brings us back to an issue I raised in the introductory chapter of this book. What is congressional intent, really? Does the statute detailing REAL ID—which was steamrolled through the legislative process by leadership without a hearing or debate and passed by large majorities in both houses—express the intent of Congress? Were the legislators who urged DHS to delay or block the implementation of the statute undermining the intent of Congress? Were they overseeing the intent of Congress? When Secretary Napolitano worked with lawmakers to delay implementation of REAL ID until legislation could be passed to replace it, was she participating in an inter-branch collusion to undermine legislative intent?

Rep. James Sensenbrenner (R-WI), the proud sponsor and advocate of the REAL ID Act, would surely say they were undermining legislative intent. In fact, he expressed his concern to the Secretary of Homeland Security about the department's failure to implement the REAL ID Act, arguing, "Rather than usurping Congress's authority in writing policy, DHS should commit to the law and fully support implementation."[8]

Can we fault the persistent lawmakers who continue to represent their constituencies even if it means undermining the intent of Congress? Are legislators who exploit the separation of powers in order to overcome the obstacles of the legislative process effective policymakers or lawless members of Congress undermining democratic representation? Amid polarization and gridlock that drive the legislative process to a grinding halt, is back-channel policymaking a necessity in order to effectively represent constituencies and tailor broad laws to serve the diversity of the nation? In fact, inter-branch cooperation may be the ideal of representative government.

The Recursive Ideal?

What I have referred to as a backdoor for policymaking may, in fact, be essential and even optimal given the strain on legislative capacity. Legislators' limited capacity is split between an overwhelming expanse of policy issues and a growing, more demanding constituency. The recursive model of representation stresses the importance of interactive communication between lawmakers and agencies for representative democracy under the challenges of the twenty-first century (Mansbridge 2019).

While recursive representation most obviously focuses on interactivity between representatives and constituents, it recognizes the indisputable dominance of administrative policymaking and the importance of intercommunication across branches of government. The defining feature of recursive representation involves "both constituents and representatives [learning] from one another through interactions in which those on each side hold open the possibility of changing their positions, concepts, and conclusions on the basis of what they learn" and should include "not only legislative representatives but also administrative and societal representatives" (Mansbridge 2019, 300). In short, the recursive ideal involves intercommunication between citizens and legislators, between agencies and citizens, and between legislators and agencies.

Recursive representation departs from traditional models of representation that assume voters communicate their preferences to legislators and that legislators translate those preferences to agencies. Related to my discussion in earlier chapters, deviation from this direction of communication is thought to be illegitimate usurpation of legislative authority by agencies requiring oversight. However, Mansbridge argues, "Such direction and oversight might have been possible one hundred, or perhaps even just fifty, years ago. With the increasing complexity of collective decision-making, it is no longer possible" (300). Instead, administrative lawmaking is a forgone conclusion:

> In the twenty-first century, we need administrative lawmaking. And we need a lot of it—much more than can be directed by the legislature, except in the most general way, and much more than can be subject to legislative oversight, except relatively superficial oversight supplemented by the "fire alarms" set off by interest groups and other observers (McCubbins and Schwartz 1994). (Mansbridge 2019, 316)

Given the inevitability of administrative lawmaking, what are the implications for representative democracy? How do democratic norms square with unelected bureaucrats' numbness to the concerns of citizens as they interact with policies on a daily basis, often with substantial variation based on geographic region, demographics, and economic and industry factors? How can we approach democratic norms given these circumstances? Recursive representation offers a response:

To approach this goal more closely, we need to stop anchoring all democratic legitimacy in elected office. Instead of deploring the "outsourcing of the law," we need to use our ingenuity to find ways of making electoral, administrative, and societal representation not only more democratic but also more communicatively thoughtful and recursive, so that as citizens and representatives together coproduce their own and the public's interests they do so in conditions close to those the citizens would approve, either hypothetically or in retrospect. (324)

The recursive ideal, then, requires that the legislator acts not only as lawmaker but as a lobbyist on behalf of the constituency. In Mansbridge's words:

> Within recursive representation, the ideal role for the representative is as interlocutor, a discursive intermediary between the representative's legal constituents and several other entities: the constituents in other districts, the legislative representatives from other districts, the "administrative representatives" who in practice make many of the laws, the organized groups that represent their own constituents' interests and sometimes help craft the laws, and the lobbyists those groups hire to represent their interests. The representative as interlocutor links the representative system together less by making policy herself than by helping those in all the other parts of the system understand one another. (299)

The legislator's role as interlocutor with administrators is not encapsulated by traditional views on legislative oversight. The recursive model of representation does not assume legislators are communicating with agencies to ensure the implementation of statute and curtail the bureaucracy's discretion. Instead, legislators are informing agencies that are understood to be creating law.

Perhaps, then, back-channel policymaking does not signal the corrosion of the separation of powers, as this book has implied thus far. Instead, back-channel policymaking may provide the preservation of democratic norms within an expanded and evolved representative system. Given the increasingly complex society, legislators' policy appeals to agencies may be a necessary approach for maintaining democratic legitimacy.

Yet, the promise of the recursive ideal assumes processes that allow for transparency and accountability. This book's findings suggest that inter-branch communications are not only opaque, but that lawmakers choose this policymaking venue because it allows them to avoid scrutiny. While this book may shed light on back-channel policymaking, members of Congress's ability to adapt to changing circumstances—whether new laws, regulations, or ethics rules—is well-documented. As I described in the opening of Chapter 3, bipartisan efforts to fight public access to the records used in this book have already begun. Afterall, FOIA was never intended to apply to Congress.

Conclusion

What is the forecast for backdoor lawmaking? The patterns described in the book might seem like a fragile equilibrium, but the predominant findings are enduring. These communications are likely to become more vulnerable to transparency through the efforts of journalists, citizens, and scholarly work like my own. Moreover, partisan organizations and interest groups have begun using the FOIA as a trove for opposition research on presidential candidates. However, congressional scholars and spectators are well aware that members of Congress are nothing if not adaptable, as we have observed lawmakers learn to circumvent ethics rules. As these records become more transparent to the public, members of Congress will look for ways to avoid the increased transparency.

We may see changes in the courts' treatment of these practices. While previous court decisions have been tolerant of legislators lobbying the bureaucracy,[9] the possible weakening of Chevron deference towards agency decisions could limit agencies'—and, by the same token, lawmakers'— ability to leverage bureaucratic discretion.[10] Indeed, the findings presented in this book could have implications for the Supreme Court's growing skepticism of agency regulations.[11] On one hand, agency policymaking may seem even more questionable if decisions are being made in response to political pressure from a few powerful lawmakers rather than the expertise of objective administrators. However, my research suggests that agencies are not insulated from the real-world concerns of the constituents on whose behalf legislators often are advocating. Agencies are not making policies in a vacuum, unaware of the unintended consequences and costs of their actions on citizens.

How should this book change the way we study and understand Congress? Given the growth of administrative lawmaking, we can no longer assume that roll-call votes are legislators' most important policymaking action. Lawmakers' behavior on the chamber floor and their Article I authority represents the tip of the iceberg.

This call to move our study of Congress beyond formal legislative action is a tall order, to be sure. In addition to assumptions about the importance of legislators' Article I powers, data availability has driven the focus on the formal activities of legislators. Likewise, the ease of publicly available data has steered a substantive focus on position-taking and credit claiming rather than on the less visible, strategic means and motivations behind representation and policymaking.

As a growing number of scholars are pointing out, lawmaking is not confined to Congress. In fact, bureaucracy scholars have recognized the rise of administrative lawmaking for decades. This rebalancing of power makes the transactional relationship between legislators and agencies of mounting importance and indicates a need to reassess how we approach the study of Congress (Carpenter and Krause 2015).

We may need to reconsider how we evaluate members of Congress and the assumptions we make about their preferences based on their behavior within the legislative venue. If a legislator is not actively sponsoring legislation on a policy issue, it does not mean she is not working on it behind the scenes. In fact, she may be strategically using other venues for propelling the issue, either because it would be costly to pursue publicly or because the issue has no chance of advancing through legislation given the political circumstances. Likewise, while legislators' formal participation is largely subsumed by party and leadership, informal channels are a means to pursue individual priorities apart from collective interests and commitments. By focusing on the legislative process, we may have underestimated the degree to which members of Congress act as free agents and active policymakers.

My findings should lead to a reassessment of the authority of the collective institutions of Congress as well. Unlike theories of congressional dominance, my framework suggests that legislators' exploitation of agency discretion showcases the inadequacies of Congress as a collective body. Lawmakers are driven to the bureaucratic venue by obstacles in the legislative process, which have been exacerbated by a gridlock that has become a more constant feature of Congress in the current era of intense polarization. Moreover, back-channel communications and the complexity of policy make it challenging for Congress to oversee the transactions between its own members and agencies, for better or worse.

What is the normative outlook suggested by this book? It is not clear. Backdoor policy transactions are off the books and depart from the lawmaking process as described in the Constitution. Yet, this inter-branch communication may offer an approach for democratic norms to endure given the inevitable dominance of administrative lawmaking and the strains for representational systems in the twenty-first century. This normative trade-off suggests that the relationship between legislators and the bureaucracy is due for increased scrutiny. Policymaking spans branches of government, and legislators' strategies for influencing policy are not confined to the legislative process. It is important that congressional scholars examine the ways legislators influence policy off the Congressional Record.

Notes

Chapter 1

1. Senator's personal writings dated June 17, 2021, referencing a diary excerpt from March 20, 1976.
2. See Bjorhus (2020) and Hemphill (2011).
3. The League of Conservation Voters (LCV) gave Klobuchar a 96% lifetime score rating, and she earned a perfect score from the Center for Biological Diversity Action Fund in 2018.
4. See Bjorhus (2020) and Keen (2019).
5. Klobuchar was listed as the most effective lawmaker in the 115th Congress according to the Center for Effective Lawmaking. See Volden (2019) and https://thelawmakers.org.
6. See Hemphill (2011).
7. See *Humane Society v. Jewell*, No. 15-5041 (DC Cir. 2017). Ralph E. Henry argued on behalf of the Humane Society that the agency succumbed to political pressure and its commitment to Klobuchar's demands. Citing Klobuchar's letters to Ken Salazar, then-Secretary of the Interior, and internal agency emails, Henry argued that "the record here shows FWS's [US Fish and Wildlife Service] ultimate decision was driven by promises made to members of Congress, rather than the enumerated listing factors of the ESA [Endangered Species Act]." See Plaintiffs' Brief, 71.
8. Approximately 90% of law is made by agency rules (Warren 2011, 7).
9. See Carpenter (2001); Ferejohn and Shipan (1990); Potter (2019).
10. See Merrill (2022); Sunstein (1990); Sunstein (2022); and White and Neblo (2021) for related discussions.
11. But see Carpenter and Krause (2015) for a discussion of the transactional authority perspective on bureaucratic politics, which departs from the traditional focus on formal mechanisms of congressional control.
12. See Carpenter (2001).
13. See Clark (2017).
14. See Ban and You (2019); Krawiec (2013); Libgober (2020).
15. See Potter (2019).
16. See Lowande, Ritchie, and Lauterbach (2019); Minta (2011).
17. Senator Kennedy's letter to then-FDA Commissioner Mark B. McClellan is dated October 15, 2003. The House bill described in the letter was H.R. 2427.
18. The DOL logged the contact on August 4, 2009. Chapter 3 describes the agency records in detail.
19. See Zwick (2010).

20. Also see Volden and Wiseman (2014).
21. See Arnold (1979).
22. See, for example, McCubbins, Noll, and Weingast (1987, 1989); Weingast and Moran (1983).
23. Moe (1987) makes a similar critique of how theories of congressional dominance (e.g., McCubbins and Schwartz (1984); Weingast and Moran (1983)) define the concept of congressional control of the bureaucracy and "an unresolved tension between the goals of individual legislators and vaguely specified notions of collectively expressed 'legislative goals'; just whose interests are being realized when Congress controls the bureaucracy is left unclear" (483–4).
24. See Carpenter and Krause (2015) for a related discussion on a transactional authority perspective to bureaucratic politics.
25. Shepsle (1992), 239.
26. But see Hall and Miler (2008) for a notable exception.
27. Formal or institutional mechanisms of oversight may be non-statutory, such as committee hearings or appropriation committee reports, for example (see Bolton 2022), but are features of legislative institutions rather than unilateral action through unconstrained, informal channels.
28. See Mansbridge (2019) and White and Neblo (2021).

Chapter 2

1. For examples, see Casas, Denny, and Wilkerson (2020); Reynolds (2017).
2. A notable exception includes research on distributive policy.
3. See Ferejohn and Shipan (1990).
4. See Foster (2022).
5. I discuss each of these examples in detail in subsequent chapters.
6. The EPA issued an update to a rule that will reduce the lead and copper in drinking water (Environmental Protection Agency, 2020).
7. See US Department of Labor, Mine Safety and Health Administration (1999).
8. The subsequent rule allowing employers to deny contraceptive coverage based on religious beliefs was also established through administrative policymaking. The Department of Health and Human Services (DHHS) announced the contraception mandate, which was an interim final rule that went into effect on August 1, 2011. The Trump administration later expanded the religious exemption for employers through rulemaking, which was upheld by the Supreme Court in 2020.
9. As I point out in Chapter 1, Shepsle (1992) uses a similar line of reasoning to argue that "legislative intent" is an oxymoron given that "Congress is a 'they' not an 'it.'"
10. See Ban and You (2019); Krawiec (2013); Libgober (2020).
11. See Mayhew (1974) and Fenno (1978, 1977) for discussions of the general goals of members of Congress.
12. I examine this pathway empirically in Chapter 6.
13. I test hypotheses derived from this argument in Chapter 7.

14. See Lesniewski and Tully-McManus (2019); Levine (2019).
15. See Willis and Reyes (2015).
16. Data obtained from https://www.govtrack.us.
17. Friedman also attributes this view to Francis Fukuyama.
18. Also see Drutman (2017).
19. Even in the Senate, where there are fewer restrictions on amendments, non-germane amendments are not permitted on appropriations bills, budget measures, and other instances. Furthermore, restrictions are not enforced uniformly (Davis 2013).
20. See table A1 in the appendix of Wolfensberger (2018).
21. See Wiseman and Wright (2020) for a discussion on the impact of the Supreme Court cases of *Chevron U.S.A., Inc., v. Natural Resources Defense Council, Inc.* (1984) and *Motor Vehicles Manufacturers Association of the U.S. v. State Farm Mutual Automobile Insurance Co.* (1983) ("State Farm") and the role of the judiciary in agency policymaking.
22. *Chevron USA, Inc. v. Natural Resources Defense Council, Inc.* 467 U.S. 837 (1984).
23. But see Chapter 9 for a discussion about the potential weakening of Chevron deference going forward (Davenport 2022; Merrill 2022).
24. The DC Circuit Court found retaliatory threats by a House member to withhold funding for a subway system if the Department of Transportation failed to meet the lawmaker's demands for a bridge to be improper. See *DC Fed'n Civil Ass'ns v. Volpe*, 459 F.2d 1231 (DC Cir. 1971).
25. See *DC Fed'n Civil Ass'ns v. Volpe*, 459 F.2d 1231 (DC Cir. 1971).
26. *Sierra Club*, 657 F.2d at 409–410. Also see Beermann (2006) for a discussion of the case law on ex parte communications.
27. As quoted in Potter (2019), 19.
28. See table 3.2 in Russell (2021).
29. Records from the DOL show that among the lawmakers were Senators Jeff Merkley (D-OR), Mark Warner (D-VA), Ben Cardin (D-MD), Barbara Mikulski (D-MD), Jeanne Shaheen (D-NH), Charles Grassley (R-IA), and Richard Lugar (R-IN).
30. The Keating Five affair may come to mind, for instance, when five senators pressured the Federal Home Loan Bank Board to let up on the businesses of Charles Keating, Jr., a campaign contributor (see Beermann 2006; Thompson 1993; Levin 1996). House Speaker Newt Gingrich faced similar accusations that he urged the FDA to approve a HIV home testing kit in a letter at the request of the kit's manufacturer. The manufacturer reportedly contributed $25,000 to a foundation that funded Gingrich's speeches shortly thereafter (see Levin 1996).
31. See *Tummino v. Torti* 4. 603 F. Supp. 2d 519 (E.D.N.Y. 2009) for an example. Senators Patty Murray and Hillary Clinton held up confirmations until the FDA moved forward on approving Plan B for over-the-counter sale. The senators believed the FDA was dragging its feet due to political pressure from the White House.
32. In fact, the use of Senator Klobuchar's appeals during internal debates are depicted in court documents related to the opening example of this book. Based on internal FWS emails: "In weighing the pros and cons of various options for the final delisting rule—that arose largely because FWS did not know what wolf species actually existed

in the Great Lakes—the FWS listed as the sole 'Con' to delisting was that attempting to resolve the issue before issuing a final delisting rule 'delays final decision on the WGL DPS beyond commitment to Sen. Klobuchar' and listed as a 'Pro' that issuing a final rule without resolving this issue '[r]etains commitment to Sen. Kobuchar [sic].' " See Plaintiff's Brief, p. 117, n. 36, *Humane Soc'y v. Jewell*, No. 15-5041 (DC Cir. 2017). Despite evidence that the agency considered Senator Klobuchar's requests in their deliberations, the court ruled that it found no improper political influence. The court rule upheld the district court's ruling vacating the FWS's 2011 rule on other grounds. See *Humane Soc'y v. Jewell*, No. 15-5041 (DC Cir. 2017).

33. Thanks to Ken Meier for this insight.
34. Senator Robert Packwood's writings dated June 17, 2021, referencing a diary excerpt from March 20, 1976, and emailed to the author by the senator.
35. *Politifact* rated the claim "Half True" and concluded Harris's statement was "technically correct, but misleading" (Nichols 2016).
36. See Nichols (2016).

Chapter 3

1. Obama (2009). Also see *FOIA Is Broken: A Report* (2016).
2. As quoted in *FOIA Is Broken: A Report* (2016).
3. The Bipartisan Legal Advisory Group ('BLAG'), comprising Speaker Paul Ryan, Majority Leader Kevin McCarthy, Majority Whip Steve Scalise, Minority Leader Nancy Pelosi, and Minority Whip Steny Hoyer, voted unanimously to take legal action to stop the release of the records (Gerstein, 2017).
4. *American Oversight v. U.S. Department of Health and Human Services, et al.*
5. See Gerstein (2017).
6. Austin Evers, executive director of American Oversight as quoted in Gerstein (2017).
7. There have been recent instances when investigative journalists have used records of communication between agencies and legislators for stories that became embarrassing headlines. For example, in the fall of 2019, *Politico* used the FOIA to obtain records and emails uncovering the potentially unethical interactions between the US Department of Transportation (DOT) and the Senate Majority Leader's office. The records suggested that Transportation Secretary Elaine Chao favored her husband, Senate Majority Leader Mitch McConnell's (R-KY) constituents. *Politico* found that Secretary Chao met with Kentucky officials far more frequently (a quarter of all her meetings) than any other state's officials, often about grants the officials were seeking from the DOT. Moreover, *Politico* obtained emails indicating that McConnell staffers alerted Secretary Chao's office to meeting requests from Kentuckians that were "friends" or "loyal supporters" and details about what they wanted to discuss and special favors. Interestingly, the records I requested during Elaine Chao's time as Secretary of the US Department of Labor—a position she held several years prior to her appointment at the DOT—include unique notation for contacts coming from Kentucky (using all capital letters in the state's name), suggesting that a similar

pattern of behavior may have occurred then as well. The notation is only present when she was Secretary of Labor, not for the previous or subsequent secretaries, and only for the state of Kentucky, suggesting that the notation is not simply an indication of home-state bias or consistent favoritism of Senate leadership (McConnell was Senate Minority Leader for part of Chao's time at the DOL). Such favoritism could be problematic because McConnell often campaigns on his ability to bring home federal grants, and ethics rules prohibit government officials from taking actions that benefit them personally or close family members. See Snyder, Doherty, and Kimbel-Sannit (2019).

8. There is some disagreement about whether congressional records in the possession of agencies are subject to the FOIA, as the case in the opening of this chapter suggests. The DC Circuit has held that a congressional document in an agency's possession is not subject to the FOIA if Congress explicitly expressed its intention to maintain control over the particular document prior to the FOIA request (Sheffner 2020). But see Beermann (2006) for a related discussion on off-the-record communication between members of Congress and agencies and the Administrative Procedures Act (APA).

9. See Gerstein (2017) and Motion to Leave, *American Oversight v. DHHS*.

10. See Georgantopoulos and Wagner (2017); Gerstein (2017).

11. P.L.89-487, 80 Stat. 250 (1966). An individual does not need to be a US citizen to make a FOIA request. Foreign nationals, businesses, political organizations, and state and local governments can make FOIA requests. Requests can be made for documents and other records including letters, photos, and films (see Halstuk and Chamberlin 2006).

12. The 1966 FOIA (s. 1160) was an amendment to Section 3 of the Administrative Procedure Act (APA), which had required agencies to disclose government information to the public but was ineffective due to broad and vaguely defined exceptions and no process for seeking judicial review of agency decisions. See Sheffner (2020).

13. See Halstuk and Chamberlin (2006).

14. See Johnson (1966). Also see *FOIA at 50* (2016).

15. See Halstuk and Chamberlin (2006); Johnson (2021).

16. Johnson (1966). Also see *FOIA at 50* (2016).

17. The FOIA is often credited to Rep. John E. Moss's (D-CA) pursuit of government transparency. He warned, "The present trend toward Government secrecy could end in a dictatorship," and argued that the "more information there is made available, the greater will be the nation's security" (Thomas, 1997).

18. See Stuessy (2015). Some agency officials expressed concerns about the costs and complications of implementation (see Halstuk and Chamberlin 2006).

19. See Rothman (2016).

20. P.L.89-487, 80 Stat. 250 (1966). Also see Sheffner (2020) and www.foia.gov/about.html.

21. Edwin Meese III, Attorney General's Memorandum on the 1986 Amendments to the Freedom of Information Act (Dec. 1987), *supra* n. 21, at 18. Also see Sheffner (2020).

22. 5 U.S.C. § 552(c)(1).

23. 5 U.S.C. § 552(c)(2).
24. 5 U.S.C. § 552(c)(3).
25. See www.hhs.gov/foia/fees/index.html. The State Department lists fees in a similar range: https://foia.state.gov/Request/Fees.aspx.
26. The four categories of requesters are "commercial use requesters," who are making a request for information to further commercial or profit interests; "education institutions and non-commercial scientific institution requesters" making requests for scholarly research; "requesters who are representatives of the news media" and are gathering information about current events or that would be of public interest (and that is likely to be published); and, in the final category, all other requesters. Commercial requesters are charged for all direct costs. Educational and news media requesters are charged reproduction costs that exceed 100 pages. All other requesters (members of the general public) are charged for reproduction that exceeds 100 pages and search time that exceeds two hours. See 5 U.S.C. § 552(a)(4)(A). Also see Ginsberg and Greene (2016).
27. 5 U.S.C. §552(a)(4)(A)(iii). The DOJ determines if a request meets the public interest criteria based on whether it provides information that contributes to the public understanding of government activities and that does not already exist in the public domain (Stuessy, 2019).
28. Agencies collected a total of $2,547,638.48 in fees. Statistics compiled from data available at https://www.foia.gov.
29. Ginsberg and Greene (2016).
30. For example, when I made a FOIA request to DOE, all of my interactions were with a private contractor.
31. *FOIA Is Broken: A Report* (2016).
32. See *FOIA Is Broken: A Report* (2016).
33. The initial response to a FOIA request can often involve an inquiry for clarification. Particularly for requesters who are new to the FOIA process or unfamiliar with the documents they are requesting, there may need to be follow-up conversations with FOIA officers to clarify, narrow, or otherwise revise a request. Once a request has been clarified, there still be extensive delays.
34. See the Justice Department's instructions for responding to requests: https://www.justice.gov/archives/open/responding-requests.
35. In fact, the FOIA process is constantly plagued by backlogs, and agencies are required to report statistics on FOIA requests and response times. For example, in FY2019, the executive branch received 858,952 FOIA requests. By the end of FY2019, there was a total of 120,436 backlogged requests. Based on agency determinations about the complexity of a request, it took agencies an average of 1 to 383 days to process simple requests, 10 to 752 days to process complex requests, and 31 to 180 days to process expedited requests. Statistics compiled from data available at https://www.foia.gov.
36. See *FOIA Is Broken: A Report* (2016).
37. The Office of Government Information Services can assist with pursuing both administrative and legal remedies.
38. See Johnson (2021).

39. After explaining to the district staffer that I was a former congressional staffer myself, I offered to draft the letter I wanted the congressional office to send to the agency. He agreed and pasted my draft onto the office's letterhead along with the congressman's signature, which he emailed to the agency. He shrugged off my appreciation pointing out that I had made it easy for him.

40. The process is detailed in an internal agency handbook intended for use by agency staff, which I discuss further in Chapter 8. For example, the Energy Department's handbook describes the agency's system of correspondence control: "The Executive Secretariat (ES) controls all correspondence addressed to the Secretary, Deputy Secretary, and Under Secretaries of Energy; all correspondence from the National Security Council and the White House; as well as all correspondence from Members of Congress and Tribal Leaders addressed to anyone at the Department. If program offices receive any of these types of correspondence directly, they are responsible for referring these documents to the Executive Secretariat for proper control and assignment. The Executive Secretariat uses an electronic document management system (eDOCS) to control, assign, route, and track executive correspondence throughout the Department"(Office of the Executive Secretariat 2007, I-1).

41. While these logs may miss some contacts that are not conducted over government email, phone lines, or meetings during the course of business, the Presidential and Federal Records Act Amendments of 2014, Pub. L. No. 113-187, 128 Stat. 2003, prohibits agency employees from creating or sending "a record using a non-official electronic messaging account unless [the employee] copies an official electronic messaging account . . . in the original creation or transmission of the . . . record" or "forwards a complete copy of the . . . record to an official electronic messaging account . . . not later than 20 days after the original creation or transmission of the . . . record." Also see Sheffner (2020). In *Competitive Enterprise Institute v. Office of Science and Technology Policy (OSTP)*, the DC Circuit decided in favor of a request for "all policy/OSTP-related email" contained in a private email account of the OSTP director, determining that "records do not lose their agency character just because the official who possesses them takes them out the door or because he is the head of the agency" and that if "the agency head controls what would otherwise be an agency record, then it is still any agency record and still must be searched or produced" (as quoted in Sheffner (2020), 9). Thus, agency records in nongovernmental electronic accounts are still subject to FOIA.

42. The dates recorded in the log are usually the date of the contact (or the date on a letter) or the date the contact was received by the agency. Alternatively, some agencies include the date the contact was logged or entered into the agency correspondence database.

43. Exemption (b)(6) allows agencies to redact identifying information (e.g., names) about individuals (usually constituents). The redaction justification is usually included in the log.

44. To review other work using similar data, see Lowande (2018, 2019); Lowande, Ritchie, and Lauterbach (2019); Mills and Kalaf-Hughes (2015); Mills, Kalaf Hughes, and MacDonald (2016); Neiheisel and Brady (2017); Ritchie (2018); Ritchie and You (2019).

45. Careful readers will notice the typographical errors in the logs. These types of spelling errors and mistakes are pervasive throughout the logs and, in addition to other reasons including the wide-ranging subjects, made hand-coding—rather than automated coding techniques—necessary.

46. Customs and Border Protection Bureau (2008).

47. Customs and Border Protection Bureau (2010).

48. Parts of this section were adapted from Ritchie (2018).

49. There was unified Republican control under the first two years of President Bush's second term (2005–2006, 109th Congress) and divided government under the final two years (2007–2008, 110th). President Obama's first two years were under unified Democratic control (2009–2010, 111th) and the second two years of his first term were during divided government (2011–2012, 112th).

50. See Ritchie (2018) for reliability statistics (Cohen's kappa scores and percentage agreement) for this coding scheme, which indicate a "substantial" or high level of agreement (Cohen, 1960).

51. See the codebook in the Appendix for coding rules and examples.

52. By "routine" I am referring to the services regularly performed by congressional caseworkers that are often advertised on a member of Congress's website under "casework" or "constituency service."

53. However, some of the arguments of back-channel policymaking likely apply to grant requests as well. For example, grant requests to the DOL increased following the earmark moratorium, which constrained legislators from pursuing earmarks in legislation. In this sense, legislators used the bureaucracy as a backdoor for earmarks.

54. See my coding procedure for bill sponsorship in Chapter 5.

55. As lawmakers co-sponsor legislation, they also collaborate on their appeals to agencies. The percentage of such collaborations is very small compared with the independent efforts of individual lawmakers, as shown in Figure 3A.1 in the Appendix. Yet, collaboration is more common when lawmakers pursue policy influence in comparison to casework (see Figure 3A.2 in the Appendix). It is also not uncommon for lawmakers to collaborate on grant requests, often with their state delegations.

56. See U.S. Department of Energy's Recover Act Investments (2013). Also see FACT SHEET: The Recovery Act Made the Largest Single Investment in Clean Energy in History, Driving the Deployment of Clean Energy, Promoting Energy Efficiency, and Supporting Manufacturing (2016).

57. The DHS was created by President George W. Bush on November 25, 2002.

58. See Lee (2001).

59. Kwoka (2016); Mullins and Weaver (2013).

60. See Galka (2017); Lee (2001); Kwoka (2016); Mullins and Weaver (2013).

61. The DOL, DHS, and DOE are included in the quantitative dataset I constructing using the coding procedures described below. In addition, I also made FOIA requests for congressional correspondence logs from several other agencies including the Departments of Agriculture, Commerce, Health and Human Services, Interior, Treasury, Transportation, and Education which are utilized in the qualitative accounts in the book.

62. There was unified Republican control under the first two years of President Bush's second term (2005–2006, 109th Congress) and divided government under the final two years (2007–2008, 110th). President Obama's first two years were under unified Democratic control (2009–2010, 111th) and the second two years of his first term were during divided government (2011–2012, 112th).

63. See Ritchie (2018) for reliability statistics (Cohen's kappa scores and percentage agreement) for this coding scheme, which indicate a "substantial" or high level of agreement (Cohen, 1960).

64. By "routine" I am referring to the services regularly carried out by congressional caseworkers which are often advertised on a member of Congress' website under "casework" or "constituency service."

65. However, some of the arguments of back-channel policymaking likely apply to grant requests as well. For example, grant requests to the DOL increased following the earmark moratorium, which constrained legislators from pursuing earmarks in legislation. In this sense, legislators used the bureaucracy as a backdoor for earmarks.

Chapter 4

1. Quoted material regarding contacts are taken from the internal agency notes in the congressional correspondence logs or, occasionally, directly from letters, emails, and faxes themselves unless otherwise noted. I refer to "logs" as a shorthand for the congressional correspondence logs.

2. The Administrative Procedure Act (APA) established rulemaking procedures. Yet less than a page of the law covers the sparse parameters for rulemaking, and it offers different procedural options and significant leeway to agencies. As Potter (2019) explains, the APA requires that agencies "(1) provide notice of the proposed policy change, (2) solicit public input, (3) publish a final rule, and (4) allow some time between the final rule's publication and the effective date" (Potter 2019, 68–9, see 5 U.S.C. § 553). However, the statute offers exceptions to some or all of these requirements (but that are not applicable when the requirements are made explicit by statute) when, for example, they are "interpretative rules, general statements of policy, or rules of agency organization, procedure, or practice" or "when the agency for good cause finds (and incorporates that finding and a brief statement of reasons therefor in the rules issued) that notice and public procedure thereon are impracticable, unnecessary, or contrary to the public interest" (5 U.S.C. § 553). Final rules must be published in the Federal Register, as established in the Federal Register Act (Pub. L. No. 74-220, § 5) (See Potter 2019, 25).

3. While the Office of Information and Regulatory Affairs (OIRA), housed within the OMB, has authority to review rules to ensure consistency with the president's agenda, OIRA only reviews a fraction of agency rules (Potter 2019, 81). OIRA's reluctance to review rules could be an equilibrium outcome if agencies do not step out of line very often because they know they would get penalized by OIRA (see Wiseman 2009).

4. The exceptional use of the CRA at the beginning of the Trump administration in the first two months of 2017 was due to the infrequent circumstance of one party

losing the White House after finalizing many midnight rules and the opposing party gaining unified control of both branches of government. Moreover, congressional Republicans were exceptionally coordinated and unified in their efforts to make use of the CRA at the time. In other words, the context in the first sixty days of 2017 was particularly and untypically fruitful for using the CRA, which was used to overturn fourteen rules (Kerwin and Furlong 2018).

5. See Chapters 2 and 8 for my arguments and findings on agency responsiveness to legislators' policy appeals.

6. Senator Robert Packwood's (R-OR) writings dated June 17, 2021, referencing a diary excerpt from March 20, 1976, and emailed to the author by the senator.

7. Also see a study by Haeder and Yackee (2022) on statutory language and regulatory timing.

8. For example, after making a floor speech in the House urging action on seat-belt warning systems in cars, Rep. Michael Bilirakis (R-FL) contacted the Department of Transportation (DOT) to request "that DOT Consider Rulemaking to Require Automobile Manufacturers to Include [more effective] Seatbelt Warning devices in Vehicles They Produce." Contact recorded in DOT log, dated May 24, 2006. While Rep. Bilirakis did not issue a press release about his contact with the DOT, he did issue one on May 10, 2006, for his floor speech on the issue.

9. Contact dated December 6, 2007, and recorded in the DOE log on December 7, 2007, at 7:46 a.m. Further details from a press release issued by Senator Dorgan on December 10, 2007.

10. Contact received on December 15, 2004, and recorded in the HHS log.

11. The contact was a letter emailed to DOE and entered in the DOE log on October 26, 2012.

12. For example, Congresswomen Carolyn Maloney (D-NY) and Thelma Drake (R-VA) wrote "to urge DHS to move forward with issuing the regulations necessary to allow victims of human trafficking and domestic violence to apply for U- visas [sic]." The letter was dated July 12, 2007, and received on July 16, 2007.

13. This information and quote are from an interview conducted on November 28, 2015, with a division chief within the agency's Washington, DC, office.

14. Also see Krawiec (2013) and Libgober (2020) for case studies of agency contacts regarding the implementation of Dodd-Frank prior to the Notice of Proposed Rule-making ("NPRM"). Such contacts are generally not subject to the APA disclosure requirements (Krawiec 2013) and may have more influence at the development stage when agency staff have greater discretion (Libgober 2020).

15. The contact was recorded in the DOT log and is dated June 27, 2008.

16. The contact was recorded in the DOT log and is dated October 31, 2005.

17. Letter and press release from Rep. Dingell's office on July 30, 2009.

18. See Corn (2010); Garner (2011); Mueller (2011a,b); Wilson (2013).

19. See Agricultural Marketing Service (2010); Flagg (2012). Specifically, the interest groups proposed a marketing order (Cord, 2012; Schumer, 2012).

20. Senator Schumer's efforts were described in a press release from his office on May 16, 2012.

21. Lawmakers oppose new guidance as well. Several lawmakers, including Senator Hillary Clinton, wrote to the Secretary of Education to "REQUEST THAT THE SEC-RETARY RECONSIDER THE DEPARTMENT'S NEW TITLE IX POLICY GUID-ANCE, ISSUED LAST WEEK." According to the log, "SHE INDICATES THE GUIDANCE APPEARS TO BE AN EFFORT TO REDUCE ATHLETIC OPPOR-TUNITIES FOR WOMEN AND GIRLS" (letter dated March 23, 2005, and recorded in the US Department of Education log). A bipartisan group of lawmakers, includ-ing Reps. Judy Biggert (R-IL), Sherwood Boehlert (R-NY), Shelley Moore Capito (R-WV), Betty McCollum (D-MN), Louise Slaughter (D-NY), and Chris Shays (R-CT), also wrote to "URGE SEC'Y TO RESCIND THE NEW POLICY" and expressed "DOUBT THAT A SURVEY ALONE CAN RELIABLY MEASURE STU-DENTS' INTEREST IN SPORTS" (letter dated March 12, 2005, and recorded in the Education Department log).

22. Excerpt from letter addressed June 29, 2005, included in Rep. Rosa DeLauro's press release issued on June 29, 2005.

23. The contact was recorded in the DHS log. The contact date is January 17, 2006, and it was received on January 30, 2006.

24. The contact was recorded in the DHS log. It was dated July 13, 2006, and received July 24, 2006.

25. Previous work traditionally focused on congressional committees and "iron trian-gles." More recent work considers legislators formal and public participation during the comment stage of rulemaking (Lowande and Potter 2021).

26. The contact was recorded in the DOE log. The contact is dated October 31, 2007, and was logged on November 2, 2007, at 9:05 a.m. The press release, titled "Democratic 'No-Energy Bill' will Eliminate Five Million American Jobs & Cost each American Family $1,700 each year," was issued by Rep. Don Young on November 14, 2007.

27. For example, Senator Hillary Clinton (D-NY) contacted Secretary Samuel W. Bod-man to request "DOE's support for legislation to ensure that New Yorkers are not gouged at gasoline pump," and for "immediate [passage of the] Energy Emergency Consumer Protection Act." The contact was recorded in the DOE log as having occurred on April 12, 2006, and was logged on April 13, 2006, at 9:29 a.m.

28. For example, "Chairman Donald Manzullo hopes Secretary Bodman support [sic] opposition to Section 6023 of the iraq/Afghanistan [sic] Emergency Supplemental Act for FY 2005 and would be happy to meet concerning this matter." The contact was recorded in the DOE log as taking place on April 28, 2005, and was recorded on April 29, 2005, at 7:54 a.m.

29. The contact was recorded in the DHS log on November 30, 2010, and dated Novem-ber 29, 2010.

30. For example, Senator Jeff Sessions (R-AL) asked the Commerce Department to "con-sider proposing legislation or promulgating a rule that will immediately amend the CZMA [Coastal Zone Management Act] routine change procedure so [that] one state cannot, under the guise of federal law, dictate the environmental laws of another" (contact was recorded in the Commerce Department log on April 11, 2007). Senate Energy and Natural Resources Committee Chair Jeff Bingaman (D-NM) faxed DOE

requesting "DOE's assistance on crafting legislation to address the risks posed by U.S. emissions of greenhouse gases; requests views on greenhouse gas emissions questions, and invites DOE to attend the Senate workshops beginning 212/2007 [sic]" (contact was recorded in the DOE log on January 29, 2007, at 9:15am and dated January 1, 2007). Rep. Chris Smith (R-NJ), Chair of the Commission on Security and Cooperation in Europe (Helsinki Commission), contacted the Commerce Department regarding "proposed legislative language to extend export controls on intercept and surveillance products." The Bureau of Industry and Security, an agency within Commerce, noted it "provided technical comments to the [Helsinki] Commission staff on proposed legislative language to extend export controls on intercept and surveillance products" (December 20, 2011).

31. For example, Rep. Michael D. Rogers (R-MI) wrote to DHS "regarding the Deputy Secretary's 1/27/2010 testimony regarding the averted terrorist attack on Northwest Airline Flight 253; requests a classified briefing regarding the increased use of canines; and would like to work collaboratively on legislation to establish a pilot program for passenger screening using detection canines" (contact recorded in the DHS log on January 27, 2010). Similarly, Senator Ted Kennedy wrote to the Secretary of Education to request "the Secretary's assistance in identifying technical changes that need to be made in the current Higher Education Act, and to provide technical drafting assistance to the Committee to make the necessary changes" (contact dated June 14, 2005, and recorded in the Education Department log).

32. See Walker (2017) for a discussion about the implications of agencies "legislating in the shadows."

33. This practice is particularly common when the US Trade Representative (USTR) is negotiating trade agreements using fast-track authority that prevents lawmakers from amending the deal, a clear illustration of how lawmakers shift to the bureaucratic venue when they are constrained in Congress. For example, prior to the up-or-down vote on the Trans-Pacific Partnership (TPP), several Republican legislators, including Reps. Pat Tiberi (OH), Devin Nunes (CA), Mark Meadows (NC), and Mick Mulvaney (SC), among others, contacted Trade Representative Froman in support of tobacco growers that were at risk of being carved out of the benefits received by other agricultural commodities in TPP. (Contact recorded in the USTR log on July 29, 2015.) These efforts to pressure the USTR to protect the tobacco industry were critical given the lawmakers' threats to vote down the TPP. Also see Becker and Neeham (2015).

34. The contact, dated February 2, 2007, was recorded in the DOE log on February 2, 2007, at 1:49 p.m.). Additional details about the correspondence can be found in press releases issued by Senator Tom Coburn on February 2, 2007 ("Dr. Coburn, Senator McCain urge Energy Department to Follow the Law and President's Direction on Earmarks") and Senator McCain on February 14, 2007 ("Senator McCain Statement on HJ Res 20").

35. Both Secretary Bodman's memorandum and his response letter to Senators McCain and Coburn can be found in the Congressional Record for February 14, 2007.

36. The DHS log characterized Rep. Reyes contact with Secretary Chertoff and Attorney General Gonzales (dated August 1, 2006): "he begins by offering congratulations regarding their plans to dedicate 25 additional Assistan[t] U.S. Attorneys to the SW border. He writes that based on his 26.5 years [as a] Border Patrol vet and [his] appreciation for their [issues], we must cont[i]nue the open dialog on these critical subjects. He then writes regardin[g] the enforcement of our federal employer sanction laws in that we are overdue in enforcing these laws. He asks the Secretary and the AG to work together over the next 30 days to identify and assign 1,000 ICE investigators [across] the country for [this] enforcement." The contact was received on August 2, 2006.

37. For example, Reps. Mark E. Souder (R-IN) and Ralph Regula (R-OH) wrote to DHS "regarding religious objections to aspects of the new WHTI rules and would like to facilitate a meeting between DHS officials and religious groups" (contact received on February 14, 2008, and recorded in the DHS log and dated February 15, 2008). Reps. Joseph R. Pitts (R-PA) and Ralph Regula wrote "to asks [sic] that something be done to help the Amish community in light of WHTI which will require them to have passport photos, which is against their religious beliefs" (contact recorded in the DHS log dated May 11, 2007, and received on May 25, 2007). Rep. Ciro D. Rodriguez (D-TX) "Writes with concerns regarding WHTI's possible effect on the Kickapoo Traditional Tribe of Texas and other border tribes which regularly cross to neighboring countries" (contact recorded in the DHS log dated April 11, 2007, and received on April 20, 2007).

38. See Manuel and Garvey (2013).

39. Muehlenbachs, Sinha, and Sinha (2011) show that the EPA strategically times the announcement of enforcement actions on Fridays and holidays to avoid public scrutiny.

40. However, prosecutorial discretion is perceived to be particularly broad in the enforcement of immigration, as stated in *United States ex rel. Knauff v. Shaughnessy* (see Manuel and Garvey 2013).

41. *Heckler v. Chaney*, 470 U.S. 821, 832-33 (1985). Also see Barkow (2016).

42. *Heckler v. Chaney*, 470 U.S. 831. Also see Garvey (2014).

43. Cuellar (2006), 230.

44. Cuellar (2006), 230.

45. *United States v. Goodwin*, 457 U.S. 368 (1982). Also see Manuel and Garvey (2013).

46. *United States v. Armstrong*, 517 U.S. 456 (1996).

47. See Manuel and Garvey (2013); also see Garvey (2014).

48. See ICE Director John Morton's memo from June 17, 2011. Also see Manuel and Garvey (2013).

49. See Scholz and Wei (1986). Also see Balla and Gormley (2018), 146.

50. The contact is recorded in the DHS log as dated April 14, 2011, and was received on May 31, 2011.

51. See ICE Director John Morton's memo from June 17, 2011. DHS Secretary Janet Napolitano issued a memorandum on June 15, 2012, which coincided with President Obama's announcement about DACA.

52. Attorney General Sessions's memorandum was issued on January 4, 2018. The Cole memo was issued on August 29, 2013, by Deputy Attorney General James M. Cole.

53. *Justice Department Issues Memo on Marijuana Enforcement* (2018).

54. See Foster (2022) for a case study of Sessions rescission of the Cole Memo.

55. The letter from Warren and Murkowski is dated March 2, 2017 (Everett, 2017). The Colorado delegation's letter is dated January 9, 2018, and was distributed with a press release by Rep. Ed Perlmutter (D-CO).

56. See Everett (2018) and Welch (2018).

57. See Everett (2018) and Jaeger (2019).

58. Contact dated March 10, 2010, and recorded in the DOE log on March 22, 2010.

59. Contact recorded in the DHS log on December 23, 2009.

60. See H.R. 3531, the Human Enforcement and Legal Protection for Separated Children Act. The bill was introduced by Rep. Woolsey on July 31, 2009.

61. Letter dated January 14, 2002, and published on Rep. Markey's website.

62. Quoted material and excerpts from Senator Robert Packwood's personal diary entries summarized in his writing entitled "French Pete" dated March 1, 2020, which was emailed to the author on March 1, 2020 and from a similar opinion piece published in the *Register-Guard* on March 18, 2018 titled, "French Pete: Birth of a Wilderness" (Packwood 2018). Also see Husk (2018) and Williams (2008). Other excerpts (as referenced) are from his diary entry summarized in his writing entitled draft #8 of "Hells Canyon—Boundaries and Real Politics" (hereafter "Hells Canyon"), dated May 11, 2020, and emailed to the author on May 18, 2020.

63. "Hells Canyon."

64. Packwood (2018).

65. Ibid.

66. Marsh (2007), 108.

67. Packwood (2018).

68. Ibid.

69. Senator Robert Packwood's personal diary entries summarized in his writing, entitled "French Pete," dated March 1, 2020, which was emailed to the author on March 1, 2020.

70. Packwood (2018).

71. Marsh (2007), 108.

72. Senator Robert Packwood's personal diary entries summarized in his writing, entitled "French Pete," dated March 1, 2020, which was emailed to the author on March 1, 2020.

73. Ibid.

74. Eugene *Register-Guard*, Thursday, May 25, 1972, as referenced in Senator Robert Packwood's personal diary entries summarized in his writing, entitled "French Pete," dated March 1, 2020, which was emailed to the author on March 1, 2020.

75. Roseburg *News-Review*, September 18, 1972, ibid. Also, according to the February 24, 1971, issue of the *Daily Astorian*, the state's senior senator, "as a member of the Senate Interior Committee, to which the bill was referred, he has the power to bottle it up if he cares to exercise it because the chairman, Senator Henry M. Jackson, D-Wash., gives committee members life or death powers over bills affecting their states."

76. Senator Robert Packwood's personal diary entries summarized in his writing, entitled "French Pete," dated March 1, 2020, which was emailed to the author on March 1, 2020. The bill referenced by Senator Packwood is Senate Bill 866, "To establish the French Pete Creek Intermediate Recreation Area."

77. Senator Robert Packwood's personal diary entries summarized in his writing, entitled "French Pete," dated March 1, 2020, which was emailed to the author on March 1, 2020.

78. Ibid.

Chapter 5

1. When a legislator contacts a department multiple times about the same issue, I count each contact as a separate correspondence.

2. See Table 5A.1 in the Appendix for descriptive statistics by committee and party.

3. For comparison, members of Congress introduce roughly one bill per month on average.

4. "Iron triangle" refers to the relationship between committees, agencies, and interest groups.

5. Parts of this section are adapted from Ritchie (2018).

6. While I argue that policy appeals are a strategic alternative to the legislative process—suggesting that they would be used differently than other legislative activities—if policy appeals are measuring policymaking efforts, they should still be positively and significantly related to legislative participation. In short, lawmakers' policy priorities are consistent across venues, but their strategic choice of venue varies based on conditions of constraint and opportunity.

7. See Table 5A.2 in the Appendix for sample characteristics.

8. Also see Ritchie and You (2021).

9. Of course, it is possible that lawmakers provide representation on a different set of issues through the backchannel than they do in the legislative process, and there may be strategic reasons for doing so, as I demonstrate in subsequent chapters. However, consistency in the priorities lawmakers pursue across venues would suggest that their inter-branch appeals are sincere signals of their policy interests. Lawmakers participate in policymaking for a variety of reasons, whether through the legislative process or the bureaucracy. One consistent motivation for their participation is to pursue their policy priorities, regardless of other strategic calculations. Their strategic choice of venue is dependent on the conditions under which they confront constraints and opportunities, as I demonstrate in the chapters to follow.

10. Bill introduction data are from the Congressional Bills Project (CBP), maintained by E. Scott Adler and John Wilkerson (2008). CBP uses the coding scheme from the Policy Agendas Project, developed by Frank Baumgartner and Bryan D. Jones (2000). Under the coding scheme, bills are coded based on 19 major topic issue areas and more than 200 subtopic issue areas. I include bills coded with the major topic, "Labor, Employment, and Immigration," and the major topic, "Macroeconomics," subtopic, "Unemployment Rate." I included homeland security bill introductions

when coded with the subtopic category, "Civil Defense & Homeland Security" (under the major topic, "Defense"); "Immigration and Refugee Issues" (under the major topic, "Immigration"); "Domestic Disaster Relief" (under the major topic, "Banking, Finance, and Domestic Commerce"); and "Terrorism, Hijacking" (under the major topic, "International Affairs and Foreign Aid"). I include energy bills coded under the major topic category for "Energy."

11. The committees with primary jurisdiction are the House Committee on Education and Labor (also referred to as the House Committee on Education and the Workforce) and the Senate Committee on Health, Education, Labor, and Pensions (HELP) for the DOL; the House Committee on Energy and Commerce and the Senate Committee on Energy and Natural Resources for the DOE; and the House Committee on Homeland Security and the Senate Committee on Homeland Security and Governmental Affairs (which is also the Senate's principal oversight committee) for the DHS. Committee membership data is from Wiseman and Volden's LES dataset and Charles Stewart's website on committee assignments.

12. Of course, legislators can claim credit for earnest policymaking efforts. This section addresses the notion that legislators' contacts with agencies are symbolic.

13. Also see Mills, Kalaf-Hughes, and MacDonald (2016).

14. See Sulkin (2011), 30–3 for a helpful discussion on this point.

15. See Mayhew (1974), 63; Schiller (2000), 55; Sulkin (2005), 36–37.

16. Much of this reasoning could also apply to membership on the committee with jurisdiction, which is also included in the models.

17. When a legislator contacts multiple times about the same issue, I count each contact separately. See Chapter 3 for a detailed description of the coding procedure.

18. The Senate Committee on Homeland Security and Governmental Affairs is the chief oversight committee in addition to its jurisdiction over the DHS.

19. Table 5.3 presents the results from ordinary least squares (OLS) regression models.

Chapter 6

1. See Lerer and Litvan (2010).

2. Despite several attempts to win over enough Republicans to overcome the 60-senator threshold for cloture, the Dream Act never surpassed 56 votes. Senate Democrats tried to include the Dream Act in the National Defense Authorization Act for Fiscal Year 2011, but the filibuster was sustained 56–44. In one last effort weeks before the Republicans took over the House, the Dream Act passed the House on December 8, 2010, but fell short with 55 votes in favor of invoking cloture in the Senate ten days later.

3. See Hulse and Herszenhorn (2010).

4. The letter, dated April 13, 2011, was recorded in the DHS congressional correspondence log on May 31, 2011.

5. See memorandum from US Immigration and Customs Enforcement Director John Morton "Exercising Prosecutorial Discretion Consistent with the Civil Immigration

Enforcement Priorities of the Agency for the Apprehension, Detention and Removal of Aliens." US Immigration and Customs Enforcement, June 17, 2011.

6. The executive order is known as DACA or Deferred Action for Childhood Arrivals. See memorandum from DHS Secretary Janet Napolitano, "Exercising Prosecutorial Discretion with Respect to Individuals Who Came to the United States as Children," June 15, 2012.

7. The nascent empirical literature on inter-branch communication is divided on the question of whether agencies are more responsive to requests from particular legislators based on committee membership and White House co-partisanship (i.e., Lowande 2019; Mills, Kalaf-Hughes, and MacDonald 2016; Ritchie and You 2019).

8. Previous success with the bureaucracy could lead legislators to continue to engage with agencies. If legislators previously found agencies to be unresponsive, they may not want to waste efforts on the bureaucracy. In this way, who tries to use back-channel policymaking can shed light on which legislators use it most successfully. If the bureaucracy is useless as a policymaking tool, we would not expect senior legislators, who have accumulated years of experience and political know-how, to continue to try to use the bureaucratic venue if it has proven to be a failure in the past. If policy contact increases with seniority, it could suggest legislators learn how to take advantage of the bureaucratic venue over time. Likewise, frequent policy contact between particular legislators and an agency might point to a relationship of reciprocity. A legislator would not spend time and effort regularly contacting an agency if she was not getting anything out of the relationship.

9. House ranking minority member status, for instance, is not correlated with LES (Volden and Wiseman 2014, n. 46, p. 40).

10. I estimate least-squares regression models with standard errors clustered by legislator to account for the possible nonindependence of legislators' contacts over time.

11. Bill introduction data are from the Congressional Bills Project (CBP), maintained by E. Scott Adler and John Wilkerson (2008). CBP uses the coding scheme from the Policy Agendas Project, developed by Frank Baumgartner and Bryan D. Jones (2000). Under the coding scheme, bills are coded based on 19 major topic issue areas and more than 200 subtopic issue areas. I include bills coded with the major topic, "Labor, Employment, and Immigration," and the major topic, "Macroeconomics," subtopic, "Unemployment Rate." I include homeland security bill introductions when coded with the subtopic category, "Civil Defense and Homeland Security" (under the major topic, "Defense"); "Immigration and Refugee Issues" (under the major topic, "Immigration") "Domestic Disaster Relief" (under the major topic, "Banking, Finance, and Domestic Commerce"); and "Terrorism, Hijacking" (under the major topic, "International Affairs and Foreign Aid"). I include energy bills coded under the major topic category for "Energy."

12. The committees with primary jurisdiction are the House Committee on Education and Labor (also referred to as the House Committee on Education and the Workforce) and the Senate Committee on Health, Education, Labor, and Pensions (HELP) for the DOL; the House Committee on Energy and Commerce and the Senate Committee on Energy and Natural Resources for the DOE; and the House

Committee on Homeland Security and the Senate Committee on Homeland Security and Governmental Affairs (which is also the Senate's principal oversight committee) for the DHS.

13. Committee membership data are from Volden and Wiseman (2014) and Charles Stewart's committee assignment dataset. Data on seniority, leadership positions, vote share, and LES scores are from Volden and Wiseman (2014). Other data are from the *Almanac of American Politics*, Tracy Sulkin, and Katherine Francis.

14. The dummy variable for subcommittee chairs is excluded from the Senate models because most (over 80%) majority members in the Senate are subcommittee chairs, but including the variable does not change the substantive findings.

15. Setting aside conceptual concerns with the definition of oversight (see the discussion of Shepsle's "Congress is a 'they' not an 'it'" in Chapter 1), some of these patterns could be consistent (although others are, notably, not consistent) with a general pattern of oversight, as commonly conceived. Committee chairs, for instance, may engage in more policy interactions with agencies as a result of their oversight duties. This certainly could be the case, and, as I emphasize in previous chapters, I am not arguing that the explanations that are the focus of this book are the only reasons why lawmakers contact agencies. Also, as I describe in Chapter 4, the content of the policy contacts are more akin to individual policy interests than concerns with standard notions of oversight (e.g., ethics abuses, spending, investigations, and standard oversight duties).

16. See Volden and Wiseman (2014).

17. The policy was introduced ten times as either a stand-alone bill or incorporated into other legislation.

18. See Lee (2016) and Green (2015, 83, 115) for a related discussion of the "deep minority."

19. To be clear, evidence lacking in support for my theory would find that legislators contact most when they are in the majority and White House co-partisans or only when they are in the majority and White House out-partisans (or null results).

20. While controlling for divided government, this model excludes Congress fixed effects because the high correlation between minority party status, White House co-partisan, and Congress leads to the omission of variables of interest due to multicollinearity when estimating a model with Congress fixed effects. The House models do not include a Congress fixed effect or divided government due to multicollinearity. To address this issue, I estimate a fixed effect model (by Congress) using ranking minority membership in place of minority party membership. The results are consistent and robust, most critically for ranking minority members.

21. Using a senator fixed effect, which controls for time-invariant differences between legislators, in a sparser model without other individual-level variables produces results that are consistent with those presented in Table 6.5 and Figures 6.1 and 6.2 and are robust. See Figure 6A.1 in the Appendix.

22. The vertical lines shown in the figures represent 90% confidence intervals.

23. For comparison, the average number of policy appeals from senators is 22.

24. Also see Figure 6A.2 in the Appendix.

25. The vertical lines shown in the figures represent 90% confidence intervals.
26. On average, House members make seven policy appeals during a Congress.
27. Additional analyses in the Appendix are consistent with this interpretation. Table 6A.1 and Figures 6A.4 and 6A.5 show that ideologically extreme White House out-partisans (in the House) engage more frequently with agencies.
28. These figures were produced from the model displayed in column 4 in Table 6A.1 and include congress and district fixed effects. The gray regions shown in the figures represent 90% confidence intervals.

Chapter 7

1. Sections of this chapter were adapted from Ritchie (2018) with permission of the Southern Political Science Association.
2. Levy (2020).
3. Others suggest nearly 200,000 jobs were directly or indirectly supported by the industry.
4. Foran and National Journal (2014).
5. For example, former Pennsylvania Governor, Republican Tom Corbett, claimed his policies led the way to the creation of 200,000 jobs in the natural gas industry (see Foran and National Journal 2014), and Senator Pat Toomey (R-PA) held a press conference with industry leaders in support of fracking (see O'Boyle 2020).
6. McGraw (2020).
7. Lustgarten (2014).
8. Sullivan (2020).
9. In fact, Joe Biden even struggled to balance environmental and economic concerns while campaigning for president in his home state of Pennsylvania (Colman 2020).
10. Levy (2019).
11. Levy (2020).
12. Senator Casey contacted the DOE a total of 72 times during the 112th Congress; 17 of these contacts were about policy issues.
13. The letter, dated October 18, 2011, was emailed to Secretary Steven Chu and was recorded on October 20, 2011, at 11:43 a.m.
14. The letter was addressed to Secretary Steven Chu from Senator Casey.
15. The letter was dated May 20, 2011, and was addressed to Secretary Steven Chu from Senator John D. Rockefeller, IV (D-WV), Senator Joe Manchin, III (D-WV), and Senator Robert P. Casey, Jr. (D-PA). The contact was recorded on May 23, 2011, at 1:41 p.m.
16. The letter to Secretary Steven Chu was dated February 29, 2012, and was recorded by DOE on March 1, 2012, at 10:35 a.m.
17. See Morrill (2002); Morrill and Johnson (2004).
18. If this line sounds familiar, it is likely because the fictional House Majority Whip Frank Underwood from *House of Cards* adopted it as well (McCalmont 2014).
19. To jointly model the effects of cross-pressures on policy communication and bill sponsorship, I use seemingly unrelated regression (SUR) models. OLS models offer

largely consistent results to the SUR approach, as shown in Figures 7.1 through 7.14. These figures were produced from OLS models with robust standard errors clustered on the individual legislator and congress fixed effects.

20. There are established ways of measuring cross-pressures on labor issues in the literature. I use similar measures to examine the relationship between cross-pressures and legislators' policy contact with the DOL.

21. The time period examined here predates the Trump campaign's protectionist platform (see Ritchie and You 2019).

22. The population of blue-collar workers has been used in previous work (e.g., Conley 1999) to examine cross-pressures on labor and trade issues and is appropriate because it measures the proportion of workers in occupations perceived to be negatively affected by trade and vulnerable due to the manual labor involved, lack of job security, and often low income of these employees (see Conley and Yon 2007; Holian, Krebs, and Walsh 1997; U.S. Bureau of Labor Statistics 2011). Thus, blue-collar workers have been a major focus of labor policy. The measure is the proportion of employees who work in production/manufacturing, construction, and transportation and was collected from the *Almanac of American Politics* and the US Census Bureau's American Community Survey data.

23. A Breusch-Pagan test of independence allows me to reject the null hypothesis that the residuals from the two equations are independent for the Senate ($\tilde{\chi}^2$=13.235, p=0.000) and the House ($\tilde{\chi}^2$=27.807, p=0.000).

24. The results are generally robust when manufacturing employment is used in place of blue-collar population. See Ritchie (2018) for results from Senate models.

25. Latino population data is from the US Census Bureau's American Community Survey.

26. A Breusch-Pagan test of independence allows me to reject the null hypothesis that the residuals from the two equations are independent for the Senate ($\tilde{\chi}^2$=28.808, p=0.000) and the House ($\tilde{\chi}^2$=129.376, p=0.000).

27. Data on oil and gas production are from the US Energy Information Administration.

28. A Breusch-Pagan test of independence allows me to reject the null hypothesis that the residuals from the two equations are independent for both the Senate ($\tilde{\chi}^2$=60.112, p=0.000) and the House ($\tilde{\chi}^2$=93.638, p=0.000).

Chapter 8

1. See https://www.opensecrets.org for the top agencies targeted by lobbying.

2. Agencies also have their own policy preferences and priorities (Carpenter 2001, 2010) that can play a role in how they respond to legislators' requests (Mills, Kalaf-Hughes, and MacDonald 2016). My analyses in this chapter are more telling of interactions with appointees, whose interests are more closely tied to presidential preferences, than civil servants. However, Chapter 4 includes a qualitative account of a career civil servant working with a like-minded senator against the interests of agency heads and others in Congress.

3. See Matishak and O'Brien (2021).

4. However, this partisanship does not appear to extend to the Senate (Kriner and Schickler 2016, 66).

5. See *A Survivor's Guide for Presidential Nominees* (2020) from the Brookings Institution.

6. See Wyden (2006).

7. Also see Chapter 4 of Kriner and Schickler (2016).

8. I am grateful to Jim Curry for this anecdote.

9. Tweet from October 18, 2019. On July 31, 2020, Rep. Ocasio-Cortez tweeted: "Abolishing ICE isn't a radical thing to do, it's a humane thing to do."

10. Tweet dated June 19, 2019.

11. See, for example, Davis and Linstedt (2006); Higgins (2010).

12. Also see Chapter 5 of Kriner and Schickler (2016) for a similar argument regarding the indirect influence of congressional investigations on presidential behavior.

13. See O'Donnell (2016).

14. Other literature has focused on agency incentives for vote-buying—that agencies favor pivotal legislators in key positions who can be won over (Arnold 1979) and that presidents distribute more federal funding and other benefits to swing states to influence the Electoral College (Hudak 2014; Kriner and Reeves 2015).

15. These collaborative appeals from large groups of lawmakers are unique to policy appeals—casework and grant requests do not include more than the state delegation and are often only from a single legislator. This is another way theoretical arguments and empirical results may differ from previous literature focusing on distributive politics.

16. The DOE's "Correspondence Style Guide" states, "The Executive Secretariat (ES) controls all correspondence addressed to the Secretary, Deputy Secretary, and Under Secretaries of Energy; all correspondence from the National Security Council and the White House; as well as all correspondence from Members of Congress and Tribal Leaders addressed to anyone at the Department." "Correspondence Style Guide." July 2007. Office of the Executive Secretariat, US Department of Energy.

17. This guidance is referred to in the handbook as the "general guidance for Executive Secretariat-assigned due dates."

18. Lowande (2019) uses the "close out date" to produce a measure of how responsive an agency was to a legislator's contact by assuming that the fewer days lapsed between the correspondence and the close out date, the more responsive the agency was to the contact (and that the agency prioritized the contact).

19. Also see Balla (2000).

20. Previous work using response time as a measure of agency prioritization calculates response time using "close out dates" rather than "due dates." It might be argued that due dates reflect the guidelines detailed in the handbook referenced in Table 8.1, which automatically set due dates that prioritize policy, committee chairs, and so on (as described in the handbook) but that these due dates do not reflect actual response times. However, the results presented in this chapter suggest that may not be the case; the analyses using "due dates" do not align with the guidance in the handbook.

For example, as shown in Figure 8.1c, agencies take longer to respond to policy communication than constituency service, which conflicts with the instructions in the handbook (and these results are consistent for Figure 8.1a, which relies on the preferred "close out date"). Also, as shown in Table 8.3, the DOE takes longer to respond to policy communication from senators, energy committee members, and committee chairs and subcommittee chairs (results for chairs not shown) despite the instructions in the handbook. While results of analyses using response time do not align with the guidance in the handbook, my measure of agency prioritization is consistent with the guidance (as shown in Figures 8.1 (right-hand panel), 8.2, and 8.3, as well as the results from the first column of Table 8.3), suggesting that the issue is not related to my coding procedure or the use of due dates as a measure of response time—but with using response time as a measure of prioritization. Moreover, the figures and tables display analyses using due dates as well as close out dates and show largely consistent substantive results (and I make note when they do not).

21. Also see Balla (2000).

22. Thus, the results in this chapter and Chapter 6 are largely consistent with the *capacity hypothesis* described in Chapter 2.

Chapter 9

1. However, this advantage does not always come down to institutional power. For instance, I do not find quantitative evidence that congressional leadership engages more with agencies or benefits from greater access to the top appointees, although qualitative accounts suggest leadership carries substantial weight with agencies. The discrepancy is likely due to leadership's demands within the chambers and their focus on the collective needs of their members.

2. But see Lowande, Ritchie, and Lauterbach (2019) for evidence of how the backchannel might promote the representation of underrepresented communities.

3. Davidson (2007).

4. Also see Curry (2015), chapter 6 for an excellent case study on the House passage of the bill.

5. See the press release on April 12, 2005, from the US Senate Committee on Homeland Security and Government Affairs titled, "Twelve Senators Urge Frist to Keep REAL ID Act off Supplemental Appropriations Bill."

6. See the announcement made by DHS on December 5, 2022.

7. See testimony of Secretary Napolitano before the Senate Committee on Homeland Security and Governmental Affairs, "Identification Security" (Oral Testimony) given July 15, 2009.

8. See House Judiciary Committee Republicans (2011).

9. See Beermann (2006) for an excellent discussion of the court's treatment of ex parte communications.

10. See Merrill (2022) for a discussion about the history and future of Chevron.

11. See Davenport (2022) for a discussion of *West Virginia v. EPA* and on the potential weakening of Chevron.

References

Aberbach, Joel D. 1990. *Keeping a Watchful Eye: The Politics of Congressional Oversight.* Brookings Institution.

Agricultural Marketing Service. 2010. "United States Standards for Grades of Olive Oil and Olive-Pomace Oil."

Aldrich, John H. 1995. *Why Parties?: The Origin and Transformation of Political Parties in America.* University of Chicago Press.

Anagnoson, J. Theodore. 1982. "Federal Grant Agencies and Congressional Election Campaigns." *American Journal of Political Science* 26 (3): 547–561.

Anderson, William D., Janet M. Box-Steffensmeier, and Valeria Sinclair-Chapman. 2003. "The Keys to Legislative Success in the U.S. House of Representatives." *Legislative Studies Quarterly* 28 (3): 357–386.

Ansolabehere, Stephen, James M. Snyder, Jr., and Charles Stewart, III. 2001. "Candidate Positioning in U.S. House Elections." *American Journal of Political Science* 45 (January): 136–159.

Arnold, R. Douglas. 1979. *Congress and the Bureaucracy: A Theory of Influence.* Yale University Press.

Arnold, R. Douglas. 1990. *The Logic of Congressional Action.* Yale University Press.

Arnold, R. Douglas. 2004. *Congress, the Press, and Political Accountability.* Princeton University Press.

Balla, Steven J. 1998. "Administrative Procedures and Political Control of the Bureaucracy." *American Political Science Review* 92 (3): 663–673.

Balla, Steven J. 2000. "Political and Organizational Determinants of Bureaucratic Responsiveness." *American Politics Quarterly* 28 (April): 163–193.

Balla, Steven J., and William T. Gormley. 2018. *Bureaucracy and Democracy: Accountability and Performance.* 4th ed. CQ Press.

Balla, Steven J., and John R. Wright. 2001. "Interest Groups, Advisory Committees, and Congressional Control of the Bureaucracy." *American Journal of Political Science* 45 (4): 799–812.

Ban, Pamela, and Hye Young You. 2019. "Presence and Influence in Lobbying: Evidence from Dodd-Frank." *Business and Politics* 21 (June): 267–295.

Bang, Insik, and Gary E. Hollibaugh. 2022. "Legislative Influence on Administrative Decision Making in Pennsylvania's Abandoned and Orphan Well Plugging Program." *Public Administration* 100 (3), 737–758.

Barkow, Rachel E. 2016. "Overseeing Agency Enforcement Annual Review of Administrative Law: Foreword." *George Washington Law Review* 84 (5): 1129–1186.

Baumgartner, Frank R., and Beth L. Leech. 1998. *Basic Interests: The Importance of Groups in Politics and in Political Science.* Princeton University Press.

Baumgartner, Frank R., Jeffrey M. Berry, Marie Hojnacki, Beth L. Leech, and David C. Kimball. 2009. *Lobbying and Policy Change: Who Wins, Who Loses, and Why.* University of Chicago Press.

Bawn, Kathleen. 1995. "Political Control versus Expertise: Congressional Choices about Administrative Procedures." *American Political Science Review* 89 (1): 62–73.

Becker, Bernie, and Vicki Neeham. 2015. "McConnell Warns Obama against Tobacco Carve-out in Trade Deal." *The Hill* (July).

Beermann, Jack M. 2006. "Congressional Administration." *San Diego L. Rev.* 43: 61.

Bernhard, William, and Tracy Sulkin. 2013. "Commitment and Consequences: Reneging on Cosponsorship Pledges in the U.S. House." *Legislative Studies Quarterly* 38 (4): 461–487.

Berry, Christopher R., Barry C. Burden, and William G. Howell. 2010. "The President and the Distribution of Federal Spending." *American Political Science Review* 104 (November): 783–799.

Bertelli, Anthony M., and Christian R. Grose. 2009. "Secretaries of Pork? A New Theory of Distributive Public Policy." *Journal of Politics* 71 (3): 926–945.

Binder, Sarah A. 1999. "The Dynamics of Legislative Gridlock, 1947–96." *American Political Science Review* 93 (3): 519–533.

Binder, Sarah A. 2003. *Stalemate: Causes and Consequences of Legislative Gridlock.* Brookings Institution Press.

Bishin, Benjamin. 2009. *Tyranny of the Minority: The Subconstituency Politics Theory of Representation.* Temple University Press.

Bishin, Benjamin G. 2000. "Constituency Influence in Congress: Does Subconstituency Matter?" *Legislative Studies Quarterly* 25 (August): 389–415.

Bjorhus, Jennifer. 2020. "Gray Wolf Loses Endangered Species Act Protections." *Star Tribune* (October 29).

Bolton, Alexander. 2022. "Gridlock, Bureaucratic Control, and Nonstatutory Policymaking in Congress." *American Journal of Political Science* 66 (1): 238–254.

Box-Steffensmeier, Janet M., Laura W. Arnold, and Christopher J. W. Zorn. 1997. "The Strategic Timing of Position Taking in Congress: A Study of the North American Free Trade Agreement." *American Political Science Review* 91 (June): 324–338.

Burstein, Paul, and April Linton. 2002. "The Impact of Political Parties, Interest Groups, and Social Movement Organizations on Public Policy: Some Recent Evidence and Theoretical Concerns." *Social Forces* 81 (December): 380–408.

Cain, Bruce, John Ferejohn, and Morris Fiorina. 1990. *The Personal Vote: Constituency Service and Electoral Independence.* Harvard University Press.

Caldeira, Gregory A., and Christopher Zorn. 2004. "Strategic Timing, Position-Taking, and Impeachment in the House of Representatives." *Political Research Quarterly* 57 (December): 517–527.

Canes-Wrone, Brandice, David W. Brady, and John F. Cogan. 2002. "Out of Step, Out of Office: Electoral Accountability and House Members' Voting." *American Political Science Review* 96 (March): 127–140.

Carpenter, Daniel P. 2001. *The Forging of Bureaucratic Autonomy: Reputations, Networks, and Policy Innovation in Executive Agencies, 1862–1928.* Princeton University Press.

Carpenter, Daniel. 2010. *Reputation and Power: Organizational Image and Pharmaceutical Regulation at the FDA.* Princeton University Press.

Carpenter, Daniel, and George A. Krause. 2015. "Transactional Authority and Bureaucratic Politics." *Journal of Public Administration Research and Theory* 25 (January): 5–25.

Carson, Jamie L., Gregory Koger, Matthew J. Lebo, and Everett Young. 2010. "The Electoral Costs of Party Loyalty in Congress." *American Journal of Political Science* 54 (July): 598–616.

Casas, Andreu, Matthew J. Denny, and John Wilkerson. 2020. "More Effective Than We Thought: Accounting for Legislative Hitchhikers Reveals a More Inclusive and Productive Lawmaking Process." *American Journal of Political Science* 64 (1): 5–18.

Clark, Krissy. 2017. "The Sentence That Helped Set Off the Opioid Crisis." The Uncertain Hour. http://www.marketplace.org/shows/the-uncertain-hour/s02-4-sentence-helped-set-opioid-crisis (Program on Marketplace, May 12, 2022).

Clinton, Joshua D., Anthony Bertelli, Christian R. Grose, David E. Lewis, and David C. Nixon. 2012. "Separated Powers in the United States: The Ideology of Agencies, Presidents, and Congress." *American Journal of Political Science* 56 (April): 341–354.

Cohen, Jacob. 1960. "A Coefficient of Agreement for Nominal Scales." *Educational and Psychological Measurement* 20 (April): 37–46.

Cohen, Linda R., and Roger G. Noll. 1991. "How to Vote, Whether to Vote: Strategies for Voting and Abstaining on Congressional Roll Calls." *Political Behavior* 13 (June): 97–127.

Colman, Zack. 2020. "Pennsylvania Tests Biden's Balancing Act on Climate, Fracking." *Politico* (July 20, 2020).

Conley, Richard S. 1999. "Derailing Presidential Fast-Track Authority: The Impact of Constituency Pressures and Political Ideology on Trade Policy in Congress." *Political Research Quarterly* 52 (4): 785–799.

Conley, Richard S., and Richard M. Yon. 2007. "The 'Hidden Hand' and White House Roll-Call Predictions: Legislative Liaison in the Eisenhower White House, 83d–84th Congresses." *Presidential Studies Quarterly* 37 (2): 291–312.

Cooper, Jasper, Sung Eun Kim, and Johannes Urpelainen. 2018. "The Broad Impact of a Narrow Conflict: How Natural Resource Windfalls Shape Policy and Politics." *Journal of Politics* 80 (April): 630–646.

Cord, Curtis. 2012. "American Olive Oil Producers Draft Federal Marketing Order—Olive Oil Times." *Olive Oil Times* (March).

Corn, Elaine. 2010. "Your Olive Oil May Not Be the Virgin It Claims." Weekend Edition Sunday (Program on National Public Radio, July 24, 2010).

Covington, Cary R. 1987. " 'Staying Private': Gaining Congressional Support for Unpublicized Presidential Preferences on Roll Call Votes." *Journal of Politics* 49 (August): 737–755.

Cox, Gary W., and Mathew D. McCubbins. 2005. *Setting the Agenda: Responsible Party Government in the U.S. House of Representatives*. Cambridge University Press.

Cox, Gary W., and Mathew Daniel McCubbins. 1993. *Legislative Leviathan: Party Government in the House*. University of California Press.

Crespin, Michael H. 2010. "Serving Two Masters: Redistricting and Voting in the U.S. House of Representatives." *Political Research Quarterly* 63 (December): 850–859.

Cuellar, Mariano-Florentino. 2006. "Auditing Executive Discretion." *Notre Dame Law Review* 82 (1): 227–312.

Curry, James M. 2015. *Legislating in the Dark: Information and Power in the House of Representatives*. University of Chicago Press.

Customs and Border Protection Bureau. 2008. "Proposed Interpretation of the Expression 'Sold for Exportation to the United States' for Purposes of Applying the Transaction Value Method of Valuation in a Series of Sales."

Customs and Border Protection Bureau. 2010. "Withdrawal of Proposed Interpretation of the Expression Sold for Exportation to the United States, etc."

Davenport, Coral. 2022. "Republican Drive to Tilt Courts against Climate Action Reaches a Crucial Moment." *New York Times* (June 19, 2022).

Davidson, Adam. 2007. "World Sock Capital Suffers from Duty-Free Imports." *National Public Radio* (November 27, 2007).

Davis, Christopher M. 2013. "The Amending Process in the Senate." Report Congressional Research Service Washington, DC.

Davis, Henry L., and Sharon Linstedt. 2006. "Despite Criticism, FEMA Moves to Aid in Cleanup." *The Buffalo News* (October 18, 2006).

Dodd, Lawrence C., and Richard L. Schott. 1979. *Congress and the Administrative State.* John Wiley.

Drutman, Lee. 2017. "House Leadership Has Been Writing Bills behind Closed Doors for Years." *Vox* (March 3, 2017).

Drutman, Lee. 2018. "Why So Many Members of Congress Are Retiring." *Vox* (February 1, 2018).

Environmental Protection Agency. 2020. "EPA Finalizes Historic Action to Better Protect Children's Health."

Epstein, David, and Sharyn O'Halloran. 1999. *Delegating Powers: A Transaction Cost Politics Approach to Policy Making under Separate Powers.* Cambridge University Press.

Eskridge, Jr., William N., and John Ferejohn. 1992. "Making the Deal Stick: Enforcing the Original Constitutional Structure of Lawmaking in the Modern Regulatory State." *Journal of Law, Economics, & Organization* 8 (March): 165–189.

Esterling, Kevin M. 2004. *The Political Economy of Expertise: Information and Efficiency in American National Politics.* University of Michigan Press.

Everett, Burgess. 2017. "Sessions Reassures Senators: No Pot Crackdown Imminent." *Politico* (March 2, 2017).

Everett, Burgess. 2018. "Colo. Senator: Trump Easing Up on Pot Crackdown." *Politico* (April).

FACT SHEET: *The Recovery Act Made the Largest Single Investment in Clean Energy in History, Driving the Deployment of Clean Energy, Promoting Energy Efficiency, and Supporting Manufacturing.* 2016.

Farina, Cynthia, Mary Newhart, Claire Cardie, and Dan Cosley. 2011. "Rulemaking 2.0." *Cornell Law Faculty Publications* (January).

Fedaseyeu, Viktar, Erik Gilje, and Philip E Strahan. 2015. "Voter Preferences and Political Change: Evidence from Shale Booms." *NBER Working Paper 21789*: 38.

Fenno, Richard F. 1973. *Congressmen in Committees.* Little, Brown.

Fenno, Richard F. 1977. "U.S. House Members in Their Constituencies: An Exploration." *American Political Science Review* 71 (3): 883–917.

Fenno, Richard F. 1978. *Home Style: House Members in Their Districts.* Little, Brown.

Ferejohn, John A. 1974. *Pork Barrel Politics: Rivers and Harbors Legislation, 1947–1968.* Stanford University Press.

Ferejohn, John, and Charles Shipan. 1990. "Congressional Influence on Bureaucracy." *Journal of Law, Economics, & Organization* 6: 1–20.

Fiorina, Morris P. 1974. *Representatives, Roll Calls, and Constituencies.* Lexington Books.

Fiorina, Morris P. 1977. *Congress, Keystone of the Washington Establishment.* Yale University Press.

Flagg, Nancy. 2012. "Three Fronts Converging in U.S. Olive Oil Industry—Olive Oil Times." *Olive Oil Times* (December 3, 2012).

FOIA at 50. 2016. *The Washington Post* (July 3, 2016).

FOIA Is Broken: A Report. 2016. Technical report US House of Representatives Committee on Oversight and Government Reform.

Foran, Clare, and National Journal. 2014. "How Many Jobs Does Fracking Really Create?" *The Atlantic* (April).

Foster, David. 2022. "Persistent Unilateral Action." Working paper, London School of Economics & Political Science.

Galka, Max. 2017. "Who Uses FOIA? : An Analysis of 229,000 Requests to 85 Government Agencies." FOIA Mapper.

Garner, Dwight. 2011. "Olive Oil's Growers, Chemists, Cooks and Crooks." *New York Times* (December 8, 2011).

Garvey, Todd. 2014. "A Primer on the Reviewability of Agency Delay and Enforcement Discretion." *Congressional Research Service* (September): 15.

Georgantopoulos, Mary Ann, and Daniel Wagner. 2017. "A House Committee Doesn't Want You to See Its Correspondence with Government Officials." *BuzzFeed News* (May 4, 2017).

Gerstein, Josh. 2017. "House Goes to Court to Protect Secrecy of Records." *Politico* (September 15, 2017).

Gilligan, Thomas W., and Keith Krehbiel. 1997. "Specialization Decisions within Committee." *Journal of Law, Economics & Organization* 13 (October): 366–386.

Ginsberg, Wendy, and Michael Greene. 2016. "Access to Government Information in the United States: A Primer." Technical report Congressional Research Service, Washington, DC.

Glazer, Amihai, Robert Griffin, Bernard Grofman, and Martin Wattenberg. 1995. "Strategic Vote Delay in the U.S. House of Representatives." *Legislative Studies Quarterly* 20 (February): 37–45.

Golden, Marissa Martino. 2003. "Who Controls the Bureaucracy? The Case of Agenda Setting." Georgetown University.

Goldstein, Rebecca, and Hye Young You. 2017. "Cities as Lobbyists." *American Journal of Political Science* 61 (October): 864–876.

Green, Matthew N. 2015. *Underdog Politics: The Minority Party in the U.S. House of Representatives.* Yale University Press.

Grimmer, Justin. 2013. *Representational Style in Congress: What Legislators Say and Why It Matters.* Cambridge University Press.

Grimmer, Justin, Sean J. Westwood, and Solomon Messing. 2014. *The Impression of Influence: Legislator Communication, Representation, and Democratic Accountability.* Princeton University Press.

Haeder, Simon F., and Susan Webb Yackee. 2015. "Influence and the Administrative Process: Lobbying the U.S. President's Office of Management and Budget." *American Political Science Review* 109 (August): 507–522.

Haeder, Simon F., and Susan Webb Yackee. 2020. "Policies That Bind? The Use of Guidance Documents by Federal Agencies." *Journal of Health & Human Services Administration* 43 (September): 87–100.

Haeder, Simon F., and Susan Webb Yackee. 2022. "Handmaidens of the Legislature? Understanding Regulatory Timing." *Journal of Public Policy* 42 (June): 298–322.

Hall, Richard L. 1996. *Participation in Congress.* Yale University Press.

Hall, Richard L., and Alan V. Deardorff. 2006. "Lobbying as Legislative Subsidy." *American Political Science Review* 100 (February): 69–84.

Hall, Richard L., and Frank W. Wayman. 1990. "Buying Time: Moneyed Interests and the Mobilization of Bias in Congressional Committees." *American Political Science Review* 84 (3): 797–820.

Hall, Richard L., and Kristina C. Miler. 2008. "What Happens after the Alarm? Interest Group Subsidies to Legislative Overseers." *Journal of Politics* 70 (October): 990–1005.

Halstuk, Martin E., and Bill F. Chamberlin. 2006. "The Freedom of Information Act 1966–2006: A Retrospective on the Rise of Privacy Protection over the Public Interest in Knowing What the Government's Up To." *Communication Law and Policy* 11 (September): 511–564.

Hansen, John Mark. 1991. *Gaining Access: Congress and the Farm Lobby, 1919–1981.* University of Chicago Press.

Harbridge, Laurel. 2015. *Is Bipartisanship Dead?: Policy Agreement and Agenda-Setting in the House of Representatives.* Cambridge University Press.

Hemphill, Stephanie. 2011. "Minn. Plans Hunting Season as Gray Wolves Come Off Endangered List." *Minnesota Public Radio* (December 21).

Higgins, Congressman Brian. 2010. "Higgins Fights FEMA on Buffalo Flood Maps." Press release (April 19, 2010).

Holian, David B., Timothy B. Krebs, and Michael H. Walsh. 1997. "Constituency Opinion, Ross Perot, and Roll-Call Behavior in the U. S. House: The Case of the NAFTA." *Legislative Studies Quarterly* 22 (3): 369–392.

House Judiciary Committee Republicans. 2011. "Smith, King and Sensenbrenner: Further REAL ID Extension Threatens National Security." Press release (February 28, 2011).

Howell, William, Scott Adler, Charles Cameron, and Charles Riemann. 2000. "Divided Government and the Legislative Productivity of Congress, 1945–94." *Legislative Studies Quarterly* 25 (May): 285–312.

Huber, John D., and Charles R. Shipan. 2002. *Deliberate Discretion?: The Institutional Foundations of Bureaucratic Autonomy.* Cambridge Studies in Comparative Politics. Cambridge University Press.

Hudak, John. 2014. *Presidential Pork: White House Influence over the Distribution of Federal Grants.* Brookings Institution Press.

Hulse, Carl, and David M. Herszenhorn. 2010. "After Bruising Session, Congress Braces for More." *The New York Times* (December 22, 2010).

Hume, Robert J. 2009. *How Courts Impact Federal Administrative Behavior.* Routledge.

Husk, Lee Lewis. 2018. "A Fifty-Year Anniversary by the Unlikely Victors Who Saved Hells Canyon." *1859 Oregon's Magazine* (July).

Jacobson, Gary C. 1987. "The Marginals Never Vanished: Incumbency and Competition in Elections to the U.S. House of Representatives, 1952–82." *American Journal of Political Science* 31 (February): 126–141.

Jaeger, Kyle. 2019. "One Year after Jeff Sessions Rescinded a Federal Marijuana Memo, the Sky Hasn't Fallen." *Marijuana Moment* (January 4, 2019).

Johannes, John R. 1984. *To Serve the People: Congress and Constituency Service.* University of Nebraska Press.

Johnson, Gbemende E. 2021. "The Law: Government Transparency and Public Access." *Presidential Studies Quarterly* 51 (September): 705–724.

Johnson, Lyndon. 1966. "Statement by the President upon Signing S.1160." Office of the White House Press Secretary (July 4, 1966).

Jones, David R. 2001. "Party Polarization and Legislative Gridlock." *Political Research Quarterly* 54 (1): 125–141.

Justice Department Issues Memo on Marijuana Enforcement. 2018. US Department of Justice. https://www.justice.gov/opa/pr/justice-department-issues-memo-marijuana-enforcement.

Kalla, Joshua L., and David E. Broockman. 2016. "Campaign Contributions Facilitate Access to Congressional Officials: A Randomized Field Experiment." *American Journal of Political Science* 60 (3): 545–558.

Keen, Judy. 2019. "Environmental Activists Fault Some of Sen. Amy Klobuchar's Moves." *Star Tribune* (August 6).

Kernell, Samuel, and Michael P. McDonald. 1999. "Congress and America's Political Development: The Transformation of the Post Office from Patronage to Service." *American Journal of Political Science* 43 (3): 792–811.

Kerwin, Cornelius Martin, and Scott R. Furlong. 2018. *Rulemaking: How Government Agencies Write Law and Make Policy.* CQ Press.

Kingdon, John W. 1973. *Congressmen's Voting Decisions.* University of Michigan Press.

Koger, Gregory. 2003. "Position Taking and Cosponsorship in the U.S. House." *Legislative Studies Quarterly* 28 (May): 225–246.

Krause, George A. 2003. "Coping with Uncertainty: Analyzing Risk Propensities of SEC Budgetary Decisions, 1949–97." *American Political Science Review* 97 (1): 171–188.

Krawiec, Kimberly. 2013. "Don't 'Screw Joe the Plummer': The Sausage-Making of Financial Reform." *Arizona Law Review* 55 (January): 53–103.

Krehbiel, Keith. 1991. *Information and Legislative Organization.* University of Michigan Press.

Krehbiel, Keith, Adam Meirowitz, and Alan E. Wiseman. 2015. "A Theory of Competitive Partisan Lawmaking." *Political Science Research and Methods* 3 (September): 423–448.

Kriner, Douglas L., and Andrew Reeves. 2015. *The Particularistic President: Executive Branch Politics and Political Inequality.* Cambridge University Press.

Kriner, Douglas L., and Eric Schickler. 2016. *Investigating the President: Congressional Checks on Presidential Power.* Princeton University Press.

Kroeger, Mary A. 2021. "Bureaucrats as Lawmakers." *Legislative Studies Quarterly* 47 (1): 257–289.

Kwoka, Margaret. 2016. "FOIA, Inc." *Duke Law Journal* 65 (April): 1361–1437.

Lapinski, John S. 2008. "Policy Substance and Performance in American Lawmaking, 1877–1994." *American Journal of Political Science* 52 (2): 235–251.

Lauterbach, Erinn. 2020. *Punishments, Incentives, and Oversight: How Legislators Turn Preference Into Policy.* Dissertation ed. University of California, Riverside.

Lee, Frances E. 2016. *Insecure Majorities: Congress and the Perpetual Campaign.* University of Chicago Press.

Lee, Raymond M. 2001. "Research Uses of the U.S. Freedom of Information Act." *Field Methods* 13 (November): 370–391.

Lerer, Lisa, and Laura Litvan. 2010. "No Congress since 1960s Has Impact on Public as 111th." *Bloomberg News* (December 22, 2010).

Lesniewski, Niels, and Katherine Tully-McManus. 2019. "Perfect Attendance? Not for Democratic Presidential Hopefuls." *Roll Call* (June 26, 2019).

Levendusky, Matthew. 2009. *The Partisan Sort: How Liberals Became Democrats and Conservatives Became Republicans.* University of Chicago Press.

Levin, Ronald M. 1996. "Congressional Ethics and Constituent Advocacy in an Age of Mistrust." *Michigan Law Review* 95 (1): 111.

Levine, Marianne. 2019. "White House Hopefuls Are Missing Senate Votes—and Nobody Cares." *Politico* (November 15, 2019).

Levitt, Steven D., and James M. Snyder. 1995. "Political Parties and the Distribution of Federal Outlays." *American Journal of Political Science* 39 (4): 958–980.

Levy, Marc. 2019. "Toomey Presses to Prevent a Future Fracking Ban." *The Express-Times* (November 9, 2019).

Levy, Marc. 2020. "Fracking Debate Causes Tremors in Battleground Pennsylvania." *AP NEWS* (February 20, 2020).

Lewis, David E. 2008. *The Politics of Presidential Appointments: Political Control and Bureaucratic Performance*. Princeton University Press.

Libgober, Brian. 2020. "Meetings, Comments, and the Distributive Politics of Rulemaking." *Quarterly Journal of Political Science* 15 (4): 449–481.

Lowande, Kenneth. 2018. "Who Polices the Administrative State?" *American Political Science Review*, 112 (4): 874–890.

Lowande, Kenneth. 2019. "Politicization and Responsiveness in Executive Agencies." *Journal of Politics* 81 (November): 33–48.

Lowande, Kenneth, Melinda Ritchie, and Erinn Lauterbach. 2019. "Descriptive and Substantive Representation in Congress: Evidence from 80,000 Congressional Inquiries." *American Journal of Political Science* 63 (3): 644–659.

Lowande, Kenneth, and Rachel Augustine Potter. 2021. "Congressional Oversight Revisited: Politics and Procedure in Agency Rulemaking." *Journal of Politics* 83 (January): 401–408.

Lustgarten, Abrahm. 2014. "New York's Gas Rush Poses Environmental Threat." *ProPublica* (December 17, 2014).

MacDonald, Jason A. 2010. "Limitation Riders and Congressional Influence over Bureaucratic Policy Decisions." *American Political Science Review* 104 (November): 766–782.

Malbin, Michael J. 1980. *Unelected Representatives: Congressional Staff and the Future of Representative Government*. Basic.

Maltzman, Forrest, and Lee Sigelman. 1996. "The Politics of Talk: Unconstrained Floor Time in the U.S. House of Representatives." *Journal of Politics* 58 (August): 819–830.

Mansbridge, Jane. 2019. "Recursive Representation." In *Creating Political Presence: The New Politics of Democratic Representation*, ed. Cario Castiglione and Johannes Pollak. University of Chicago Press.

Manuel, Kate M, and Todd Garvey. 2013. "Prosecutorial Discretion in Immigration Enforcement: Legal Issues." *Congressional Research Service* (December): 31. Washington, DC.

Marsh, Kevin R. 2007. *Drawing Lines in the Forest: Creating Wilderness Areas in the Pacific Northwest*. First ed. University of Washington Press.

Matishak, Martin, and Connor O'Brien. 2021. "GOP Uses Threats Hearing to Air Political, Personal Grievances." *Politico* (April 15, 2021).

Matthews, Donald R. 1960. *U.S. Senators and Their World*. University of North Carolina Press.

Mayhew, David R. 1974. *Congress: The Electoral Connection*. Yale University Press.

Mayhew, David R. 1991. *Divided We Govern: Party Control, Lawmaking and Investigations, 1946–2002*. Yale University Press.

McCalmont, Lucy. 2014. "McCarthy: Spacey Stole My Line." *Politico* (July 31, 2014).

McCarty, Nolan, and Rose Razaghian. 1999. "Advice and Consent: Senate Responses to Executive Branch Nominations 1885–1996." *American Journal of Political Science* 43 (4): 1122–1143.

McCubbins, Mathew D., Roger G. Noll, and Barry R. Weingast. 1987. "Administrative Procedures as Instruments of Political Control." *Journal of Law, Economics, & Organization* 3 (2): 243–277.

McCubbins, Matthew D., Roger G. Noll, and Barry R. Weingast. 1989. "Structure and Process, Politics and Policy: Administrative Arrangements and the Political Control of Agencies." *Virginia Law Review* 75 (2): 431–482.

McCubbins, Mathew D., and Thomas Schwartz. 1984. "Congressional Oversight Overlooked: Police Patrols versus Fire Alarms." *American Journal of Political Science* 28 (February): 165–179.

McGrath, Robert J. 2013. "Congressional Oversight Hearings and Policy Control." *Legislative Studies Quarterly* 38 (August): 349–376.

McGraw, Meridith. 2020. "Trump's Final Pitch to Pennsylvania: I Love Fracking." *Politico* (October 26, 2020)

Merrill, Thomas W. 2022. *The Chevron Doctrine: Its Rise and Fall, and the Future of the Administrative State*. Harvard University Press.

Miler, Kristina C. 2007. "The View from the Hill: Legislative Perceptions of the District." *Legislative Studies Quarterly* 32 (4): 597–628.

Miler, Kristina C. 2010. *Constituency Representation in Congress: The View from Capitol Hill*. Cambridge University Press.

Miller, Susan M., and L. Marvin Overby. 2010. "Parties, Preferences, and Petitions: Discharge Behavior in the Modern House." *Legislative Studies Quarterly* 35 (May): 187–209.

Miller, Warren E., and Donald E. Stokes. 1963. "Constituency Influence in Congress." *American Political Science Review* 57 (1): 45–56.

Mills, Russell, and Nicole Kalaf-Hughes. 2015. "The Evolution of Distributive Benefits: The Rise of Letter-Marking in the United States Congress." *The Journal of Economics and Politics* 22 (1).

Mills, Russell W., Nicole Kalaf-Hughes, and Jason A. MacDonald. 2016. "Agency Policy Preferences, Congressional Letter-marking and the Allocation of Distributive Policy Benefits." *Journal of Public Policy* 36 (December): 547–571.

Minta, Michael D. 2011. *Oversight: Representing the Interests of Blacks and Latinos in Congress*. 1st ed. Princeton University Press.

Moe, Terry M. 1987. "An Assessment of the Positive Theory of 'Congressional Dominance'." *Legislative Studies Quarterly* 12 (November): 475–520.

Montgomery, Jacob M., and Brendan Nyhan. 2017. "The Effects of Congressional Staff Networks in the US House of Representatives." *Journal of Politics* 79 (April): 745–761.

Morrill, Jim. 2002. "Candidates Skirmish Over Trade Policy—Dole, Bowles Blame Each Other for Loss of Textile Jobs Both Point Fingers over Fast-Track Authority and Smuggled Imports." *The Charlotte Observer* (October 31, 2002).

Morrill, Jim, and Mark Johnson. 2004. "Senate Hopefuls Criticize Trade Pact—Bowles Calls CAFTA a Mistake Burr Wants Textile Protections Critics Say Central American

Free Trade Agreement Could Wipe Out Carolinas Jobs." *The Charlotte Observer* (May 29, 2004).

Muehlenbachs, Lucija, Elisabeth Newcomb Sinha, and Nitish Ranjan Sinha. 2011. "Strategic Release of News at the EPA." *Resources for the Future* Discussion Paper 11–45, (October 26, 2011): 33.

Mueller, Tom. 2011a. "Can American Virginity Be Saved?." *Wall Street Journal* (December 30, 2011).

Mueller, Tom. 2011b. *Extra Virginity: The Sublime and Scandalous World of Olive Oil.* Norton, W. W. & Company, Inc.

Mullins, Brody, and Christopher Weaver. 2013. "Open-Government Laws Fuel Hedge-Fund Profits." *Wall Street Journal* (September 23, 2013).

Neiheisel, Jacob R., and Michael C. Brady. 2017. "Congressional Lettermarks, Ideology, and Member Receipt of Stimulus Awards from the US Department of Labor." *Research & Politics* 4 (3).

Nichols, Chris. 2016. "Claim Loretta Sanchez 'Passed One Bill in 20 Years': Technically Correct, but Misleading." *Politifact* (October 6, 2016).

Obama, President Barack. 2009. "Memorandum from President Barack Obama for the Heads of Exec. Departments and Agencies, Freedom of Information Act." (July 21, 2009).

O'Boyle, Bill. 2020. "Toomey 'Pushes Back' on Dems' Efforts to Ban Fracking." *Times Leader* (February 19, 2020).

O'Donnell, Katy. 2016. "Jordan Says He Will Continue Push for IRS Chief's Impeachment." *Politico* (November 14, 2016).

Office of the Executive Secretariat. 2007. "Correspondence Style Guide."

Packwood, Bob. 2018. "French Pete: Birth of a Wilderness." *The Register-Guard* (March 17, 2018).

Parker, Glenn R. 1980. "Sources of Change in Congressional District Attentiveness." *American Journal of Political Science* 24 (1): 115–124.

Poole, Keith T., and Howard Rosenthal. 1991. "Patterns of Congressional Voting." *American Journal of Political Science* 35 (1): 228–278.

Potter, Rachel Augustine. 2017. "Slow-Rolling, Fast-Tracking, and the Pace of Bureaucratic Decisions in Rulemaking." *Journal of Politics* 79 (May): 841–855.

Potter, Rachel Augustine. 2019. *Bending the Rules: Procedural Politicking in the Bureaucracy.* University of Chicago Press.

Quirk, Paul J. 2014. *Industry Influence in Federal Regulatory Agencies.* Princeton University Press.

Reynolds, Molly E. 2017. *Exceptions to the Rule: The Politics of Filibuster Limitations in the U.S. Senate.* Brookings Institution Press.

Ritchie, Melinda N. 2018. "Back-Channel Representation: A Study of the Strategic Communication of Senators with the US Department of Labor." *Journal of Politics* 80 (1): 240–253.

Ritchie, Melinda N., and Hye Young You. 2019. "Legislators as Lobbyists." *Legislative Studies Quarterly* 44 (1): 65–95.

Ritchie, Melinda N., and Hye Young You. 2021. "Women's Advancement in Politics: Evidence from Congressional Staff." *Journal of Politics* 83 (April): 421–438.

Rohde, David W. 1991. *Parties and Leaders in the Postreform House.* University of Chicago Press.

Rothman, Lily. 2016. "FOIA at 50: How American Views of Transparency Have Changed." *Time* (July 21, 2016).

Russell, Annelise. 2021. *Tweeting Is Leading: How Senators Communicate and Represent in the Age of Twitter.* Oxford University Press.

Sances, Michael W., and Hye Young You. 2022. "Voters and Donors: The Unequal Political Consequences of Fracking." *Journal of Politics* 84 (July): 28.

Schiller, Wendy J. 1995. "Senators as Political Entrepreneurs: Using Bill Sponsorship to Shape Legislative Agendas." *American Journal of Political Science* 39 (February): 186–203.

Schiller, Wendy J. 2000. *Partners and Rivals: Representation in U.S. Senate Delegations.* Princeton University Press.

Scholz, John T., and Feng Heng Wei. 1986. "Regulatory Enforcement in a Federalist System." *American Political Science Review* 80 (December): 1249–1270.

Schumer, Charles. 2012. "Schumer: Fed Ruling Could Put Hundreds of Rome Workers Out of Work—Urges Feds Not to Adopt Costly Olive Oil Regs That Would Be a Blow to Sovena and Raise Prices for Consumers." Press release (May 16, 2012).

Sellers, Patrick. 2010. *Cycles of Spin: Strategic Communication in the U.S. Congress.* Cambridge University Press.

Sheffner, Daniel J. 2020. "The Freedom of Information Act (FOIA): A Legal Overview". Technical report Congressional Research Service, Washington, DC.

Shepsle, Kenneth A. 1992. "Congress is a 'They,' not an 'It': Legislative Intent as Oxymoron." *International Review of Law and Economics* 12 (June): 239–256.

Shipan, Charles R. 2004. "Regulatory Regimes, Agency Actions, and the Conditional Nature of Congressional Influence." *American Political Science Review* 98 (August): 467–480.

Sinclair, Barbara. 1986. "Senate Styles and Senate Decision Making, 1955–1980." *Journal of Politics* 48 (November): 877–908.

Sinclair, Barbara. 1989. *The Transformation of the U.S. Senate.* Johns Hopkins University Press.

Snyder, Tanya, Tucker Doherty, and Arren Kimbel-Sannit. 2019. "Elaine Chao Favored Kentuckians in Meeting with Officials Seeking Grants." *Politico* (October 7, 2019).

Stein, Robert M., and Kenneth N. Bickers. 1997. *Perpetuating the Pork Barrel: Policy Subsystems and American Democracy.* Revised ed. Cambridge University Press.

Stuessy, Meghan M. 2015. "The Freedom of Information Act (FOIA): Background, Legislation, and Policy Issues." Technical report Congressional Research Service, Washington, DC.

Stuessy, Meghan M. 2019. "Freedom of Information Act Fees for Government Information." Technical report Congressional Research Service, Washington, DC.

Sulkin, Tracy. 2005. *Issue Politics in Congress.* Cambridge University Press.

Sulkin, Tracy. 2011. *The Legislative Legacy of Congressional Campaigns.* Cambridge University Press.

Sullivan, Sean. 2020. "Union Leaders Have Biden's Back on Fracking. But in Pennsylvania, Their Members Aren't So Sure." *Washington Post* (October 23, 2020).

Sunstein, Cass R. 1990. "Law and Administration after Chevron." *Columbia Law Review* 90 (8): 2071–2120.

Sunstein, Cass R. 2022. "Who Should Regulate?" *The New York Review of Books* (May).

Taylor, Andrew J. 2013. *Congress: A Performance Appraisal.* 1st ed. Routledge.

Thomas, Jr., Robert Mcg. 1997. "John E. Moss, 84, Is Dead; Father of Anti-Secrecy Law." *The New York Times* (December 6, 1997).

Thompson, Dennis F. 1993. "Mediated Corruption: The Case of the Keating Five." *American Political Science Review* 87 (2): 369–381.

U.S. Department of Energy's Recover Act Investments. 2013. Technical report, The Center for Climate and Energy Solutions.

US Department of Labor, Mine Safety and Health Administration. 1999. "Health Standards for Occupational Noise Exposure." *Federal Register* 64 (September).

U.S. Bureau of Labor Statistics. 2011. "Fatal Occupational Injuries and Nonfatal Occupational Injuries and Illnesses, 2008." Technical report U.S. Department of Labor. https://www.bls.gov/iif/oshwc/osh/os/oshs2008.pdf.

Volden, Craig. 2019. "Highlights from the New 115th Congress Legislative Effectiveness Scores." *Center for Effective Lawmaking* (February).

Volden, Craig, and Alan E. Wiseman. 2014. *Legislative Effectiveness in the United States Congress: The Lawmakers*. Cambridge University Press.

Volden, Craig, and Alan E. Wiseman. 2018. "Legislative Effectiveness in the United States Senate." *Journal of Politics* 80 (April): 731–735.

Walker, Christopher. 2017. "Legislating in the Shadows." *University of Pennsylvania Law Review* 165 (January): 1377.

Warren, Kenneth F. 2011. *Administrative Law in the Political System*. 5th ed. Westview Press.

Weingast, Barry R., and Mark J. Moran. 1983. "Bureaucratic Discretion or Congressional Control? Regulatory Policymaking by the Federal Trade Commission." *Journal of Political Economy* 91 (October): 765–800.

Welch, Matt. 2018. "How a Lone Republican Changed Trump's Position on Pot." *Los Angeles Times* (June 14, 2018).

West, William F., and Connor Raso. 2013. "Who Shapes the Rulemaking Agenda? Implications for Bureaucratic Responsiveness and Bureaucratic Control." *Journal of Public Administration Research and Theory* 23 (3): 495–519.

White, Avery, and Michael Neblo. 2021. "Capturing the Public: Beyond Technocracy & Populism in the U.S. Administrative State." *Daedalus* 150 (July): 172–187.

Williams, Larry. 2008. "Memories of an Oregon Conservationist." (January 1, 2018). Blog post. Oregon Environmental Council. https://oeconline.org/larry-williams/.

Willis, Derek, and Cecilia Reyes. 2015. "The Dog Ate My Vote: How Congress Explains Its Absences." *ProPublica* (November 10, 2015).

Wilson, Jacque. 2013. "5 Things You Might Not Know about Olive Oil." *CNN* (February 26, 2013).

Wilson, Rick K., and Cheryl D. Young. 1997. "Cosponsorship in the U. S. Congress." *Legislative Studies Quarterly* 22 (February): 25–43.

Wiseman, Alan E. 2009. "Delegation and Positive-Sum Bureaucracies." *Journal of Politics* 71 (July): 998–1014.

Wiseman, Alan E., and John R. Wright. 2020. "Chevron, State Farm, and the Impact of Judicial Doctrine on Bureaucratic Policymaking." *Perspectives on Politics*: 20 (3): 901–915.

Wolfensberger, Donald R. 2018. *Changing Cultures in Congress: From Fair Play to Power Plays*. Columbia University Press.

Woon, Jonathan. 2009. "Issue Attention and Legislative Proposals in the U.S. Senate." *Legislative Studies Quarterly* 34 (1): 29–54.

Wyden, Ron. 2006. "Wyden Blocks Interior Department Nominee over Funding for Rural Schools and Roads." Press release (May 26, 2006).

Yackee, Susan Webb. 2012. "The Politics of Ex Parte Lobbying: Pre-Proposal Agenda Building and Blocking during Agency Rulemaking." *Journal of Public Administration Research and Theory* 22 (April): 373–393.

Yackee, Susan Webb. 2020. "Hidden Politics? Assessing Lobbying Success during US Agency Guidance Development." *Journal of Public Administration Research and Theory* 30 (September): 548–562.

You, Hye Young. 2017. "Ex Post Lobbying." *Journal of Politics* 79 (October): 1162–1176.

You, Hye Young. 2020. "Foreign Agents Registration Act: A User's Guide." *Interest Groups & Advocacy* 9 (September): 302–316.

Zwick, Jesse. 2010. "Old Senator, New Tricks." *The New Republic* (January).

Index